Countdown to 2000

Editors

Simon Halberstam

Jonathan D.C. Turner

Co-Authors

Jonathan Berman

Caroline Bramley

Christopher Davis

Simon Halberstam

Owen Keane

Ian Lloyd

Eoin O'Shea

William Rees

Malcolm Stirling

Butterworths
London, Edinburgh and Dublin
1998

United Kingdom	Butterworths a Division of Reed Elsevier (UK) Ltd, Halsbury House, 35 Chancery Lane, LONDON WC2A 1EL and 4 Hill Street, EDINBURGH EH2 3JZ
Australia	Butterworths, SYDNEY, ADELAIDE, BRISBANE, CANBERRA, MELBOURNE and PERTH
Canada	Butterworths Canada Ltd, TORONTO and VANCOUVER
Ireland	Butterworth (Ireland) Ltd, DUBLIN
Malaysia	Malayan Law Journal Sdn Bhd, KUALA LUMPUR
New Zealand	Butterworths of New Zealand Ltd, WELLINGTON and AUCKLAND
Singapore	Butterworths Asia, SINGAPORE
South Africa	Butterworths Publishers (Pty) Ltd, DURBAN
USA	Michie, CHARLOTTESVILLE, Virginia

© Reed Elsevier (UK) Ltd 1998

A CIP Catalogue record for this book is available from the British Library.

ISBN 0 406 899 282

Printed by Antony Rowe, Chippenham, Wiltshire.

Visit our website on http://www.butterworths.co.uk

Halberstam Elias & Co

Countdown to 2000

A guide to the legal issues

THE AUTHORS

Jonathan Berman LLB (Lond) is head of Internet law and joint head of the Year 2000 Law Group at Halberstam Elias & Co, Solicitors

Caroline Bramley is Corporate IT Client Manager at Cambridgeshire County Council and has the role of Milleniunm Co-ordinator across the Council

Christopher Davis LLB heads the Due diligence Department at Davis & Co and was formerly in charge of the Due diligence Group at McKenna & Co

Simon Halberstam LLB (Lond), Maitrise en Droit (Sorbonne) is head of IT law and joint head of the Year 2000 Law Group at Halberstam Elias & Co, Solicitors

Owen Keane is a barrister specialising in IT. In addition to normal practice he participates on the Bar Council's Bar Services and Information Technology committees and the Lord Chancellor's Civil Litigation Working Party to ITAC

Ian Lloyd is Professor of Information Technology Law and Director of the Centre for Law, Computers and Technology at the University of Strathclyde

Eoin O'Shea BA (NVI), BA (Cantab) is a barrister practising at 4 Field Court, Gray's Inn

William Rees is a barrister practising at 4 Kings Bench Walk and is Standing Counsel to Davis & Co and Halberstam Elias & Co. He has also held Fellowships at various universities in Britain and the USA

Malcolm Stirling is the Director responsible for KPMG's Year 2000 services in the United Kingdom

Jonathan D.C. Turner MA (Cantab), Lic Sp Dr Eur (Brussels) is a barrister practising at 4 Field Court, Gray's Inn

Dedication

In memory of my parents, Marilyn Wigoder Halberstam and Alfred Peter Halberstam

Simon Halberstam

Table of Statutes

Table of Statutory Instruments

ix

Table of Community Conventions and Treaties

Table of Cases

xiii

Table of Cases

Contents

7 Escrow, copyright and data protection   113

8 Company directors' duties in the context of the system of corporate governance   119

1 Foreword

The impact of the millennium on software and hardware has been dominating the computer press for about a year. The national press has become increasingly interested as the potential enormity of the chaos has become more and more obvious. The first wave of attention focused on computers and software. More recently, industry has been worrying about the effect on machinery containing embedded chips.

The millennium, unlike EMU was never unforeseeable. Hence, the relatively late hour at which industry has become aware of the probably catastrophic proportions of the effect of the Year 2000 is almost incredible. If the crystallisation of awareness of the technical issues was slow in coming, then the appreciation of the legal ramifications has been, at best, partial and sluggish.

At the start, legal work centred on drafting questionnaires for IT users who wanted suppliers to reassure them that their IT systems would continue to work in the next century. More recently, activity has focused on auditing existing software and hardware contracts, outsourcing agreements and machinery supply agreements to advise on how to minimise legal exposure to customers and maximise potential legal recourse against suppliers should equipment fail in the Year 2000. However, the whole legal position relating to Year 2000 issues should be addressed *now* by all who may be affected. There may already be circumstances giving rise to substantial claims which may be statute-barred by the time that their effects are felt.

Despite the valiant efforts of David Atkinson MP (considered in Chapter 8), the Year 2000 problem has not produced new law. It has instead created the challenge of applying many different areas of existing law to a unique problem. Its uniqueness centres on the fact that although the potential damage is foreseeable, it has not yet occurred and those affected must act to mitigate their losses in advance of sustaining them.

Since the Year 2000 problem impacts on so many different areas of law, and it is not practicable to write a volume on each, we have instead endeavoured to address some of the more significant legal ramifications in the most important areas. This work is not intended to replace existing textbooks on each of these areas but merely to complement them by focusing on the main issues arising in this particular sphere.

In order to bring these to life we have included in Chapter 2 a fictional case study concerning the Thrombodirect group of companies and its various relationships.

Whilst this is a legal and not a technical treatise, we could not ignore the technical roots of this problem and are grateful to Caroline Bramley of Cambridgeshire County Council for Chapter 3.

Businesses which do not address the impact of the Year 2000 run the risk of having their accounts qualified. We are indebted to Malcolm Stirling of KPMG who has vast experience of the financial implications of the Year 2000 for his analysis of this area in Chapter 4.

Despite the contributions from Caroline and Malcolm, this is a book by lawyers for lawyers. In this context, thanks are due to Jonathan DC Turner who, besides an extensive written contribution, co-ordinated the substantial part of this book which considers the contractual aspects of the Year 2000.

Jonathan Berman, my colleague and joint head of the Year 2000 Law Group at Halberstam Elias also burned the midnight oil in bringing this book to fruition.

We are grateful, too, for the assistance of co-authors Eoin O'Shea, Owen Keane , Ian Lloyd, Chris Davis and Bill Rees, and for valuable information provided by the National Computing Centre and the Office of the Data Protection Registrar.

A website has also been developed to complement the printed text of this book. This can be accessed at the following URL:

http://www.butterworths.co.uk/content/y2k/default.htm

The site contains news items, articles and links to important Year 2000 resources. The site will also be used as a means to update users on the legal issues surrounding the Year 2000 problem and will be closely linked with the book.

Finally, a special word of thanks to Sabina Smith and her colleagues at Butterworths, not least for stiffening our resolve to address these issues before it is too late.

Simon Halberstam
Halberstam Elias & Co.
March 1998

2 A Fictional Case Study—Is time ticking away for Thrombodirect?

(1) STRUCTURE AND OPERATIONS

The Thrombodirect group manufactures and supplies medical equipment, including dialysis machines and time-controlled drug delivery mechanisms. It also formulates, packs and supplies various analgesic and other medical preparations.

The parent company, Thrombodirect plc ("Plc"), has been listed on the AIM since its flotation in 1995. Most of the shareholders are UK-based but 10 per cent of the equity is held by Marvin Hick Junior, a US investor. The management of Plc suspect that Hick holds some or all of these shares as a nominee, but have no specific information. Plc has four full-time directors - Sir Magnus Millichip (Managing Director), Jack Curite (Sales Director), Manny Coin (Finance Director) and David Wytook (Information Technology) - each of whom holds 5 per cent of the company shares. It also has 2 non-executive, part-time directors who do not have any shares in the company.

Plc's UK subsidiary, Thrombodirect Manufacturing Limited ("Manufacturing") manufactures or formulates the products and handles UK sales. It has various customer groups, including hospitals, health trusts and general practitioners, typical examples of which are the Millshire Health Trust, the Ennium Hospital and Dr Justin Time. The group also supplies customers in France and Italy through its subsidiaries Thrombodirect SA ("SA") and Thrombodirect SRL ("SRL") respectively.

Plc operates the head office and general administration of the group, but the group's IT is operated by another UK subsidiary, Thrombodirect Systems Limited ("Systems"). There are no formal contracts between the companies in the group regarding administrative or IT services, but service charges are transferred from Manufacturing, SA and SRL to Plc and Systems. The subsidiaries are wholly owned by Plc, with the exception of Systems, in which Plc has 75 per cent of the shares and Wytook's girl-friend, Izza Lipia, holds the balance. Wytook and Lipia are also the directors of Systems. The directors of Manufacturing are Millichip and Coin. The directors of the other subsidiaries are Millichip and Curite.

The group's main suppliers include Chipsrus, a supplier of electronic components with a head office in Hong Kong and a factory in Shenzen, and Drugsulike, which holds patents for Ceniocaine, an analgesic which is the active ingredient in various preparations formulated by Manufacturing.

Plc has outsourced group marketing to Fontanel plc, which carries out various functions including the publication and despatch of *Thrombonews*, a weekly newsletter sent out to customers to update them on developments in the medical industry and the group's product range. The contract commenced in June 1997 and has a three year term, renewable on 6 months' advance notice.

Plc wishes to expand the group's operations and is considering various bolt-on acquisitions. It is looking to double its authorised shared capital and hopes to place the shares with Gregorian Trust, an investment trust which focuses on the medical sector. Gregorian is looking into Thrombodirect's financial situation and awaiting its next annual report with interest. Plc's year-end is approaching and its auditors, Anomerge, are about to carry out their annual audit.

(2) IT AND YEAR 2000 STRATEGY

The Thrombodirect group is heavily dependent on IT for its operations. David Wytook has an IT background and is responsible for selecting and procuring systems for the group. Wytook took "A" level law, distrusts lawyers and consults them as rarely as possible. He negotiates all of the IT contracts himself.

Wytook is endeavouring to ensure that the operation of software used by the group will be unaffected by the change of millennium but does not have sufficient time to vet it all himself. The other directors consider that the fears about the inability of computer systems to cope with the change of millennium are mostly the result of media hype.

However, because of Wytook's concerns, Systems has engaged the services of B&W Agon Ltd to assist in this process. B&W Agon is a small company relying on consultants which it sources from India through an informal arrangement with an Indian recruitment consultancy based in New Delhi. There is no formal agreement between Systems and B&W Agon. Wytook feels that this would have resulted in unnecessary legal expenditure and, in any case, he plays bowls with B&W Agon's managing director, Jonathon Jumpon, and feels that Jumpon is a decent sort of fellow.

Some of the software used by the group was written in-house by Kevin Culater, who has just given in his notice for personal reasons. However, much of the software was sourced from software suppliers. The main software programs on which the group's operations depend are:

* *Debtpay 3.0*

    This is an off-the-shelf debt management package. Its features include automatic production of a summons if a debt is six months overdue and writing off debts which are more than 3 years overdue. The package was acquired by Wytook at his previous company, Hardman & Co. When Hardman and Co ceased to trade and Wytook joined the Thrombodirect group, he brought the package with him. Thrombodirect handed over the operation of Debtpay to Julian Associates as part of a facilities management agreement which has been in place since 1995.

- *Medinvent*

   This is a bespoke stock control system which was developed by Anocomp Inc (a Delaware corporation based in Boston) for Systems in 1995. It is maintained by Anocomp and the source code is held in escrow by Futurerisk plc, a specialist escrow agent. The contracts with Anocomp are on Anocomp's standard terms which specify that they are governed by Delaware law.

- *Manucont*

   This is an off-the-shelf manufacturing control program which is the market leader and was acquired by Systems from Sofchoice, a large software retailer with branches all over England.

The group's hardware systems comprise a mainframe, which Thrombodirect Limited (now Plc) bought from Legacy Limited in 1983, and a miscellany of PCs. Legacy is no longer in business. Wytook is currently negotiating a contract with Nogar Antis Ltd for the replacement of most of the existing PCs.

3 Introduction to the technical issues

Whether it is a time-bomb, a bug, or simply a program design error, the millennium problem can no longer be ignored by any business, large or small, public or private. Two years ago knowledge of the problem was confined to a few forward-thinking souls in the Information Technology industry. Now we are terrified on a regular basis by prophecies of disaster as the century draws to its close. The problem is a very simple one - the implications complex and far-reaching.

(1) COMPRESSION OF DATA

For those of us programming over twenty years ago one of the most valuable and expensive of IT resources was space. Early computers had little storage or memory - any technique which reduced the amount of data to be processed was to be adopted. Dates were an easy target for compression. Clearly the century would always start with '19', so this did not need storing. Only the last two digits of the year needed to be stored - the '19' could be assumed by the program doing the processing. Thus the date:

15 February, 1955 is stored as: 150255 or more usually as: 550215

(storing the date as year, month, day makes calculations easier as will be seen below).

As long as the programs would process only dates in the 20th Century, i.e. with years starting with '19', this would work perfectly. This practical technique was adopted across the industry.

In the Year 2000, however, things are not so convenient. So . . .

31 December, 1999 is stored as: 991231

but

1 January, 2000 is stored as: 000101.

The first problem with this will be clear. Because the century is implied rather than explicitly stated, the programs processing the data cannot know that the century is '20' and will assume that the date is 1 January, 1900. This simple misunderstanding by the computer will have implications in almost every area of our lives.

The millennium problem will cause difficulties to at least three categories of technology:

software;

hardware; and

embedded chips.

(2) SOFTWARE

The easiest case to consider first is that of software. It is clearest to consider software in three main categories: operating systems; applications; and 'tailoring'. Operating Systems control the computer's functions such as reading files, outputting to printers, and running other programs. Applications programs run on top of operating systems and mainly carry out particular functions, such as printing cheques or doing particular calculations. These are typically the packages which can be bought off-the-shelf, or systems which are written specially for a particular business or institution, and are usually written by programmers rather than by the end-users. 'Tailoring' is the user-applied layer, which consists of formulae and data entered into proprietary applications such as databases and spreadsheets. Such tailoring is typically entered by the user rather than an IT specialist.

Applications are the simplest type to consider first. Take, for example, a program printing out cheques. Most will print today's date on the cheque - the computer will think that this is 1 January, 1900 and the cheque will instantly be 100 years old. A program registering births will age new-born babies equally quickly, and one registering deaths may well register the date of death as before the birth date. As an added problem, the days of the week in 2000 are different from those in 1900 (1 January, 1900 was a Monday, in 2000 it is a Saturday.) Thus a process programmed to occur every Wednesday, weekly payrolls for instance, will get itself into a muddle over the century change. Lastly, and easily forgotten, the Year 2000 is a Leap Year, whereas 1900 was not. (Centuries are Leap Years if divisible by 400, not by 4. The last century which was a Leap Year was 1600.) The programs that assume that they are in 1900 will process their dates completely incorrectly after 28 February.

The problem of the date being mistaken for 1900 has, however, more complex repercussions than those outlined above. Computers use dates for a wide range of processes: displaying and printing, comparing, sorting and validating. Think of any process which has to assess how long something has been happening, e.g. calculating the length of time that a library book has been out on loan, or working out somebody's age, or calculating the interest due on a bank loan. All these processes require calculations to be made to work out the number of days between two dates, and they will be badly affected by the millennium problem. Computers assume that dates tend to get 'larger' numerically, because the year numbers step up in ones. When they are calculating the difference between two dates the first thing they tend to do is to work out the number of years between them. Thus if I was born in 1955 and it is now 1999, 55 taken from 99 will give 44 as the correct number of years. In 2000, however, 55 taken from 00 will produce a very curious result. I will in fact be 45, but for the computer I will be -55 or, because programmers quite reasonably do not usually allow for negative ages, I will be 55 or the program will fail. (If this calculation was for a bank loan we might be pleased that we would have the loan for a negative number of years and would therefore incur negative interest. For a savings plan, however, the opposite would be the case.)

A particular form of date comparison is sorting data. Frequently programs need to display data in date order. When the year ticks over to '00', the data relating to early 21st Century dates will sort before all the data relating to late 20th Century dates and appear as the earlier, not the later information.

Another very common process is comparing dates to validate data. Perhaps you take out a loan on 20 December, 1990 (stored by the computer as 901220). If you make a payment on 20 December, 1999 (991220), the computer will check that the payment is being made after the loan has started, and it does this by simply subtracting one date from the other. In 1999 this will work successfully - in 2000 the date will appear to be before the start of the loan (001220) and will be invalid.

As can be seen, application programs will suffer badly from the millennium problem. But it is too easy to fall into the trap of assuming that they will be the only, or the worst, affected. Operating systems are equally badly hit. At the very least these programs may store the date in the format indicated above and this means that application systems running under them, even if they are themselves compliant, will process incorrectly because they will be passed an incorrect date from the operating system. Some operating systems may not be able to cope with the date change at all, and may crash as soon as the date ticks over to 2000.

The 'highest' level of software is the layer added onto proprietary programs such as databases and spreadsheets - the 'tailored' layer. In this case the user inputs data and programming statements into the program. Even if the database or spreadsheet is itself compliant, the user may input data which does not allow for the century change and the program will function incorrectly or fail.

(3) HARDWARE

One of the greatest myths surrounding the millennium problem is that it will only affect software, that is what people consider to be 'programs', 'packages' or 'systems'. All computers, from the smallest laptop to the largest mainframe, contain microcode which stores the configuration of the machine and also, except for the very earliest models, stores and updates the current date. Many machines store this date in the standard format, i.e. without the century. These machines will assume that it is 1900, and pass this incorrect date to any programs running on them, irrespective of whether those programs are themselves millennium-compliant. But some hardware will be more severely affected than this. Some computers may simply not be able to handle the change from '99' to '00' and will fail to work at all. Other machines will decide that the date that they are trying to process is invalid, and will default to another date, typically 1 January, 1980 or 1 April, 1980. (There is nothing mysterious about this date - this was when the microcode was written, and if it encounters a date before this, (e.g. it mistakes 1 January 2000 for 1 January 1900) it defaults to the first date it is happy with, i.e. 1 April, 1980). To summarise, a large percentage of computer hardware will either report the wrong date or simply fail to run at all.

(4) EMBEDDED CHIPS

Traditionally, when people talk about computers or about IT, they are talking about hardware and the programs that run upon it. There is, however, a third category of technology which will be severely affected by the millennium problem, and that category consists of all the items we use today which contain an embedded chip. This refers to all that equipment which relies on some level of computerisation to control it, but would not be regarded as a 'computer'. A quick scan around your home or office will typically highlight many items which fall into this category: videos, mobile phones, pagers, washing machines, photocopiers and fax machines may all contain this sort of technology. Looking further afield, anything which is computer-controlled, such as pump control systems, or has a timing system which is not controlled by clockwork, is liable to be affected.

Although this category of items is affected in the same way as hardware and software, there are two particular problems with it. The first is that, on the whole, the owners of these items are completely unaware of whether there are chips in them or not. In many cases, there is no evidence of the fact for the users. Take for example a computerised servicing system for a car or a lift. This may have very complex chip technology, but the driver may be unaware of it. Even if the user is aware of the embedded chips in the item, how can he tell if there are any implications arising from the date changing? Does the chip store dates? What format does it store them in? Does it matter if the chip thinks it is 1900? How can the date be changed, or even tested?

If we theorise about what problems this category of items might encounter, our thoughts may be very scary indeed. Lifts are often used as an example. Some modern lifts may have servicing data stored on chips inside their controls, and if they have not been serviced for a certain period of time they either sound a warning or stop altogether. If presented with a current date which is 99 years before the last serviced date they could perform very unpredictably. A similar effect might be seen in cars with a computerised servicing history. At the very least the date might cause some sort of upset. The more worrying thought is that the equipment, on encountering a date which appears to precede the date it had registered on the previous day, will simply fail altogether. If we give a moment's thought to all the pumping systems controlled by microchips, the medical equipment, the guidance systems, it is difficult even to think of how widespread and catastrophic the problem could be.

(5) PROBLEMS ARISING BEFORE YEAR 2000

It should by now be clear that the change of century could cause immense problems everywhere. For any users of any of the categories of technology discussed above time is running out if they wish to put the problem right. But the situation could be even worse than might be thought. As IT workers have studied the use of dates in programs, it has become clear that there will be problems before 01/01/00.

The first type of problem will be encountered by programs that use dates in the future as part of the processing. Typically these would be mortgage processors or pension plans. But these will have already had to cope with the Year 2000. Programs that will more recently have started to fail are those such as budgeting programs which typically profile five years or so ahead. Errors will begin to creep into programs as the months go by and their particular functionality calls for forward date processing.

More common, will be programs which fail on 1 April, 1999. This problem is caused by the way in which many programs process financial years. It is very common practice to input or store the financial year in the format 95/96 or 1997/98. Many programs check the validity of this by ensuring that the second year is greater than the first by a factor of one. In 98/99 this is fine - in 99/00 the check will fail, and many financial systems will cease to function.

A third problem date is when the year number is 99, or perhaps when it is 9 September, 1999 (or 9/9/99). Especially in the most common business mainframe programming language, COBOL, and also in some other languages, it is common practice to use '00' and '99' for very specific purposes. They are frequently used to denote the beginning and end of processes, because they are the least and largest value that a positive two digit numeric field can have. Take, for example, a file which is sorted on date. Programmers may construct a dummy record with '99' in the year which will always be the end of the file, and then write a statement into the program which says something like 'if year = 99 then end'. In this program the first record with a date in 1999 will end the program. Similarly '99' is sometimes used in the retention date for files. Instead of specifying a particular date, programmers simply specified the largest year the field would hold as the time when the file would be deleted, i.e. '99'. Such files will disappear on 01/01/1999.

(6) SOLUTIONS

Having dwelt on the cause of the 'bug', and the many problems caused by it, it is worth looking at some solutions, starting again with software.

For programmers there are two main solutions. Either they lengthen the year field to four characters ('date expansion') or they code round the problem ('windowing').

Date expansion is a technique whereby the programmer must examine every occurrence of a date within the program, either stored on a file or manipulated in memory, and change it so that four characters are used for the year rather than two. This technique has one major advantage. It makes the program completely future proof and, as long as it can process leap years correctly, it could happily go on through the 22nd Century. It has, however, some disadvantages, as it is the technique that causes the most disruption to programs. Changing the date field means changing every file and storage layout. Files and databases, which in some systems can be huge, need to be completely reorganised and will take up far more space. (This seems trivial but in fact one study was made of the amount of space saved over the years by storing two character years, and the cost saved was compared with the projected cost of putting the problem right, with the result that the original method of storage was deemed cost effective.) All files interfacing to these systems will probably need changing too. The other major disadvantage is that the program is still dependent on being fed the right date. If presented with 1900 or '00' it will still process incorrectly.

Windowing or *coding round* is quite a different technique. In this case the programmer assumes, for example, that any year ending, say, '00' to '49' is going to be in the 21st Century, i.e. 2000 to 2049, and that any year ending '50' to '99' is in the 20th, i.e. 1950 to 1999. Then, instead of reorganising and expanding fields, the programmer adds statements into the program to supply the missing century when it is required. This technique has obvious advantages - files and storage areas need not be reorganised, and the program can handle being presented with '00' as a year. There is, however, one major drawback to this technique. It cannot be used in any situations where the program needs to be able to handle dates from 1900 to 1949 as well as 2000 to 2049. Many programs will need to do this - any storing birthdays for example. Indeed some programs may need to use three centuries to function correctly. (The story, albeit apocryphal, of the old lady born in 1895 and sent to school in 2000 because the program thought that it was 1900 and that she was 5 years old and not 105, is nonetheless salutary.)

The choice of solution depends on the individual system and its requirements, and also on the requirements of any interfacing systems. Whichever choice is made the exercise requires every occurrence of date processing to be found, examined and amended if necessary. Herein lies the enormity of the Year 2000 problem. More about this later, but it is worth considering that many systems have millions of lines of code to be examined.

Hardware manufacturers have similar choices to make. They can replace the microcode with code which handles four character years, or they can add code which codes round the problem. Both systems are being used, and, as hardware usually only has to deal with the current date, the problems outlined above when 'windowing' are not relevant.

When looking at embedded chips, the choices are again much the same. The original problems outlined, however, are also still the same. Knowing what the date format is, finding it, and putting it right are all far more difficult than making a choice between the two techniques.

The problem, then, is simple and the solution, apart from the case of embedded chips, clear. So what is all the fuss about? It is about three basic things - size, risk and time.

(7) TIME AND RISK

Taking these in reverse we can start with time. Any Year 2000 project has an immovable end date - 1 January, 2000. Many have an earlier end date than this, as can be seen above when we were considering other problem dates. This is not a desirable or useful date, it is all or nothing - meet this date or the project will be pointless. Those who have worked in the IT industry for any length of time will know that projects tend to come in over time and over budget, and working to an immovable end date is an unusual state of affairs in many IT Departments. Because it is driven by time rather than by business requirements, the Year 2000 projects will require a quite different type of project management from usual IT projects.

The second factor - risk - is a very major consideration. No-one has ever tackled the Year 2000 problem before - there are no precedents. This, coupled with the potential to affect every aspect of IT, makes the risk of failure enormous. Even where programs are very well known and ample resource is available to change them, it is by no means certain that the full implications of the date change are fully understood. For many systems the resource and knowledge to amend them may no longer be available - many companies no longer retain staff for maintaining so called 'heritage' systems, i.e. those written in older style languages. Staff wished to learn more modern techniques, and the skills to maintain the older systems became rare and expensive. Many companies rely on third parties to maintain these systems if necessary, and will need to continue to rely on them over the Year 2000. This actually compounds the risk - because everybody has the same problem, skills are at a premium and costs soaring. Some companies run the risk of not being able to secure the resource they need.

The risk is greatest, of course, where the problem is unknown, and here we return to the problem of embedded chips. The risk of missing those which will go wrong, or being unable to correct them, is huge. Managers are extremely exposed in this area and the industry itself still has not the knowledge to scope the problem.

There is one further element of risk emerging, especially for businesses. Those which have started their own Year 2000 projects have realised that, not only their own systems will need investigating, but also those of their subcontractors or trading partners, and they will be requiring assurances from these people that they are working to become compliant. Any companies unable to give those assurances run a severe risk of being shunned as business partners.

(8) SIZE OF THE PROBLEM

The final factor is the size of the problem. Every program, every piece of hardware, every piece of machinery likely to contain an embedded chip must be examined. Taken globally this is a huge undertaking. Estimates, which, it must be said, could be wildly inaccurate, are currently running at a world-wide cost of £400 billion. Whatever the cost to an individual company, this will certainly mean that all other IT work will need to be completely stopped and, probably, considerable extra resource will be required to help in the projects. Most companies will also be facing the prospect of having to change their programs to cater for EMU before the millennium, a fact which can only put more strain on IT resource. In the case of embedded chips, the staff required will cover many areas and they will also probably have to defer all new work and stop all work in progress. For businesses this could be devastating, and many small companies may well not be able to take the strain and keep their businesses running. Because of the size of the problem, most people will have to prioritise the areas which can be worked on, and manage the risk of the others going wrong.

So, what hope is there for IT past the millennium? Despite the risks, size and finality of the problem there are some sound techniques being proved as IT Departments start their work. It would be inappropriate to go into detail about these in this introduction, but they can be condensed into a few points:

- Find out what you have got. (If you don't know you cannot fix it.)

- Use these inventories to plan your projects including continuity plans if your projects go wrong.

- Make a time-line plan covering ALL the work you will have to do, and check your progress regularly against it.

- Understand that the project is going to cost you money and budget for it.

- Book third party help very early if you think that you are going to need it, and ensure that your contracts are watertight.

- Stop any non-essential IT work until your projects are finished.

- Check out all your contracts with anybody - firms may be unwilling to renew as the Year 2000 looms.

- Ensure that everything you buy in the future is millennium-compliant.

A bug, a time-bomb or a design error? Or a plot by the IT industry to keep itself in business? The answer to this does not really matter. The important thing is to understand the problem, and start to tackle it immediately.

4 Year 2000 and the Auditor

(1) PURPOSE OF THIS CHAPTER

In this Chapter we will discuss the duties and responsibilities of the auditor. We will look at the review process the auditor is likely to adopt and how the directors of Thrombodirect plc ("Plc") may benefit from and contribute to this process.

(2) INTRODUCTION

The auditor is appointed by the shareholders of a limited company. It is to the shareholders, therefore, that the auditor owes his duty of care and responsibility, and not to potential investors such as Gregorian in our case study.

The auditor, as a member of the accountancy profession, is in a good position to understand the nature of the Year 2000 problem. He is also able to raise awareness with his clients and so spread the word. This is an activity that the Department of Trade and Industry has suggested accountants undertake. Accountants have access to almost every company in the UK through the process of accounts preparation or annual audit.

Accountants often act as business advisers to their clients. In this role, which is separate from their audit role, they may wish to help their clients in preparations for the Year 2000. It is not, however, within the auditor's remit to solve the problem, although it may be within his firm's capability to do so. Any such work would, by necessity, be covered by a separate letter of engagement.

The effects of the Year 2000 issue can be widespread throughout a company and may be far removed from the accounting system. It may be that the most significant effects will be business risks relating to the efficiency of the company's operating functions. The Year 2000 issue may have an effect on a company's products, its services or its competitive position. If this is likely then the auditor will want to see a disclosure from the directors of the company.

In essence the Year 2000 problem is a business risk that must be resolved by the directors of Plc. The auditor will want to understand how much of a business risk the Year 2000 presents to Plc and, if he believes that the directors' response to this threat is inadequate, he should bring this to the attention of the shareholders.

(3) DUTIES OF THE AUDITOR

(i) What responsibilities does the auditor have?

Technically there is no additional audit responsibility relating to the Year 2000. Auditors will, however, be mindful of the duty of care they owe to their clients and consequently would be unlikely to neglect the Year 2000 issue just because it is not included in the Auditing Standards[1]. Auditors will recognise that the financial statements of almost any organisation could be materially affected, since assets may be revalued, significant costs may be incurred or the ability of a company to continue as a going concern may be under threat. The auditors' initial opinion will stem from the view the directors themselves place on the importance of the Year 2000 to the business and its impact on the financial statements and business plans.

(ii) How will the auditor obtain his information?

Auditors will need to assess the reliability of the information supporting the directors' opinions concerning the impact the Year 2000 will have on the financial statements. The objective will be a high-level enquiry. This should be of sufficient depth to meet reasonable expectations of what a professional auditor should know about this topic and make enquiries of management. Auditors are not expected suddenly to become computer experts or to have the skills that are needed to solve the Year 2000 problem.

Auditors will need to form a preliminary view on whether there is a specific audit risk requiring an audit response. If the auditor has confidence in the information obtained then there would seem to be no requirement to make further enquiries, but he should still remain alert to further information that could impact on the preliminary conclusions. If the management's conclusions appear unreliable and the auditor believes the impact could be significant, he should ask management to focus on the uncertainties before the audit is completed.

(iii) What should be expected from the auditor?

The auditor cannot be expected or required to be proficient in areas or disciplines that are remote from his main competencies of accounting and auditing. Further, the auditor is not responsible for ensuring that his client is prepared for the Year 2000 date change. Strictly speaking, the issue will be considered only in so far as it affects the auditor's general audit responsibilities under statute and the Auditing Standards. It is important that there is no misunderstanding of the respective responsibilities of management and the

---

[1] A reference guide produced by the accounting profession which contains the basic principles and essential procedures with which auditors are required to comply.

auditors, so that no expectation gap arises. A written record of the scope of his responsibilities, which would make clear that it is not the purpose of an audit to give assurance in relation to the Year 2000, would be good practice. It would also be helpful, when communicating to the management any Year 2000 issues, that the auditor comes across in the course of the audit, if the auditor stipulated that he is not providing any assurance with respect to the client's Year 2000 exposure. The auditor may make his position clear to his client in writing either in his letter of engagement or by way of a specific management letter. Examples might be:

> *A reminder of the directors' responsibilities;*

> For example, 'The Year 2000 issue is presenting challenges to many businesses. The directors must satisfy themselves that appropriate enquiries are made within Plc to identify and deal with consequential business risks. These include systems risks, both financial and operational, including the impact of difficulties of third parties such as suppliers and customers [, and risks arising from Plc's products failing to cope with the problem].'

> *A statement of the auditors' responsibilities;*

> For example, 'As part of our assessment of the risk of error in the financial statements, we consider whether the directors are addressing the Year 2000 issue and the effect of their plans on the audit of the financial statements. However, we are not responsible for identifying problems, or for expressing an opinion on the sufficiency of the plans for addressing the issue, or for monitoring progress.'

It can be seen that the auditor is not responsible for Plc achieving millennium compliance although he does owe a duty of care to the shareholders. The auditor will, therefore, wish to raise the issue with the management. He will want to know that the management is aware of the Year 2000 issue and that it has researched the potential operational and financial reporting implications. Further, he will enquire whether the management has set aside sufficient funds and is taking appropriate actions.

(iv) What will the auditor do if he is concerned?

In the first instance, he will bring his concerns to the attention of the management. If he is not satisfied with the directors' response he may well escalate the issue to his ultimate recourse which would be to qualify the accounts. The two most likely areas for which accounts may receive a qualification regarding the Year 2000 are:

- the accuracy of the financial statements, and
- the ability of Plc to continue as a going concern.

Both areas will be discussed in more detail later in this chapter.

A qualification will not be undertaken lightly for it may have an impact on the share price, Plc's ability to borrow money and the willingness of suppliers to continue trading with Plc.

(v) Auditors of subsidiary companies

Thrombodirect plc has four reporting entities; Thrombodirect Manufacturing Limited ("Manufacturing"), Thrombodirect SA, Thrombodirect SRL and Thrombodirect Systems Limited ("Systems"). In our case study both Thrombodirect SA and Thrombodirect SRL are audited by seperate firm of accountants.

The principal auditors will, therefore, wish to verify that the auditors of Thrombodirect's other divisions have also made enquiries about the Year 2000 issues. The amount of emphasis the auditor will place on the reporting divisions will relate to contribution each division makes to the business as a whole.

(4) INTERNAL AUDITORS

Just as the external auditor is in a good position to raise awareness of the Year 2000 issue within Plc so too is the internal auditor. The internal auditor reports to Plc's own management and not to the shareholders. Internal audit should be involved in reviewing Plc's preparedness for the Year 2000 and it should also have a number of assessment processes in place that the external auditor may benefit from. If these processes are rigorous and well documented, it will be extremely beneficial to the external auditor. It would be prudent for the internal audit function to prepare an information pack for the external auditor explaining the work done to date and the processes that have been established.

(5) DUTIES OF THE DIRECTORS

It is the directors' responsibility to run the business. Part of their duties will be to take reasonable steps to ensure that the group will cope with the Year 2000 date change and that the business will not be materially affected. Where it can be shown that the directors have been negligent in their duties, and the shareholders incur losses, then the directors and officers of that company may find themselves liable (see Chapter 8, post). The directors, therefore, need to review the impact on the business and make appropriate plans to ensure the business continues as a going concern. They should also consider any specific impact on the financial statements. Their review should encompass all significant business units, including all of Plc's divisions.

It is also the directors' responsibility to ensure that financial statements reflect any financial changes caused by the Year 2000 problem where these changes would have a significant effect on the figures and disclosures contained within the financial statements. Examples of such changes might be:

- the write down of assets such as software or computer-controlled equipment that may be rendered inoperable;

- disclosure and treatment of costs that can be foreseen or disclosure of commitments;

- capitalisation of costs, though this would only be on new equipment and software or where the life was enhanced or extended;

- disclosure of contingent liabilities such as for litigation or compensation;

- consequential taxation adjustments.

(6) HOW WILL THE AUDITOR MAKE HIS ASSESSMENT?

It is likely that he will gather information from management. Examples of the kind of questions that could be asked are:

- have you identified all of the hardware and software used by the group?

- how significant do you believe the risk posed by the Year 2000 problem to be, assuming no changes are made to your IT systems?

- has a Year 2000 steering group been established?

- has a project manager been assigned to the Year 2000 project?

- have all systems been reviewed to assess whether there is a problem?

- to what extent does the awareness programme cover customers and suppliers?

- does the plan to resolve the problem include estimates for:

    costs?

    time?

    hardware capacity?

    other resources?

- has an appropriate budget been committed?

- does the plan take into account:

    resource availability?

    realistic plans to secure further resources if necessary?

- is the project plan reviewed and updated in line with actual progress?

- does the group have enough staff with experience of large scale testing and / or a plan in place to acquire / retain these skills?

(7) HOW WILL THE AUDITOR ASSESS IF THERE MIGHT BE A PROBLEM?

The auditor will consider the responses to the above questions in the context of the overall likelihood that Plc will be at risk due to its use of IT. There are a number of factors to consider that affect risk, such as:

Dependence on IT - The more dependent the group is on IT, the higher the risk that the Year 2000 issue will affect it.

Changes in IT - If the group is finding it difficult to adapt its current systems, there could be a risk that it cannot effectively solve the Year 2000 issue. Even if it changes systems, the auditor will need to be satisfied that the new systems are adequate. There is no guarantee that just because a system is new it is not at risk. For example:

- modified and new systems may contain new defects unrelated to the Year 2000 issue;

- new systems may not function as intended;

- the environment in which the systems are modified and the new systems are installed may not be adequately controlled. This in turn may create the risk of unauthorised activity that may result in the theft of data, misappropriation of assets and fraudulent financial reporting.

- testing for Year 2000 compliance may of itself render previously compliant software non-compliant.

External IT - If Systems outsources some of its IT function then the auditor will need to be satisfied that the providers of the service are contractually obliged to and have a strategy for tackling the Year 2000 issue. The problem can be compounded where Plc interfaces directly with suppliers or customers. If they have not considered the issue, then problems will emerge in day-to-day transactions with them. An example of how seriously companies take the issue is British Telecommunications plc which has written to its 1,800 core suppliers warning them that unless they can show that they are equipped to deal with the millennium problem, they will no longer be used by the company.

IT reliability - The auditor will need to consider the complexity of the systems, the adequacy of documentation, the degree of interrogation errors and the use of manual intervention. If systems are not well documented and are complex it makes it more difficult to make the necessary corrections.

IT skills and resources - The auditor will need to consider whether the skills, resources, calibre, quality, workload and turnover of staff is such that the problem can be effectively tackled.

Business focus - The auditor will need to consider the strategy and awareness of the Year 2000 issue and IT matters in general.

(8) WHAT ARE THE AUDIT IMPLICATIONS IF THERE IS A PROBLEM?

(i) Audit report

On completing his review of the annual accounts, the auditor will prepare a report for the shareholders. Potential effects on the auditor's report are:

- a statement that proper accounting records have not been kept (Companies Act 1985, s 237[1]).

- qualification due to material misstatements of account balances;

- qualification due to going concern uncertainties.

(ii) Accuracy of financial statements.

When an auditor is considering the methods a company uses to process accounting information he will consider whether data processing errors caused by the Year 2000 issue could result in a material misstatement of the accounting records under audit. That is: are there likely to be errors that adversely affect the organisation's ability to record, process, summarise and report financial data in conformity with the assertions of management in the financial statements?

The extent to which the auditor considers this risk will require professional judgement. The auditor is responsible for planning and performing the audit to obtain reasonable assurance about whether the financial statements are free from any material misstatement, whether caused by error or fraud. Thus, the auditor's responsibility relates to the detection of any material misstatement in the accounts being audited, which results from the Year 2000 issue or from any other cause. Once the final accounts of a limited company have been produced and approved by the auditor, the auditor will put his name to these accounts and state that they represent a 'true and fair' view of the company's financial status. In most modern companies, these accounts will have been produced using computer systems. If these systems fail as a result of the millennium bug, then the accounts may not represent a true and fair view. Examples of financial reporting implications are:

---

[1] 8 *Halsbury's Statutes* (4th edn).

- proper accounting records may not have been kept;

- account balances could be misstated;

- ageing of balances may be inaccurate;

- stock valuations may be incorrect;

- any business applications using any algorithm involving dates (e.g. interest calculations) will be suspect;

- it may be appropriate for directors to comment on how they are addressing the issue in the operating and financial review or in their statement on compliance with Cadbury[1] requirements;

- additional disclosure may be necessary.

It might be the case that errors in systems may not occur until the Year 2000. Some may hold the view that the auditor should confine his comments to failures that have actually happened and have his say in the Audit Report for the year ending in 2000. This would be a short-sighted approach. If, in the auditor's opinion, it is likely that proper accounting records will not be produced, he should bring it to the attention of the shareholders as a matter of urgency.

The diagram below illustrates the thought process required to establish whether a qualified audit report should be issued.

[1] The Cadbury Committee expanded the disclosure requirements of directors to make them more accountable to non-executive directors: *The Cadbury Report on the Financial Aspects of Corporate Governance System* (1992).

Qualified audit thought process

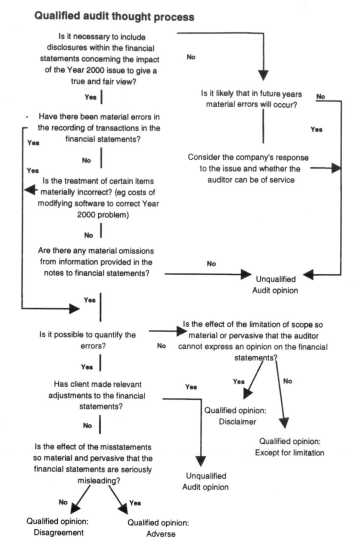

(iii) Considerations in respect of going concern

This is one of the most significant areas that the auditor will wish to review. He will be evaluating the use the group makes of computer-based technology, the level of dependency and the impact of failure. The auditor will also be looking at the costs of achieving Year 2000 compliance and the potential financial impact of any failures. Examples might be:

- Where embedded chips are used as part of the production mechanism. The concern here is that if there is no production then there is no product which in turn means no revenue. How long could the group survive without production taking place is a critical question for the auditor.

- There may be insufficient funds for some companies to replace or repair their computer systems. Banks might be unwilling to lend money if they see that profit levels are so low that interest repayments could be a challenge for a company. The Year 2000 may be the last straw that forces a struggling company to close.

The diagram below illustrates the thought process required to establish whether there are any uncertainties regarding a company's ability to continue as a going concern.

Going concern thought process

(9) DISCLOSURES AND OTHER FINANCIAL REPORTING ISSUES

(i) What disclosure should directors make?

A In general

It may be appropriate for the directors to consider explaining how they are dealing with the Year 2000 issue to a wider audience. There is a growing practice in the United States for management to make statements to their shareholders on the impact the Year 2000 issue may have on their business. In the United Kingdom, directors may also wish to make disclosures, for example in the Operating and Financial Review, on how they perceive the impact the Year 2000 will have on their business.

The Institute of Chartered Accountants in England and Wales ("ICAEW"[1]) issued a warning, in October 1997, to finance directors that their accounts could be qualified if they cannot satisfy their auditors that the accounts properly reflect the impact the Year 2000 issue may have on the business. Disclosure may be required in areas such as:

- impairment or amortisation of capitalised software costs
- inventory valuation
- long term contract accounting
- warranty reserves
- reserves for sales returns and allowances

B Contingencies

The auditor may consider it prudent to establish contingency funds to cover certain situations, for example:

- Manufacturing sells a product that contains a timer that it warrants is Year 2000 compliant. If this proves not to be the case and the product fails, Manufacturing may face the costly exercise of a product recall.

- The testing of the existing systems failed to discover errors in the billing systems, resulting in overcharging and underpayments. On discovery, clients and suppliers demand to be reimbursed.

---

[1] The ICAEW has produced a guide, for Audit Faculty members, entitled *The Year 2000 Systems Issue: Audit Implications* Thanks is expressed to the working party responsible for producing this guide together with appreciation for the contribution it has made to this chapter.

C Commitments

Companies may enter into contracts with software suppliers for the replacement or repair of computer systems. The contracts may either be for resources to fix existing systems or for the purchase of new applications. If these commitments are significant then they should be disclosed in a note to the financial statements.

D Revenue and loss recognition

The auditor will want to understand where there may be uncertainty relating to customer acceptance, customer cancellation privileges, upgrades, enhancements and post-contract support. The Year 2000 issue could affect one or more of these factors and have an unexpected effect on the timing of revenue recognition.

With Systems, the auditor will want to understand any product warranty or product defect liability or product return issues for software or hardware that Systems has supplied. The auditor will then want to ensure that adequate contingencies are made and, if the liability is material, appropriate disclosure takes place.

(ii) How should costs be treated in financial statements?

A Modifying software

An issue arises on the treatment of the modification of software correctly to process dates including the Year 2000 and other events.

In most cases the costs should be dealt with in a similar way to the way repairs and maintenance expenditure is treated. Costs should be written off as they are incurred since they are the result of modifying a fault in the programs in order to prevent the systems from breaking down. The Urgent Issues Task Force ("UITF"[1]) has already indicated that it would expect this approach to be followed.

When software is capitalised, it can be argued that modification costs extend the useful life of the software and hence should be capitalised as an enhancement.

The auditor will carefully consider any request for not writing costs off as incurred.

---

[1] The UITF's main role is to assist the Accounting Standards Board with important or significant accounting issues where there exists an accounting standard or a provision of companies legislation (including the requirement to give a true and fair view) and where unsatisfactory or conflicting interpretations have developed or seem likely to develop.

The UITF is likely to issue a draft abstract that will costs incurred in rectifying systems that are not able to cope with the Year 2000 to be capitalised where a company has a policy of capitalising software costs and where the relevant capitalised systems have been written down to reflect the loss.

B Impairment

The Year 2000 issue may result in the value of fixed assets that contain software or hardware components (for example, microchips) being reassessed. The auditor will want to review this type of asset in recognition of the fact that the software, hardware or other equipment may have been impaired and should be subject to accelerated depreciation or other form of write down.

C Provisions

There are also issues concerning what provision should be made for the correction costs. Under the principles of FRED 14[1], this would only be necessary when the reporting entity becomes committed to incurring them i.e. when the expenditure actually takes place. At present, however, companies have some flexibility about the timing of any provision. Auditors generally support the 'as incurred' approach, as there is a future benefit to be derived from the expenditure and it therefore seems unnecessary to accelerate the charge.

A policy of providing for all costs of rectification may be prudent, but it carries risks in that a company will be representing that the financial consequences of the problem have been dealt with. It is an area in which it will be difficult for the directors - and even more so, for the auditors - to be satisfied that this is a representation that can be made. The auditor will need to be careful to ensure that he does not find that he has implicitly approved the directors' plans in this area.

(iii) Keeping an eye on the issue

Even if there is currently considered to be no material effect on the financial statements, the auditor should consider whether there could be an impact in the future. If material errors could arise as the Year 2000 draws nearer then the auditor should consider Plc's response to the problem and discuss it with the directors to see if it is adequate.

---

[1] *Financial Reporting Exposure Draft* produced by the Accounting Standards Board.

(10) CONCLUSION

In summary:

- the diligent auditor will bring the Year 2000 issue to management's attention and assess the impact that failure to achieve compliance will have on Plc;

- the auditor is able to qualify the accounts if he believes that either the accuracy of the accounting records is jeopardised or that the ability of Plc to continue as a going concern is in some doubt;

- Plc's share price and net worth can be affected by investors' responses to an auditor's qualification;

- the auditor may be able to assist with the Year 2000 issue but has no legal obligation to do so;

- the auditor will be looking at how the costs incurred for Year 2000 remedial work are treated in the financial statements.

5 Contracts

(1) INTRODUCTION

Contracts both create rights and liabilities and modify the rights and liabilities arising under other areas of law, such as tort. In considering the legal position in a commercial situation, it is invariably necessary to establish what contracts exist between which parties with what valid terms. It is then possible to determine:

- liability in contract: whether any party to a contract has failed to comply with a valid contractual term; whether its liability is excluded or limited by any of the terms; and what remedies other parties may have;

- liability in tort: whether any liability for failure to comply with a non-contractual duty is affected by the existence of any contract or excluded or limited by any valid contractual terms.

Year 2000 issues may arise from a wide variety of contractual relationships, and in many cases several different relationships may be relevant. These may include:

- software development agreements, which commonly include provisions for acceptance testing, exclusions of implied terms as to quality and fitness for purpose, and significant limitations of liability;

- software maintenance agreements, frequently agreed with a software provider to come into effect on completion of acceptance testing, and often providing also for incremental upgrading and support;

- hardware procurement and maintenance agreements;

- facilities management agreements, under which the manager normally operates hardware and software provided by the user, who is likely to retain responsibility for its Year 2000 compliance, although the manager may be responsible for invoking any relevant provisions in maintenance agreements and co-ordinating third parties;

- outsourcing agreements, usually specifying service levels to be provided by the supplier using its own equipment, whose Year 2000 compliance is likely to be the responsibility of the supplier;

- shrink-wrap licences of package software, where producers of standard software seek to ensure that users accept their terms, which often include substantial exclusions and limitations of liability, by applying them to sealed packages containing a copy of the software;

- agreements for the supply of non-computer goods and services by suppliers whose systems may not be Year 2000 compliant and whose goods may contain chips with non-compliant embedded programs - some customers now insist that their suppliers are Year 2000 compliant, and warranties required to this effect may prove to be onerous;

- solution provider contracts, in which engineers undertake to investigate and resolve Year 2000 problems.

In order to establish what contracts exist between which parties with what terms, it is necessary first to establish which law applies. In many cases, the identification of the applicable law is straightforward. However, issues as to the applicable law can arise in relation to Year 2000 problems, as the Thrombodirect example illustrates. Where such issues arise, their resolution is the first step in a proper legal analysis, and they are therefore considered first in this chapter.

(2) APPLICABLE LAW

(i) Introduction

In relation to contracts made on or after 1 April 1991, questions in UK courts as to which law applies must be decided in accordance with the Rome Convention.[1] In relation to contracts prior to this date, common law rules apply. The position under the Rome Convention will be considered first.

(ii) Applicable law for contracts made on or after 1 April 1991

Under the Rome Convention, a contract (or possibly a particular part of a contract[2]) is governed by an "applicable law". Most issues are determined under the applicable law,[3] including:

- whether a contract exists

- what its terms are

- what the terms mean

- whether the terms are valid

- assessment of damages

- limitation periods.

---

[1] Convention on the Law Applicable to Contractual Obligations, Rome 1980 ("Rome Convention"), incorporated into UK law by the Contracts (Applicable Law) Act 1990, 11 *Halsbury's Statutes* (4th edn).
[2] See Dicey & Morris, *The Conflict of Laws (12th ed., 1993)*, Rule 174.
[3] Rome Convention, art 10, Dicey & Morris, *Ibid*, Rule 178, 180.

However, other laws may apply to certain issues, for example:

- "Mandatory rules" of the country where a legal action is tried,[1] or to which all relevant matters relate[2] or where a consumer resides[3] may prevail over the applicable law. It appears that "mandatory rules" may well include rules controlling the exclusion and limitation of liability and rules applying international conventions.[4] Thus in the Thrombodirect example, the contract with Anocomp may contain limitations of liability which are valid under the governing Delaware law. However, these limitations could be invalid in English courts if they are not compatible with the Unfair Contract Terms Act 1977.[5]

- The power of a company to enter into a contract is subject to the law of the jurisdiction in which the company is incorporated.[6] The personal liability of officers and members for the contractual obligations of the company is also governed by the law of incorporation.[7] Thus, Millichip and Curite could be personally liable under French law on the contracts of Thrombodirect SA, even if these are expressly subject to English law.

- A person can rely on the rules of his country to establish that he did not consent if it would be unreasonable to impose the applicable law.[8] This might be applied in relation to exclusion or limitation of liability clauses incorporated by reference under English law where a party did not have a real opportunity of considering them.

- Rules of the place of performance may apply in relation to matters such as public holidays and the examination of goods.[9]

- With regard to formal requirements, it is sufficient for a contract to comply with the applicable law or the law of the country where it is made or of one of the parties.[10]

The applicable law is often agreed between the parties as part of the contract, and a choice of law by the parties which is expressed or demonstrated with reasonable certainty by the circumstances is respected by the Rome Convention (subject to exceptions of which the most relevant are identified above).[11]

If the applicable law is not agreed, it is normally the law of the country with which the contract is most closely connected.[12] This is presumed to be the

---

[1] Rome Convention, art 7(2), Dicey & Morris, *Ibid,* Rule 183.
[2] Rome Convention, art 3(3), Dicey & Morris, *Ibid,* Rule 183.
[3] Rome Convention, art 5, Dicey & Morris, *Ibid,* Rule 183.
[4] *The Hollandia* [1983] 1 AC 565.
[5] 11 *Halsbury's Statutes* (4th edn).
[6] Dicey & Morris, *Ibid,* Rule 156; Rome Convention, art 1(2)(e), (f).
[7] *Ibid.*
[8] Rome Convention, art 8, Dicey & Morris, *Ibid,* Rule 178.
[9] Rome Convention, art 10, Dicey & Morris, *Ibid,* Rule 180; Giuliano-Lagarde Report, OJEC (1980) C282, pp 32-33.
[10] Rome Convention, art 9, Dicey & Morris, *Ibid,* Rule 179.
[11] Rome Convention, art 3, Dicey & Morris, *Ibid,* Rule 175.
[12] Rome Convention, art 4, Dicey & Morris, *Ibid,* Rule 176.

country of the party which is "to effect the performance characteristic of the contract". Where goods or services are supplied in return for money, this means the supplier, since the payment of money is generic to contracts generally. Where the contract is entered into in the course of trade, the country of a party is the country of its principal place of business, except where the performance is to be effected under the terms of the contract through a place of business in another country, in which case it is the latter.

Thus in the Thrombodirect example, if there is no express choice of law clause in the contract for the supply of components to Manufacturing by Chipsrus, the applicable law is that of the Hong Kong Special Autonomous Region, unless the contract specifies that the chips are to be supplied from the plant in Shenzen, in which case the applicable law would probably be that of metropolitan China.

The general presumption (that the country with which the contract is most closely connected is that of the party who is to effect the performance characteristic of the contract) does not apply if it is unclear which party is to effect the characteristic performance or if it appears from the circumstances as a whole that the contract is more closely connected with another country. In the case of a consumer contract, the applicable law is that of the consumer's country, if not otherwise agreed.[1]

The Rome Convention does not prejudice the application of other international conventions,[2] e.g. on international sale of goods. Under English law, the rules of the 1964 Hague Convention apply to international sales of goods if, and only if, the parties expressly agree.[3] The UNCITRAL Vienna Convention on international sales of goods has not been incorporated into English law.

(iii) Applicable law for contracts made before 1 April 1991

The general approach of the common law, applicable to contracts prior to 1 April 1991, is similar to the Rome Convention. Most issues are governed by the "proper law", which can be agreed between the parties, or (in default of agreement) is the law with which the contract has the closest connection. However, there are some differences, including the following:

- Under the common law, an "agreed" choice of law may be express or implied[4] (for example by an agreed place of arbitration[5]). On the other hand, it must be bona fide, legal and not contrary to public policy.[6]

[1] Rome Convention, art 5, Dicey & Morris, *Ibid,* Rule 183. For this purpose, a consumer contract is one where goods or services are acquired for purposes other than the customer's trade or profession.
[2] Rome Convention, art 21.
[3] Uniform Laws on International Sales Act, 1967, s 1(3), 39 *Halsbury's Statutes* (4th edn).
[4] *Amin Rasheed v Kuwait Insurance* [1984] AC 50.
[5] *Hamlyn v Talisker Distillery* [1894] AC 202.
[6] *Vita Foods v Unus Shipping* [1939] AC 277.

- In the absence of any express or implied agreement, the governing law is the law with which the contract has the closest connection. However, the criteria for determining this are different from those applicable to the corresponding concept in the Rome Convention. Under the common law, relevant matters are: the places where the contract is made and performed, the locations of the parties, the terms of the contract and the law governing any related transactions.[1] Thus in the case study, if the terms for the supply of chips by Chipsrus were agreed before 1 April 1991 and use terminology characteristic of English law, it might well be found that the governing law is English and not that of Hong Kong or metropolitan China.

(3) ELEMENTS CONSTITUTING THE CONTRACT

(i) Outline

Having identified the applicable law, it is necessary to consider under that law what contracts exist between which parties with what terms. Since this work is limited to English law, reference must be made to other sources of information if and to the extent that other laws may be applicable.

In identifying the contracts and their terms, it is always necessary to keep the basic principles in view. Under English law the following elements are required to constitute a legally binding contract:

- offer;

- acceptance of the offer;

- intention to create a legally binding relationship;

- consideration or execution as a deed;

- compliance with requirements as to:

    capacity;

    form;

    substantive law and public policy.

The offer and the acceptance are also of fundamental importance in defining the parties and establishing the basis of the terms of the contract.

[1] See *Chitty on Contracts* (27th edn, 1994) para 30-009 et seq.

(ii) Offer and acceptance

The offer and acceptance can be in any form, written or oral. A valid contract can exist even though there is no formal written document. However, informality can sometimes indicate that there was no intention to create a legally binding relationship.

Under English law, the offer and acceptance are objective acts, not subjective intentions. In determining whether, and (if so) what, offer or acceptance has been made, it is necessary to consider how the communications or other acts of the parties would reasonably be understood in the circumstances by a person in the position of the opposite party. Since understanding a communication typically involves discerning the intention of the person making it, reference is frequently made to the intention of a communication or even the intention of the party. However, it is important to keep firmly in mind that, save in exceptional circumstances, the issue is the meaning of the acts, not the actual, subjective intention of the actor. The interpretation of contractual terms in the light of this fundamental principle and the exceptions to it are discussed further below.

There has to be an acceptance of the offer, i.e. the acceptance must correspond to the offer. A communication which is described as an acceptance, but does not accept all material terms of the offer, is not an acceptance, and normally constitutes a counter-offer, which may or may not be accepted by the party making the original offer. The consequences for identifying the contractual terms are discussed in section (5) below.

(iii) Intention to create a legally binding relationship

There has to be an intention to create a legally binding relationship. Sometimes this is expressly excluded in the communications between the parties, for example by the phrase "subject to contract". However, the phrase "without prejudice" does not preclude the formation of a legally binding contract; it merely means that the correspondence is not to be used generally in legal proceedings, but can be used to show that an agreement was reached and its terms.

If not expressly excluded, an intention to create a legally binding relationship will readily be inferred in commercial matters, even if they are carried on in an informal way. Thus, in the Thrombodirect example, English courts would be likely to hold that there is a valid contract between Systems and B&W Agon, even though the relationship is an informal one based on mutual trust. The conclusion could be affected by evidence as to the circumstances which led to the arrangements. It would also be a difficult issue to determine whether there were any binding contracts between the different companies in the Thrombodirect group.

Even where there is a legally binding contract between parties, there are often questions as to whether particular statements are to be treated as terms of it. For example, Jumpon might have mentioned to Wytook (perhaps on the bowling green) that one of his staff was familiar with Legacy computers and there would be no difficulty in making any necessary changes to the operating system, and he would be happy to include this in the work being done for Thrombodirect. One issue would be whether such a statement is incorporated into any offer and acceptance constituting a contract: this is discussed further in section (5) below. However, there may also be a question as to whether there was an intention to create a legally binding relationship by this statement. (There is also a possibility of a claim for misrepresentation, as to which see Chapter 6.)

The decision in *Evans v Merzario*[1] may be relevant in this connection. In this case, a statement by a freight forwarding agent to a regular customer that goods would henceforth be packed in containers stowed under deck was held to be binding in relation to a consignment a year later.

(iv) Consideration or execution as a deed

For a contract to be legally binding, it must be supported by "consideration" or executed by deed. The requirement of consideration is that each party must provide something to the other party - either a benefit to the other party or a detriment to the party desired by the other party. As long as there is some consideration, the courts will not investigate its sufficiency, however small it is.

In a commercial context, this requirement can be relevant where a party requires further payment in order to carry out existing obligations. Even if the other party agrees, he may not be bound on the ground that there was no consideration for the additional payment. Thus if Anocomp were to demand an additional payment for ensuring that the stock control system is Year 2000 compliant, and Thrombodirect were to agree with this, Thrombodirect might still be in a position subsequently to refuse or even to recover this payment, on the ground that Anocomp was already bound to design the software to be compliant in the first place and additionally bound to ensure its continuing operability under the maintenance contract. However, it has been held that there may be consideration where ensuring performance of the original obligation confers a practical benefit on the opposite party (as it usually does),[2] and the current position is unclear.

Suppliers may well avoid the difficulty under this rule by combining rectification of Year 2000 problems with other upgrading not already required under the contract. This would provide good consideration except in the case where a determined customer declines the offer to upgrade. Alternatively, a supplier could try to ensure that the customer signs an agreement to pay the additional charge as a deed.

---

[1] [1976] 1 WLR 1078.
[2] *Williams v Roffey* [1991] 1 QB 1.

The consideration requirement can also be relevant where a party tries to incorporate additional terms, such as exclusions or limitations of liability, after the contract has been made. Even if the other party agrees to these terms, they may not be binding for lack of consideration.

As indicated above, a contract by deed does not have to be supported by consideration. Since 31 July 1990, the requirements have been very simple: the document must be expressed to be signed as a deed and be signed:

- in the case of a company, by two directors or one director and the company secretary;[1]

- in the case of an individual, by the individual in the presence of a witness.[2]

One significant consequence of making a contract by deed is that the limitation period is twelve years instead of six.

(v) **Requirements of capacity, form, substantive law and public policy**

A Introduction

The final element is that the contract must meet various requirements regarding capacity, form, substantive law and public policy. Although these are unlikely to be issues in relation to Year 2000 problems, the main requirements will be identified briefly so that the issues can be recognised if they do arise.

B Capacity

A contract must be within the legal powers of the parties as determined under the law of their incorporation or domicile. In principle, the powers of a company incorporated under English law are defined by its memorandum of association, but the validity of its acts cannot now be challenged on the basis of the memorandum.[3] The powers of a statutory body are defined by the statute which created it. The powers of the UK national government are determined in part by statutes and in part by the common law applicable to the royal prerogative. The contracts of minors under 18 are binding on the other party but not on the minor unless they are for "necessaries" or are ratified by him after becoming 18. A computer game is probably not a "necessary", but a computer might be.

---

[1] Companies Act 1985 (as amended), s 36A, 8 *Halsbury's Statutes* (4th edn); Law of Property (Miscellaneous Provisions) Act 1989, s 1, 37 *Halsbury's Statutes* (4th edn)..
[2] Law of Property (Miscellaneous Provisions) Act, 1989, s 1, 37 *Halsbury's Statutes* (4th edn).
[3] Companies Act 1985 (as amended), s 35, 8 *Halsbury's Statutes* (4th edn). Provisions applicable prior to this date protected parties dealing in good faith with the company: Companies Act 1985, s 35. In the case of charitable companies, the other party is only protected if it gave full consideration without notice of the company's charitable status and the limitation of its powers: Charities Act 1993, s 65(3), 5 *Halsbury's Statutes* (4th edn).

Even where a contract is within the powers of a party, there can be a further question as to whether a director, employee or other person representing the party had power to bind it. The powers of the board of directors of an English company are deemed to be free of any limitation in favour of a person dealing with the company in good faith.[1] However, this does not cover the position in relation to personnel who are not directors. For example, a programmer working for a supplier (possibly as a freelance sub-contractor) may agree to resolve a particular problem pointed out to him when he visits the customer, but management at the supplier may have a different view. If this agreement meets the other requirements for a valid contract, it will be binding if the programmer had actual or apparent authority to commit the supplier.[2] Whether he had apparent authority would depend on the circumstances and this issue can be difficult to resolve.

C Form

There are very few formal requirements under English law applicable to contracts for the supply of goods or services. However, the following may possibly be relevant in some cases where Year 2000 issues arise:

- hire purchase and other regulated consumer credit transactions have to be in writing and signed by the consumer;[3]

- assignments of copyright,[4] debts and other obligations[5] have to be in writing and signed by the assignor to be valid in law.[6]

D Substantive law and public policy

Contracts or particular provisions of them can be invalid under various statutes or on grounds of public policy. Sometimes the objection may relate to the entirety of the contract. However, in most cases, the objection concerns particular provisions of the contract and the rest of the contract may remain valid if the invalid provisions can be severed without frustrating the main objects of the contract.[7] Traditionally, English courts have applied a "blue pencil" test, notionally striking through the invalid provisions, and then considering what is left. However, there is high authority in relation to subordinate legislation for preferring a test of "substantive severability" to

---

[1] Companies Act 1985 (as amended), s 35A, 35B, 8 *Halsbury's Statutes* (4th edn).
[2] Cf *Royal British Bank v Turquand* (1856) 6 E&B 327, *Freeman and Lockyer v Buckhurst Park Properties* [1964] 2 QB 80.
[3] Consumer Credit Act 1974, 11 *Halsbury's Statutes* (4th edn).
[4] Copyright Designs and Patents Act 1988, s 90(3), 11 *Halsbury's Statutes* (4th edn).
[5] Law of Property Act 1925, s 36, 37 *Halsbury's Statutes* (4th edn).
[6] Informal assignments may have effects under equitable principles; this is not explored here in view of its complexity and peripheral relevance. Assignments on sale also have to be stamped, following payment of stamp duty: Stamp Act 1891, Sch 1, unless they are duly certificated as having a value of less than £60,000.
[7] *Chemidus Wavin v TERI* [1977] FSR 181.

"textual severability",[1] so that obligations which are independent as a matter of substance can be severed, even if they cannot be separated in the wording.

Rules of law and public policy which may potentially be relevant to Year 2000 problems include the following:

- The right of a lawful user of a program to decompile it for the purpose of creating an interfacing program cannot be excluded by a contractual term.[2] This may be relevant to certain Year 2000 fixes, as discussed in Chapter 7 below.

- Various restrictions on competition are contrary to the Treaty of Rome, arts 85, 86, the Restrictive Trade Practices Act 1976[3] and the common law on restraint of trade. These may be relevant to provisions restricting customers' choice of assistance in remedying Year 2000 deficiencies.

- Exclusion and limitation of liability are subject to statutory control, as discussed in section (7) below.

(4) PARTIES TO THE CONTRACT

(i) Introduction

Under current English law, a contract does not create or alter the rights or obligations of persons which are not parties to it[4]; this is known as the doctrine of privity. Scots law allows for third party rights and the implications in relation to shrink-packaged software were discussed in *Beta Computers v Adobe*.[5] The Law Commission has also proposed that English law be amended to allow a third party to enforce a contract for its benefit.[6] However, as matters stand, the English rule of privity remains applicable to contracts governed by English law. It is therefore fundamental to identify the parties to a contract governed by English law.

(ii) Identification of the parties

The parties to a contract are those who made the offer and acceptance constituting the contract. However, these acts can be done by a person as agent for another person. If so, a contract is formed between the principal and the other party, whether or not the existence of the principal was disclosed. A

---

[1] *DPP v Hutchinson* [1992] 2 AC 783.
[2] Copyright Designs and Patents Act 1988, s 296A, 11 *Halsbury's Statutes* (4th edn) (implementing EC Directive 91/250, art 6).
[3] This is expected to be replaced in the near future by a new statute modelled on the Treaty of Rome, arts 85, 86.
[4] *Beswick v Beswick* [1968] AC 58.
[5] [1996] FSR 367.
[6] Report No 242 (1996).

person can contract both as principal and also, in relation to part or all of the subject-matter, as agent for another person. Thus in *New Zealand Shipping v Satterthwaite*,[1] it was held that a carrier agreed a term limiting the liability of dockers (amongst others) as an agent for the dockers, which were therefore able to rely upon it. Similarly, a distributor of package software could act as agent for the original supplier of the software, resulting in a contract between the original supplier and the customer. This could, for example, enable the original supplier to rely on its clauses excluding or limiting liability for defects (which may include lack of Year 2000 compliance). Other ways in which a contract may be formed between an original supplier and a customer are discussed in section (5) below.

For the purposes of the law, companies in the same group are different persons from each other and from their employees, directors or shareholders.[2] Accordingly, a company does not normally have any contractual claims against a supplier which contracted with another member of the group. In the Thrombodirect example, Manufacturing cannot in principle claim for breach of contract by Anocomp, because Anocomp's contract is with Systems. On the same principle, an employee or director may be sued for unlimited damages by a company's customer for misrepresentation or negligence, even if liability of the company is excluded or limited by a contractual provision.[3] Thus individuals such as Magnus Millichip, Jack Curite, David Wytook and Jonathan Jumpon could all be personally at the receiving end of Year 2000 claims.

However, in such circumstances it may be possible to establish or infer that a company contracted as agent for other members of the group and/or for its employees or directors. In the Thrombodirect example, contracts with IT suppliers have been made by Systems, but it could be argued that Systems was acting as agent for Manufacturing and other group companies.

Partners acting in the course of partnership business are agents for all the other partners. However similar points arise as above in relation to their employees.

(iii) Effects and limits of the privity rule

As stated above, the privity rule means that persons who are not party to a contract do not in principle acquire rights under it and cannot claim relief in respect of breaches of it. A further corollary of the rule is that a party to a contract cannot normally claim damages in respect of the loss suffered by a non-party as a result of the other party's breach.[4] Thus, in principle, Thrombodirect Systems Limited would not be able to claim against a supplier such as Anocomp for losses suffered by Manufacturing as a result of a failure

---

[1] [1975] AC 154.
[2] *Prudential v Newman* [1982] Ch 204, [1982] 1 All ER 354; *Scrutton v Midland Silicones* [1962] AC 446, [1962] 1 All ER 1.
[3] *Scrutton v Midland Silicones* [1962] AC 446, [1962] 1 All ER 1.
[4] *Beswick v Beswick* [1968] AC 58.

to ensure Year 2000 compliance in breach of a contract between Systems and Anocomp.

As indicated above, this difficulty might be overcome on the ground that Systems entered into the contract as agent for Manufacturing, in which case Manufacturing could claim against Anocomp directly. Alternatively, Systems might be able to claim that the deficiency of the software supplied by Anocomp put Systems in breach of its obligations to Manufacturing. Systems might then be able to include its liability to Manufacturing or its costs of complying with its obligations to Manufacturing in its claim for damages from Anocomp. However, there are potential difficulties in this route: it may not be possible to establish the existence of intra-group contracts or obligations, e.g. for lack of intention to create a legally binding relationship; and the intra-group liability, even if established, may be too remote to be recoverable as damages. On the other hand, recent decisions have upheld claims by contracting parties in respect of damage to third parties which they had an interest in reimbursing even though they were not legally bound to do so.[1]

The benefits intended to be conferred on the non-party may also be secured where the contract can be enforced by one of the parties by injunction. This may be the case where the contract is specifically enforceable[2] or where breach of a negative covenant can be restrained by injunction. As discussed below, specific performance is unlikely to be available for failure to provide Year 2000 compliance, except perhaps in the case where a compliant upgrade is available and the argument is merely whether an additional payment should be charged. It is possible that an exclusion or limitation of liability, phrased as a covenant not to sue, might be enforceable by negative injunction, although there appears to be no precedent for this.[3] The availability of injunctive relief is discussed further below.

Another possible way round the privity rule exists where contractual rights can be said to be held on trust for a non-party whom they benefit, so that the non-party can enforce them directly under the equitable jurisdiction.[4] However, it has been held that this concept is not applicable to the benefit of exemption clauses.[5]

Finally, where a contractual exclusion clause does not confer a contractual right on a third party, the latter may still be able to rely on it as qualifying its duty of care to one of the parties to the contract. This principle has been applied particularly in relation to construction contracts,[6] and it should be equally applicable in the context of IT projects. However, it is more difficult to see how this analysis could enable a third party to benefit from a limitation (as opposed to exclusion) of liability clause.

---

[1] *Linden Gardens Trust v Lenesta Sludge Disposals* [1994] AC 85, *Darlington BC v Wiltshier Northern* [1995] 1 WLR 68.
[2] As in *Beswick v Beswick* [1968] AC 58.
[3] See Chitty on Contracts, para 14-039.
[4] *Les Affréteurs Réunis v Leopold Walford* [1919] AC 901.
[5] *Southern Water Authority v Carey* [1985] 2 All ER 1077.
[6] *Pacific Associates v Baxter* [1990] 1 QB 993.

(5) TERMS OF THE CONTRACT

(i) Introduction

It is a fundamental rule of English contract law that the rights and obligations created by a contract are to be found in its terms and nowhere else. Where the law imposes contractual rights or obligations on the parties it does so by inserting implied terms or limiting the effects of express terms of the offer and acceptance. The terms of a contract accordingly comprise:

- express terms contained in the offer and acceptance;
- implied terms imposed by law or implicit in the offer and acceptance.

A correct legal analysis requires identification of these terms and their interpretation so far as relevant to the issues to be resolved.

(ii) Express terms

A Identification

In order to identify the express terms of a contract, it is necessary first to isolate the offer and acceptance constituting the contract. Sometimes these comprise separate communications between the parties, for example a letter making an offer and a letter in reply accepting. In other cases, there is a single document, as where the parties sign a written contract which is taken as being both an offer and an acceptance. In some circumstances the acceptance can be constituted by conduct, for example unwrapping or using package software[1] may be regarded as equivalent to using the smoke ball in the well-known case *Carlill v Carbolic Smoke Ball*,[2] which was held to constitute an acceptance of the manufacturer's offer to pay £100 to any person who contracted influenza despite using it.

The communications and conduct of the parties must therefore be examined to identify communications constituting unconditional offers to be contractually bound and communications or conduct accepting such offers. In carrying out this exercise, it is necessary to distinguish between unconditional offers to be contractually bound on the one hand and mere invitations to put forward an offer or proposals on the other. In determining the character of a communication, it is necessary to interpret it objectively, in terms of what it means to a reasonable recipient in the circumstances.[3] As mentioned above, the term "subject to contract" is normally taken as negating an intention to be contractually bound.

---

[1] Cf. *Beta Computers v Adobe Systems* [1996] FSR 367.
[2] [1893] 1 QB 256.
[3] *Reardon Smith Line v Hansen-Tangen* [1976] 1 WLR 989.

There can be a difficulty where each of the parties has sought to impose its own terms on the other in a "battle of forms". For example, an offer may be made by a supplier incorporating its standard terms. A potential customer may purport to accept the offer by placing an order on its own standard terms. Normally this will rank as a counter-offer. The supplier may then dispatch the goods with a delivery note and invoice bearing its terms. This may be regarded as a counter-offer by the supplier which the customer accepts on taking delivery of the goods.

Even where a communication does not form part of the main contract between the parties, it may still be regarded as giving rise to a collateral contract,[1] for example that in return for the other party entering into the contract, the party making a statement about the software warrants that the statement is true, or based on reasonable grounds[2] or that it is able and has a genuine intention to carry out some operation. Collateral contracts may also be found in the common situation where representations are made by a sales company, but the equipment is sold by a finance company. The sales company may argue that it is not party to any contract and the finance company may disclaim any responsibility for the representations by the sales company. However, the sales company may be bound by a collateral contract under which it warrants that the representations are true in return for the customer entering into the main contract with the finance company.[3] There is often room for argument as to whether there is a collateral contract, and if so what its terms are, and the conclusion may well depend on the general merits of the case.

Communications prior to the offer and acceptance constituting the contract may also be relevant in the following ways:

- They may make the supplier aware of the purposes for which software or hardware is to be acquired. As discussed below, there is an implied term in contracts for the supply of goods and similar contracts that the goods are fit for purposes made known to the supplier.

- They constitute part the factual matrix which is to be taken into account in interpreting the terms of the contract: see below.

- They may be relevant in determining whether exclusions or limitations of liability were reasonable, as in the *St Albans*[4] case, where ICL's ultimatum to sign the contract figured largely in the decision: see below.

- They may provide the basis for a claim of misrepresentation. This is discussed generally below. However, it should be noted here that contracts frequently contain provisions seeking to exclude liability for any representation not incorporated in the contract. Such clauses

---

[1] See *Esso v Mardon* [1978] QB 801; *Howard Marine v Ogden* [1978] QB 574; *City of Westminster Properties v Mudd* [1959] Ch 129.
[2] As in *Esso v Mardon* [1978] QB 801.
[3] See e.g. *McKenzie Patten v British Olivetti*, QBD 11/1/84, noted 48 MLR 344.
[4] *St Albans v ICL* [1997] FSR 251.

are subject to the legislation controlling exclusion clauses as discussed below.

- They may be relevant to a claim for negligence against the supplier: see below.

The offer and acceptance may contain in themselves the full terms or they may incorporate some other document or statement by reference. The incorporation may be express or implied by a consistent course of previous dealing between the parties on the terms in question[1] or a practice of the trade.[2] Incorporation by express reference can be effective even if one of the parties never examined the terms so incorporated,[3] although the more stringent the terms, the more they must be emphasised to be effectively incorporated.[4] It is sufficient under English law that the other party accepted an offer which referred to terms which it could have examined. On the other hand, additional terms are not incorporated by reference if no reference is made to them until after the contract has been made.[5] Such additional terms are only contractually binding if they are incorporated into an offer and acceptance constituting a further contract meeting the requirements outlined above, including the existence of consideration.

Software or hardware which is not Year 2000 compliant may have been supplied in a variety of circumstances. While the above principles must be applied with regard for the circumstances of each case, it may be helpful to consider some of the issues which arise in two common situations:

- the supply of "shrink-wrapped" package software;
- bespoke IS developments

B Shrink-wrapped package software

Package software is commonly supplied from its producer to the eventual user through other parties, such as software distributors, or manufacturers or distributors of hardware onto which the software is loaded. Producers of software normally wish to impose their terms on the ultimate user, including restrictions on the use of the software and exclusions or limitations of liability. They often seek to achieve this by enclosing the software in sealed packaging bearing their terms and a statement that opening the packaging will constitute an acceptance of these terms. This is commonly reinforced by further notices which are caused to appear on the screen when the software is installed, and the installer may be required to press a key or click a mouse indicating "acceptance" of the terms.

---

[1] *Spurling v Bradshaw* [1956] 1 WLR 461, *McCutcheon v David MacBrayne* [1964] 1 WLR 125.
[2] and cf. the Scots case, *Beta Computers v Adobe Systems* [1996] FSR 367.
[3] *Parker v South Eastern Railway* (1877) 2 CPD 416.
[4] *Interfoto* [1989] 1 QB 433.
[5] *Olley v Marlborough Court* [1949] 1 KB 532; *Thornton v Shoe Lane Parking* [1971] 2 QB 163.

In some cases, it is made clear to the customer in advance of any transaction that the software is supplied subject to the producer's conditions. For example, this may be stated (with sufficient prominence) in an advertisement inviting telephone orders or on the exterior of packaging of products displayed for self-service. If so, there seems little doubt that the contract for supply either incorporates the producer's conditions or contains a term that the customer will accept those conditions. However, in other cases, the distributor has not specified this in advance of the supply of the software and the payment for it. In these cases, the contract between the customer and the distributor may have been made when the customer's order was accepted by the distributor, hence before the customer received the software package including the producer's terms. The question arises as to whether these terms are binding and, if so, as between which parties.

In the Scots case, *Beta Computers v Adobe Systems*[1] it was held that an agreement for the supply of an upgrade of package software was subject to the *ius quaesitum tertio* of the producer of the software, and the contract was not complete until the customer had accepted the producer's terms. In the result, the customer (which had not accepted the producer's terms) was not obliged to pay for the upgrade. A significant factor in this case was that by the date of the transaction there was an established trade practice that standard software was supplied in packaging bearing the producer's terms and conditions. It would seem that the analysis would have been different in relation to contracts before this trade practice became established and well known, as could be the case in relation to Year 2000 deficient software.

A similar result could be reached under English law in the circumstances of the *Adobe* case on the basis that the contract is conditional upon the customer accepting the producer's terms and the distributor acts as agent for the producer for this purpose. However, the position is not at all clear, and it is possible that an agreement for the supply of package software would be regarded as unconditional in the absence of any express reference by the distributor to the producer's conditions.

If so, the question then arises as to whether there is a separate contract between the producer and the customer constituted by the customer's acceptance of the producer's terms in opening the package and using the software (and perhaps confirming acceptance in the course of installation). On one view the customer is merely exercising its entitlement to use the software, and there is no consideration for any additional terms. On another view, the customer is accepting the producer's offer of a licence on the terms set out, in the same way as Miss Carlill accepted the offer of the Carbolic Smoke Ball company.

In deciding between these two possibilities, the following factors appear to be important:

- whether the customer would be entitled to use the software if it did not accept the producer's terms; and

[1] [1996] FSR 367.

- (as in the *Adobe* case) whether a normal customer would expect that its use of the software would be subject to the producer's terms.

These issues may be related in practice, in that if the customer is not entitled to use the software without further licence, the court may readily infer that the customer accepts terms by virtue of which its use is lawful; while if a further licence is in fact unnecessary, the court may suppose that the reasonable customer would not accept stringent terms for little or no benefit. Indeed if there is no benefit to the customer beyond the entitlement which it has already acquired, the existence of a contract would be excluded for lack of consideration.

Thus, whether the customer is entitled to use the software without further licence is a critical issue. The determination of this issue involves an examination of the intellectual property position under English common law and EC law. At common law, where the owner of intellectual property controlling the use of goods in the United Kingdom sells such goods subject to conditions restricting their use or resale, these conditions are in principle binding on a subsequent purchaser who acquires the goods with notice of the conditions, but not binding on a purchaser who acquires without notice of them.[1] It is a controversial question as to whether goods become free of the conditions once they have been acquired by a purchaser without notice so that such a purchaser can transfer an unencumbered entitlement.[2] On the other hand, the position under the common law is different where the goods were originally sold by a person other than the owner of the intellectual property in the United Kingdom, for example a licensee under a limited licence or an assignee of the intellectual property in another country. In this case, the purchaser of goods can acquire no right to use them in the United Kingdom which the licensee or assignee did not have.[3]

However, the common law position is affected by EC law. For the purpose of the provisions in the Treaty of Rome on the free movement of goods between member states (articles 30-36[4]) and competition (articles 85-86), where intellectual property rights are exploited by the commercialisation of physical supports bearing copies of the protected work, the rights are exhausted once such goods have been placed on the market by or with the consent of the owner of the rights. The owner of the rights is then not entitled to control the further distribution or use of the goods. The rights are considered to be exhausted in accordance with this principle where the goods are placed on the market under a licence granted by the owner of the rights, but not where they are placed on the market by an assignee of the rights in another member State.[5] However, rights are not exhausted where they are exploited by reference to the extent of use, and additional rights controlling such use are not necessarily exhausted by placing the goods on the market.[6] The case law of the European court appears

---

[1] *National Phonograph v Menck* (1911) 28 RPC 229.
[2] *Roussel Uclaf v Hockley* [1996] RPC 441; David Wilkinson [1997] EIPR 319.
[3] *Manufactures des Glaces v Tilghman* (1883) 25 Ch D 1.
[4] Using the pre-Amsterdam Treaty numbering.
[5] *IHT v Ideal Standard* [1995] FSR 59.
[6] *Warner v Christiansen* [1988] ECR 2605; *Basset v SACEM* [1987] ECR 1747; *Ministère Public v Tournier* [1989] ECR 2921; *Coditel v Ciné Vog* [1980] ECR 881.

to have developed in later cases away from the original strict rule of exhaustion.

EC Directive 91/250 provides that "in the absence of specific contractual provisions", acts which would otherwise infringe rights in a computer program do not require authorisation where they are necessary for the use of the program "by the lawful acquirer in accordance with its intended purpose". Section 50C of the Copyright Designs and Patents Act 1988, which came into force on 1 January 1993, purports to implement this provision of the Directive by providing that it is not an infringement of copyright for a "lawful user" of a computer program to copy it, provided that this is "necessary for his lawful use and is not prohibited under any term or condition of an agreement regulating the circumstances in which his use is lawful". It is further provided that "a person is a lawful user of a computer program if (whether under a licence to do any acts restricted by the copyright in the program or otherwise), he has a right to use the program".

Section 50C therefore differs from the Directive in referring to a "lawful user" rather than a "lawful acquirer", and to "term or condition of an agreement regulating the circumstances in which his use is lawful" rather than "specific contractual provisions". The implementing legislation should be interpreted so far as possible to mean the same as the Directive, and if this cannot be achieved as a matter of interpretation, it is arguable that section 50C as a whole is invalid, in that the Statutory Instrument enacting it[1] would be ultra vires the European Communities Act under which it was adopted. It is thought that the courts would prefer to give section 50C an interpretation consistent with the Directive.

Thus in the case of a sale after 1 January 1993, it appears that the customer does not need any further licence for normal use of the software, and hence is not likely to be bound by the producer's terms which were not drawn to its attention before the contract. In the case of a sale prior to that date, there may be some room for argument that the producer's terms confer a benefit in clarifying what would otherwise be a complicated and doubtful position. However, it is thought that in most cases the conclusion may still be that the producer's terms confer no advantage on the customer that it does not already enjoy, and that accordingly the customer should not be bound by them.

It might still be possible to resist this conclusion in circumstances where the producer's terms offer the customer an additional benefit beyond the minimum entitlement to reproduce the program so far as necessary for use for its intended purpose, for example a licence to load the software onto a laptop as well as a desktop provided the two are not used at the same time. However, if such benefits are not desired by many customers, there may be difficulties in using them as a reason for finding a binding contract on the producer's terms.

Finally, even if the producer's terms are not contractually binding, they could still be relevant to some issues in tort such as the duty of care owed by

---

[1] Copyright (Computer Programs) Regulations 1992, SI 1992/3233, 5 *Halsbury's Statutory Instruments*.

the producer and the risks assumed by the customer; these issues are discussed in Chapter 6 below.

C Bespoke IS developments

IS projects commonly proceed by an invitation to tender ("ITT"), a tender and then a formal written contract. Usually there is also correspondence and discussions in between these stages. The ITT may have been preceded by the preparation of a functional specification. The question may arise as to whether statements or "promises" prior to the written contract are contractually binding.

Sometimes the functional specification, ITT and/or tender are expressly incorporated in the contract, as in the *St Albans* case,[1] and in such cases their provisions form part of the contract. Where this is not the case, the general principle is that the terms of the contract are to be found in the contract and not in earlier reports, negotiations or discussions. This is often reinforced by an express provision of the written contract that it constitutes the entire agreement and understanding between the parties. The presence of such a provision makes it difficult to find a collateral contract, but does not completely rule it out. In addition, as mentioned above, earlier documents can still be relevant as part of the factual matrix, or in relation to the implied term of fitness for purpose, or as giving rise to a claim for misrepresentation[2] or negligence.

Contracts for bespoke IS development typically contain provisions governing amendments to the specification or any other aspect of the parties' obligations. It is commonly provided that any amendment must be in writing signed off by personnel of appropriate seniority. In many cases a detailed change control procedure is set out and it is provided that no change to the obligations is to be effective or acted upon unless it has been adopted in accordance with the procedure. Provisions such as these may limit the apparent authority which the personnel of a party might otherwise have to agree to variations on behalf of that party. However, it is thought that it is not possible to prevent a contract being varied by a subsequent agreement supported by consideration on both sides and made between personnel having actual authority, even if a previously prescribed procedure has not been followed.[3]

D Interpretation

Having identified the contractual terms, it is necessary to determine their meaning and hence the scope of the parties' obligations and rights. Under English law, the meaning of contractual terms is in general determined objectively on the basis of what they would mean to a reasonable person in the

---

[1] *St Albans v ICL* [1997] FSR 251.
[2] See *Thomas Witter v TBP Industries* [1996] 2 All ER 575.
[3] Cf *Berry v Berry* [1929] 2 KB 316, where an agreement by deed was varied by a subsequent agreement in writing.

circumstances; not what was in fact intended or understood.[1] Accordingly, the course of negotiations between the parties and their subsequent conduct are in general irrelevant to the interpretation of the contractual terms.[2] However, the terms are interpreted against the factual background or "matrix" known to all parties, and communications prior to the contract may be relevant to this extent.[3] They may also be relevant to further factors affecting the contractual terms, such as rectification and estoppel, discussed in section (6) below.

Some more recent contracts contain express provision that the software to be supplied will be Year 2000 compliant. Where this is the case, it is (one hopes) unlikely that the system will lack compliance in itself, and if it does, there should be no difficulty of contractual interpretation. However, issues might still arise, for example from problems of interfacing with older software or hardware. It may then be necessary to determine whether the express term covered interfacing with other software or hardware. This will be easier if the parties anticipated that the new software would have to interface with older systems.

On the other hand, until recently contracts did not normally contain Year 2000 clauses. In many cases they contained express terms that the software or system would have specified functionalities - often by incorporation of a specification of requirements, functional specification, ITT and/or tender - usually without specifying for how long the software or system must maintain such functionality. It seems that such provisions should be interpreted as requiring the delivery of the specified functionality for a reasonable period of time, subject perhaps to reasonable maintenance.[4]

The difficult question in many such cases will be how long this period should be. It is relevant that the computer industry has been undergoing rapid development over the last 30 years or more and in many cases it may have been reasonably anticipated that software would be replaced after a few years. On the other hand, it would be more difficult to say that software required to meet, e.g. specified requirements of stock control, complies with this requirement if it only does so for two years following its supply.

Contracts commonly contain *force majeure* clauses, providing that obligations are suspended if their performance is prevented[5] or delayed[6] due to acts beyond the control of the parties. Sometimes such clauses use the wider word "hindered" as well as "prevented".[7] The scope of such clauses depends on their particular terms and the circumstances. The advent of the millennium could be said to be in the nature of an Act of God, beyond the parties' control. However, it is thought that in most cases the event does not make performance impossible or delayed, since it will generally be possible to achieve Year 2000

---

[1] *Smith v Lucas* (1881) 18 Ch D 531; *Prenn v Simmonds* [1971] 1 WLR 1381; *Reardon Smith Line v Hansen-Tangen* [1976] 1 WLR 989.
[2] *Inglis v Buttery* (1878) 3 App Cas 552; *Prenn v Simmonds* [1971] 1 WLR 1381.
[3] *Reardon Smith Line v Hansen-Tangen* [1976] 1 WLR 989.
[4] Cf *Saphena Computing v Allied Collection Agencies* [1995] FSR 616.
[5] *Tennants v Wilson* [1917] AC 495.
[6] *Fairclough Dodd v Vantol* [1957] 1 WLR 136.
[7] *Tennants v Wilson* [1917] AC 495.

compliance if adequate steps are taken in advance. On the other hand, there could be provisions in contracts for facilities management which become impossible to carry out in the Year 2000; and Year 2000 problems might well fall within wider *force majeure* provisions which cover hindrance as well as impossibility.

The significance of terms requiring a party to use "best endeavours" is sometimes overlooked. Where such terms refer to a particular objective, they are in principle enforceable and require the party to take all steps which would be taken by a prudent, determined and reasonable person, acting in his own interest and desiring or anxious to achieve that objective.[1] Accordingly, if a party is obliged, for example by a maintenance or facilities management contract, to use best endeavours to ensure that a computer system remains operable, this could be an onerous obligation come the Year 2000.

Provisions excluding or limiting liability are discussed in section (7) below. Escrow provisions are discussed in Chapter 7.

(iii) Implied terms

A In general

Contractual terms may be implied under English law

- by statute;

- by common law:

    as a matter of law;

    as the obvious intention of the parties;

    as necessary to make the contract commercially effective.

Terms which would otherwise be implied by law may be excluded by express terms of the contract,[2] subject to certain restrictions, in particular relating to

- exclusions and limitations of liability;

- the making of back-up copies of software;[3]

- anti-competitive provisions.

---

[1] *Simpson v Clayton* 4 Bing NC 748; *Sheffield District Railway v Great Central Railway* (1911) 27 TLR 451; *Terrell v Maby Todd* (1952) 69 RPC 234; *IBM v Rockware* [1980] FSR 335; *Transfield v Arlo* [1981] RPC 141.
[2] Sale of Goods Act 1979, s 55, 39 *Halsbury's Statutes* (4th edn); Supply of Goods and Services Act 1982 s 11,16, 39 *Halsbury's Statutes* (4th edn).
[3] Copyright Designs and Patents Act, s 296A(1)(a), 45 *Halsbury's Statutes* (4th edn).

B Terms implied by statute

(a) Historical development

The statutory provisions implying terms in contracts have been extended and amended in a number of stages. It is necessary to consider the legislation applicable when the contract was made. Changes were made:

- on 3 January 1995 by the Sale and Supply of Goods Act 1994;[1]

- on 19 May 1985 by the Sale of Goods Act 1979;[2]

- on 4 January 1983 and 4 July 1983 by the Supply of Goods and Services Act 1982;[3]

- on 18 May 1973 by the Supply of Goods (Implied Terms) Act 1973.[4]

This text will consider the current position and the position prior to the 1994 Act since the last major change in 1985. Many of the changes in the recent legislation appear to be improvements or modernisations of style, and the House of Lords has observed that the more recent legislation is not to be construed as "virginal text".[5] Therefore, it is probably the case that the law on many points has not in fact been changed by the more recent legislation. Nevertheless, some caution should be applied and, if necessary, other works consulted if the contract was made before 1985.

(b) Distinction between goods and services

The statutory provisions for implied terms differentiate between:

- contracts for the supply of goods (i.e. sale of goods,[6] hire purchase,[7] other contracts for the transfer of property in goods,[8] and hire of goods[9]);

- contracts for the supply of services[10];

- other contracts.

In consequence, the obligations on a supplier implied by statute are generally rather stricter in the case of a supply of goods than in the case of a supply of services. However, as discussed further below, it is not clear whether or in what circumstances the supply of software is to be regarded as the supply of goods or

---

[1] 39 *Halsbury's Statutes* (4th edn).
[2] 39 *Halsbury's Statutes* (4th edn).
[3] 39 *Halsbury's Statutes* (4th edn).
[4] 11 *Halsbury's Statutes* (4th edn).
[5] *Slater v Fining* [1996] 3 All ER 398.
[6] Sale of Goods Act 1979, ss 1, 13–15, 39 *Halsbury's Statutes* (4th edn).
[7] Supply of Goods (Implied Terms) Act 1973, ss 8–12A 11 *Halsbury's Statutes* (4th edn).
[8] Supply of Goods and Services Act 1982, ss 1–5, 39 *Halsbury's Statutes* (4th edn).
[9] Supply of Goods and Services Act 1982, ss 6–11, 39 *Halsbury's Statutes* (4th edn).
[10] Supply of Goods and Services Act 1982, ss 12–16, 39 *Halsbury's Statutes* (4th edn).

services or some other type of contract. The inconsistency of treatment which would result from the statutory distinction between these categories may well be mitigated by implying terms under the common law in contracts for the supply of software similar to those implied by statute in contracts for the supply of goods, even where it is considered to be a supply of services rather than goods.[1] However, this does not altogether eliminate inconsistency, because:

- One cannot be sure that such terms will be considered by the court to be implied at common law.

- Such terms are unlikely to be implied at common law if there are express terms of differing scope. By contrast, the terms implied by statute are excluded by express terms only if these are inconsistent with the implied terms,[2] and difference in scope does not amount to inconsistency.[3]

- In addition, there are particular provisions regulating attempts to exclude or limit liability for breach of the statutory implied terms which do not apply to similar terms implied at common law.

Accordingly, it may be important to establish whether there is a supply of goods or services. Clearly hardware is goods, even if it includes embedded programs, and it has been held in Australia that a computer system comprising hardware and software is also to be treated as goods.[4] However, the position regarding software is more controversial.

In *St Albans v ICL*, the Court of Appeal concluded that the supply of a tangible article containing software is a supply of goods, while the supply of software by electronic transfer without any transfer of a physical medium is to be regarded as the supply of services.[5] However, these observations were not necessary for the decision and are therefore not strictly binding as a precedent. By contrast, in the Scottish case *Beta Computers v Adobe Systems*,[6] Lord Penrose held that contracts for the supply of proprietary software are not properly regarded as for the supply of goods, but rather are *sui generis*, since their principal object is to allow the use of the intellectual property in the programs. However, it is submitted that the reasoning of this decision is in part unsatisfactory. The use of many products (which would undoubtedly be regarded as goods) is subject to intellectual property rights of greater or lesser importance. The fact that such rights exist in software does not provide a tenable basis for distinction.

The point is controversial, but it is thought that English courts are likely to follow *St Albans* on this point.

---

[1] *St Albans v ICL* [1997] FSR 251.
[2] Sale of Goods Act 1979, s 55(2), 39 *Halsbury's Statutes* (4th edn).; Supply of Goods and Services Act 1982, ss 11(2), 16(2), 39 *Halsbury's Statutes* (4th edn).; Supply of Goods (Implied Terms) Act 1983, s 12, 11 *Halsbury's Statutes* (4th edn)..
[3] *Salvage Association v CAP Financial Services* [1995] FSR 654.
[4] *Toby Construction Products v Computa Bar* (1983) 2 NSWLR 48.
[5] [1997] FSR 251. This point was only discussed in the judgment of Sir Iain Glidewell at 264–6, but it should noted that Nourse and Hirst LJJ agreed with this conclusion: see ibid at 259, 264.
[6] [1996] FSR 367.

C Terms implied in contracts for the supply of goods

The terms implied by statute into contracts for the supply of goods can be summarised as follows:

- That the goods are of merchantable quality / satisfactory quality;

- That the goods are fit for a particular purpose made known to the supplier;

- That the goods will correspond to description;

- That the supplier has a right to transfer the goods and the customer will enjoy quiet possession.

(a) Merchantable quality / Satisfactory quality

The term implied by statute in contracts for the supply of goods which is likely to be most relevant to Year 2000 issues is that goods supplied in the course of business must be of "merchantable quality" in the case of contracts prior to 3 January 1995 or "satisfactory quality" in the case of contracts on or after 3 January 1995.[1]

The condition that the supply is in the course of business should not be overlooked. "Business" is defined as including a profession or the activities of a public authority.[2] However, a one-off project might not constitute a business for this purpose, even if payment is made.[3]

Goods are of "merchantable quality" under the pre-1995 provisions if they are as fit for the purposes for which such goods are commonly supplied as is reasonable to expect in the circumstances, including the price and any description. There may be a breach of this term even though the supplier used reasonable skill and care; in this important respect this implied term is more stringent than the term implied in a contract for the supply of services discussed below.

Whether lack of Year 2000 compliance breaches this term would depend on the circumstances, including the date of the contract and the reasonably expected lifetime of the software. As mentioned above in relation to express terms as to functionality, there have been enormous developments in the computer industry over the last three decades and it has been reasonable to anticipate that software would be replaced after a few years. Accordingly, lack of Year 2000 compliance in a package supplied in 1980 may well not

---

[1] Sale of Goods Act 1979, s 14, 39 *Halsbury's Statutes* (4th edn); Supply of Goods and Services Act 1982, ss 4,9, 39 *Halsbury's Statutes* (4th edn); Supply of Goods (Implied Terms) Act 1973, 11 *Halsbury's Statutes* (4th edn).
[2] Sale of Goods Act 1979, s 61(1), 39 *Halsbury's Statutes* (4th edn); Supply of Goods and Services Act 1982, s 18(1), 39 *Halsbury's Statutes* (4th edn); Supply of Goods (Implied Terms) Act 1973, 11 *Halsbury's Statutes* (4th edn).
[3] See *Chitty on Contracts*, para 41-071.

contravene this term; while a similar problem in software supplied after 1997 probably would. Clearly, the issue is more difficult in relation to software supplied at various points between these dates. The technical difficulty and expense (or lack of them) involved in achieving Year 2000 compliance at the date of the contract would also be relevant. As discussed in Chapter 3 above, when computer memory was a scarce and expensive resource, it was probably reasonable to compress dates by providing only two digits for the year. Parties contesting the point would be well advised to muster evidence relating to the commercial and technical circumstances of the computer industry at the date of the contract.

In *Saphena Computing v Allied Collection Agencies*[1] it appears to have been held by Recorder Havery QC and the Court of Appeal that it was not a breach of the implied term of fitness for purpose to supply bespoke software still containing bugs which the supplier was able and willing to rectify as and when it was notified during or after acceptance testing. It could be argued that a remediable Year 2000 deficiency should be treated similarly in relation to the implied terms of merchantable quality and fitness for purpose. However, it appears that in *Saphena*, the relationship between the parties was terminated before the date on which the supplier was bound to complete the development (which had been delayed due to the modifications of the customer's requirements).

The position would appear to be different where software still has bugs after the date on which the supplier was bound to complete the development. While a supplier may be able to avert damage to its customer by remedial action before Year 2000, it is thought that this possibility does not make the software of merchantable quality if (on the basis of the above principles) it is not. Furthermore, it would be unsatisfactory if the customer did not have a remedy against the supplier until after the millennium. Many things might have happened by then, including the possibility that the supplier might have gone out of business.

The 1994 Act substituted a requirement of "satisfactory quality" for "merchantable quality". Goods are of "satisfactory quality" under the new provisions if they meet the standard that a reasonable person would regard as satisfactory in the circumstances, including the price and any description. Thus far there appears to be little difference between the new provisions and the previous ones. However, the new provisions go on to state that the quality of goods may include in appropriate cases the following (among other) aspects:

- fitness for all the purposes for which goods of the kind are commonly supplied;
- appearance and finish;
- freedom from minor defects;
- safety;
- durability.

[1] [1995] FSR 616.

While these criteria may have been inserted in contemplation of consumer goods marred by blemishes or having poor durability[1] and may have been relevant in any event under the old provisions,[2] the emphasis given to them by the 1994 Act could assist a complaint about software with fixable Year 2000 bugs, which might be characterised "minor defects", or software with limited durability in that it is unsuitable for use after 1999.

Both the new and the old provisions are inapplicable to the extent that defects are specifically drawn to the customer's attention before the contract is made. It appears that disclosure in small print may not be enough to draw a defect to the customer's attention. Both the new and the old provisions are also inapplicable, if the customer examines the goods *before* the contract is made, to defects which that examination ought to reveal. In many cases these provisos do not apply because the contract is made without prior examination of the software, even if there is provision for subsequent acceptance testing. However, in some cases there may be a demonstration of the software in advance of the contract or a customer may perhaps be caught out if the contract is not tied up at the proper time. There would then be a question as to whether the customer's examination ought to have included inputting post-1999 dates.

Where goods are supplied by reference to a sample, there is an implied term that they will be free from any defect making them unmerchantable (pre-1995 contracts) or making their quality unsatisfactory (post-1994 contracts) which would not be apparent on reasonable examination of the sample. The new provisions confirm the corollary, that the requirement of satisfactory quality does not extend to any defect which would have been apparent on reasonable examination of the sample. Again, there could be a question as to whether lack of Year 2000 compliance should have been apparent on reasonable inspection of a sample of a software package, e.g. a demonstration copy.

(b) Fitness for a particular purpose

Where goods are supplied in the course of business, and the customer makes known expressly or by implication to the supplier[3] a particular purpose for which the goods are being obtained, there is an implied term that the goods are reasonably fit for that purpose.[4] However, this does not apply where the circumstances show that the customer does not rely, or it is unreasonable for him to rely, on the skill or judgment of the supplier.

The purpose made known to the supplier may be that the goods are to be used in conjunction with certain other equipment of the customer. However, this does not mean that the goods supplied must be compatible with abnormal

---

[1] See the English and Scottish Law Commissions' Report on the Sale and Supply of Goods, Cm 137 (1987), Pt 3.

[2] See *Rogers v Parrish* [1987] QB 933.

[3] This includes the real supplier where the goods are sold to a finance company and then to the customer: Sale of Goods Act 1979, s 14(3)(b), 39 *Halsbury's Statutes* (4th edn).

[4] Sale of Goods Act s 14(3), 39 *Halsbury's Statutes* (4th edn); Supply of Goods and Services Act 1982, 39 *Halsbury's Statutes* (4th edn); Supply of Goods (Implied Terms) Act 1973, 11 *Halsbury's Statutes* (4th edn).

features of that other equipment not disclosed to the supplier.[1] This point may be very relevant where a serious Year 2000 problem results from the combined use of separate software packages.

(c) Correspondence to description

If goods are supplied by reference to a particular description, there is an implied term that the goods correspond with the description.[2] Accordingly, where software supplied in 1997 is described as a "debt management package", it is arguable that it does not correspond with this description if it cannot continue to manage after the beginning of Year 2000 debts incurred prior to this date.

(d) Right to transfer and quiet possession

There are further statutory implied terms that the supplier has or will have a right to transfer property or possession in the goods and the customer will have undisturbed possession of them.[3] These terms are breached if the transfer or use of the goods infringes an intellectual property right.[4] Accordingly, it seems likely that these terms would be breached if fixing a Year 2000 defect to allow continued use of the software supplied would infringe copyright. However the position may well be different where software is altered in breach of copyright in order to allow continued use of other software supplied under a different contract.

These terms do not apply to the extent that the encumbrance is disclosed or known to the customer before the contract is made.

(e) Terms implied in contracts for the supply of services

The terms implied by statute in contracts for the supply of services which are likely to be relevant to Year 2000 issues are that where the supplier is acting in the course of business, it must carry out the service with reasonable care and skill and in a reasonable time (if this is not specified in the contract).[5]

The reasons for the practice of programmers not to provide for the transition to the Year 2000 are discussed in Chapter 3. Although it may have been justified at one time, its application in more recent software may be found to involve a lack of reasonable skill and care. However, it is thought that it would

---

[1] *Slater v Finning* [1996] 3 All ER 398.

[2] Sale of Goods Act ss 13, 39 *Halsbury's Statutes* (4th edn); Supply of Goods and Services Act 1982, ss 3,8, 39 *Halsbury's Statutes* (4th edn);Supply of Goods (Implied Terms) Act 1973, 11 *Halsbury's Statutes* (4th edn).

[3] Sale of Goods Act ss 12, 39 *Halsbury's Statutes* (4th edn);Supply of Goods and Services Act 1982, ss 2,7, 39 *Halsbury's Statutes* (4th edn);Supply of Goods (Implied Terms) Act 1973, 11 *Halsbury's Statutes* (4th edn).

[4] *Niblett v Confectioners Materials Co* [1921] 3 KB 387, *Microbeads v Vinhurst Road Markings* [1975] 1 WLR 218.

[5] Supply of Goods and Services Act 1982, ss 13, 14, 39 *Halsbury's Statutes* (4th edn).

be more difficult to establish liability on this basis than under the merchantable quality/satisfactory quality term implied in contracts for the supply of goods. Again, the evidence as to the technical and commercial considerations applicable at the relevant time will be important.

(f) Exclusion of terms implied by statute

As mentioned above, the terms implied by statute in contracts for the supply of goods or services can be excluded by express terms only if these are inconsistent with the implied terms. "Inconsistent" means "incompatible". Thus it was held that a term requiring a supplier to remedy faulty work free of charge, if demonstrated to result from a serious failure to exercise proper skill and reported within one month, did not displace the broader implied term to use reasonable care and skill.[1] Nor was this implied term excluded by an integration clause ("this Agreement is the complete and exhaustive statement of the agreement between the parties") or a provision for acceptance of deliverables.

The exclusion or limitation of liability for breach of the implied terms is in any case restricted by the provisions of the Unfair Contract Terms Act 1977, discussed in section (7) below.

D Terms implied by common law

(a) Terms implied as a matter of law

Some terms are implied as a matter of law into contracts of particular types. In particular, it seems that in the case of a contract for the bespoke creation of a product, involving a combination of supply of services and goods, the common law is ready to imply a term that what is supplied will be reasonably fit for the purpose for which it supplied.[2] This principle has been applied in particular in relation to software.[3]

In a contract for the sale of goods, a licence under the seller's intellectual property rights to repair the goods is normally implied; this may be relevant to fixing Year 2000 defects, as discussed below.

In contracts of employment, the common law implies various terms which may be indirectly relevant to Year 2000 issues, including:

- that the employee will not disclose confidential information acquired in the course of his employment, e.g. by telling the medical press that Thrombodirect is in serious difficulties with Year 2000 compliance;[4]

---

[1] *Salvage Association v CAP Financial Services* [1995] FSR 654.
[2] *Samuels v Davis* [1943] KB 526.
[3] *St Albans v ICL* [1997] FSR 251.
[4] However, the defence of disclosure in the public interest might apply: see *Lion Laboratories v Evans* [1985] QB 526, but cf *Schering v Falkman* [1982] QB 1.

- that the employee will serve the employer faithfully, e.g. that he will not moonlight for a competitor;[1]

- that intellectual property rights created in the course of employment belong to the employer.[2]

(b) Terms implied as the obvious intention of the parties

Terms may also be implied in particular circumstances if it is the obvious intention of the parties that they should apply. The well-known "officious bystander" is pressed into service here to ask the parties if they meant the term in question; if the honest answer of both parties would be "of course", the term is to be implied.[3] Thus in one case, structural engineers were commissioned to design a warehouse for oil drums; it was held that there was an implied warranty that the floor would be suitable for the movement of the drums.[4]

Similarly, where a person is commissioned to design and/or write software for a particular purpose which might reasonably be expected to extend beyond 1999, there may well be an implied term that the software will be suitable for that purpose,[5] and lack of Year 2000 compliance would be a breach of such a term.

(c) Terms implied as necessary to make the contract commercially effective

A term may also be implied on the ground that it is necessary to make the contract commercially effective.[6] It is important to note that the term must be necessary; it is not enough that it would appear to be more fair or reasonable. There is a substantial overlap between terms implied on this ground and those implied by the "officious bystander" test. However, some cases may rest more easily on this footing.

For example, if Thrombodirect's contract with Anocomp provides for Anocomp to maintain the stock control system for five years from 1995, it must be a necessary term that Anocomp would ensure that it would be Year 2000 compatible, either when developing the software or by subsequent enhancement.

---

[1] Although in practice it is very difficult to control programmers such as Kevin Culater if they have found something more interesting to do.
[2] This is buttressed by provisions of intellectual property statutes which specify that the employer is the first owner of the right where the subject-matter was created in the course of employment: e.g. Copyright Designs and Patents Act 1988, s 1, 11 *Halsbury's Statutes* (4th edn); Patents Act 1977, s 39, 33 *Halsbury's Statutes* (4th edn).
[3] *Shirlaw v Southern Foundries* [1939] 2 KB 206.
[4] *Greaves v Baynham Meikle* [1975] 1 WLR 1095.
[5] As in *St Albans v ICL* [1997] FSR 251.
[6] *The Moorcock* (1889) 14 PD 64.

(6) FACTORS ALTERING CONTRACTUAL RIGHTS AND OBLIGATIONS

(i) In general

The rights and obligations provided by the express and implied contractual terms can be altered by various matters, which must be considered in order to complete an analysis of the contractual position.

(ii) Termination

Contracts may be terminated in accordance with their express or implied terms, or by agreement of the parties, or where a repudiation of the contract by one of the parties is accepted as discharging the contract. Termination in principle discharges the parties from further performance of the primary terms of the contract, but does not normally affect their accrued rights, for example to remedies for breaches, or the operation of secondary provisions intended to govern the relationship on termination, such as arbitration of disputes or exclusions or limitations of liability.[1] Thus in the *Saphena* case,[2] although the software did not meet the contractual requirement of fitness for purpose at the date of termination by mutual agreement, the customer was not entitled to complain, since the date by which the fitness for purpose had to be achieved had not yet arrived, and the supplier was discharged from further performance by the termination. The remedy of termination is discussed further below.

(iii) Variation

Contracts can be varied at any time by further agreement. The legal effect of an agreed changed control procedure is discussed above.

(iv) Frustration

Where an event creates a fundamental change in the relevant circumstances, a contract is frustrated and the parties are in principle discharged from further performance,[3] although statute has provided for quantum meruit payments in various circumstances.[4] The question arises as to whether lack of Year 2000 compliance might frustrate a contract for maintenance or facilities management. However, the doctrine of frustration does not normally apply to events which are foreseen,[5] and it is thought that it would be unlikely that it would be held to

---

[1] *Suisse Atlantique*; Unfair Contract Terms Act 1977, 11 *Halsbury's Statutes* (4th edn).
[2] [1995] FSR 616.
[3] *Davies v Fareham* [1956] AC 696.
[4] Law Reform (Frustrated Contracts) Act 1943, 11 *Halsbury's Statutes* (4th edn).
[5] *Paal Wilson v Hannah Blumenthal* [1983] 1 AC 854.

apply in relation to events which are bound to occur as in the case of the millennium.

(v) Mistake

Contractual rights and obligations may be adjusted in various circumstances where one or both parties have made a mistake, and this area constitutes an exception to the general principle that the subjective intentions of the parties are irrelevant to the contractual obligations assumed by their objective acts.

A contract is generally considered to be void if the parties make a fundamental mutual mistake as to the quality of the subject-matter.[1] It could thus be argued that a maintenance contract is invalidated on this principle where there is a mutual mistake that the system is capable of continuing to function in the Year 2000 when it is not.[2] A contract may also be void where one party knows that there is only an appearance of agreement because the other party has made a mistake in relation to the terms of an offer or acceptance.[3] The signature of an agreement or other contractual document may be regarded as a nullity if the party signed it under a fundamental mistake as to its nature not attributable to his own negligence.[4]

A written contract may be rectified or rescinded if:

- the document does not accurately record the agreement between the parties[5]; or

- one party knows that the other party has made a mistake in relation to the terms of the document and does not point it out, so that it is inequitable for the first party to take advantage of the mistake.[6]

A contract may also be rescinded if there is a fundamental mutual mistake, and it appears that rescission on this basis may be more readily available than a finding that the contract is void on this ground.[7]

(vi) Misrepresentation

A party induced to enter into a contract by a misrepresentation may rescind it, provided that it is still possible substantially to restore the status quo before the contract and that the party has not affirmed the contract. A contract may be affirmed for this purpose by lapse of time even if the party had no knowledge of the true facts.[8] It is thought that rescission is unlikely to be available in most

---

[1] *Bell v Lever Brothers* [1932] AC 161.
[2] Cf *Sheikh v Ochsner* [1957] AC 136.
[3] *Hartog v Colin and Shields* [1939] 3 All ER 566.
[4] This is the doctrine of *non est factum* as discussed in *Saunders v Anglia* [1971] AC 1004.
[5] *Joscelyne v Nissen* [1970] 2 QB 86.
[6] *Thomas Bates v Windham* [1981] 1 WLR 505.
[7] *Associated Japanese Bank v Credit du Nord* [1989] 1 WLR 255.
[8] *Leaf v International Galleries* [1950] 2 KB 86.

Year 2000 cases, because of lapse of time and/or impossibility of restoration of the status quo ante.

Remedies for misrepresentation in tort are discussed in Chapter 6.

(vii) Estoppel

Where a party has assumed a supposed state of affairs, either because the other party allowed or encouraged the first to do so[1] or both parties have proceeded on the same basis,[2] the second may be prevented from denying that state of affairs, to the extent that this would be inequitable. Statements between contracting parties before or after the contract which are not incorporated as terms of the contract may have legal effects on the basis of this principle. Thus, for example, if a party has led the other party to believe that it is obliged by the contract to ensure Year 2000 compliance, and in reliance on this the other party has not made alternative arrangements to secure the compliance of its system, the first party may be estopped from denying the assumed obligation.

(viii) Control of exclusion /limitation of liability

Finally, provisions excluding or limiting liability may be invalid under the Unfair Contract Terms Act 1977[3] or under the Unfair Terms in Consumer Contracts Regulations 1994[4] which implement EC Directive 93/13. This subject is covered in detail in the following section.

(7) EXCLUSION AND LIMITATION OF LIABILITY BY CONTRACTUAL TERMS

(i) Introduction

It is very common for contracts for the supply of computer hardware and software to contain provisions excluding and limiting liabilities which might arise under contract or tort. It is likely that the validity and effect of such provisions will be a significant issue in many cases arising out of lack of Year 2000 compliance.

It has been a basic principle of English law that parties are free to choose the terms on which they contract, and this principle has been applied where the

---

[1] The encouragement may relate to an existing state of affairs (estoppel by acquiescence) as in *Crabb v Arun DC* [1976] Ch 179; or as to future conduct (promissory estoppel) as in *Hughes v Metropolitan Railway* (1877) 2 App Cas 439.

[2] Estoppel by convention, as in *Amalgamated Investment & Property v Texas Commerce International Bank* [1982] QB 84.

[3] 11 *Halsbury's Statutes* (4th edn).

[4] SI 1994/3159, 17 *Halsbury's Statutory Instruments*.

choice has been more theoretical than practical. There is no general principle of good faith or fairness in English contract law.[1] However, in recent years, first the courts, then the British Parliament and most recently the Council of the European Communities have mitigated the rigour of the traditional English approach to exclusions and limitations of liability.

The courts resisted the application of such terms by:

- applying strict standards for the incorporation of such terms into contracts;

- interpreting such terms restrictively;

- holding that such terms were no longer applicable where the contract had been terminated as a result of a fundamental breach of the party seeking to invoke them.

In the period prior to the legislation, the courts, and particularly the Court of Appeal under Lord Denning MR, stretched these principles in order to do justice. However the third principle was ultimately rejected as a proposition of law by the House of Lords[2] and legislation;[3] and while the first two principles remain in the law, following the introduction of comprehensive legislation it is no longer necessary to stretch them.[4] Accordingly some of the decisions on the interpretation of exclusion and limitation clauses in the period prior to the legislation should now be viewed with caution.

The issue of incorporation has been discussed above. Here the following issues will be addressed:

- the interpretation of such clauses excluding or limiting liability; and

- the statutory control under:

  the Unfair Contract Terms Act;[5] and

  the Unfair Terms in Consumer Contracts Regulations.[6]

(ii) Interpretation

Clauses excluding or limiting liability are interpreted restrictively,[7] applying two principles, both referred to as *contra proferentem*:[8]

---

[1] *Interfoto* [1989] 1 QB 433.
[2] *Suisse Atlantique* [1967] 1 AC 361.
[3] Unfair Contract Terms Act 1977, s 9, 11 *Halsbury's Statutes* (4th edn).
[4] *George Mitchell v Finney Lock* [1983] QB 284 per Lord Denning MR, apparently approved by Lord Diplock on appeal [1983] AC 803.
[5] 11 *Halsbury's Statutes* (4th edn).
[6] SI 1994/3159, 17 *Halsbury's Statutory Instruments*.
[7] *Ailsa Craig Fishing v Malvern Fishing* [1983] 1 WLR 964.
[8] *Pera Shipping v Petroship* [1984] 2 Lloyd's Rep 363; *Salvage Association v CAP Financial Services* [1995] FSR 654.

- if the provision is capable of more than one meaning and other factors are finely balanced, the interpretation less favourable to the party introducing the term into the contract will be preferred[1]

- doubts and ambiguities are resolved against the party benefiting from the term, particularly where the benefit runs counter to that party's normal obligations.[2]

It has been held that these principles are applied more strictly to exclusion clauses than clauses limiting liability[3]

The decision in *Salvage Association v CAP Financial Services*[4] illustrates the continuing applicability of these principles of interpretation to contracts for IS projects:

- By clause 11 of the contract, CAP (the supplier), warranted that the services would be provided by competent persons exercising appropriate skills; that it would remedy without charge any defect arising from a serious failure to exercise such skills if it was notified within one month of formal acceptance of the system; and that if it remedied such work within a reasonable time it would have no other liability for faulty work except under a maintenance and support agreement.

- Clause 11 concluded "If CAP fails to perform its obligations under this Condition, then the provisions of Condition 12 shall apply".

- Clause 12 specified that CAP's liability under Condition 11 was in lieu of any warranty or condition of any kind; that except as provided in Conditions 11 and 12, CAP and its employees would not be under any liability including for any injury, damage, expense or loss of any kind resulting from the supply of the services; that CAP would not be liable for any indirect or consequential losses, damage, injury or costs; and that CAP's total liability in connection with the contract would be limited to £250,000 in respect of physical damage to or loss of tangible property and £25,000 in any other case apart from negligence resulting in death or injury.

- It was held that clause 12 could be interpreted as applying generally, or only in the event of a failure to carry out the provisions of clause 11. The latter was to be preferred since:

  - otherwise the last sentence of clause 11 was unnecessary;

  - it was the interpretation less favourable to the supplier.

- On this basis, since the customer had properly terminated the contract for fundamental breach before the system had been

---

[1] *John Lee v Railway Executive* [1949] 2 All ER 581.
[2] *Photo Production v Securicor* [1980] AC 827.
[3] *George Mitchell v Finney Lock* [1983] AC 803.
[4] [1995] FSR 654.

completed and accepted, the limitations and exclusions in clause 12 were not applicable.

It is common to exclude liability for "consequential loss or damage". It has been held that this does not cover loss resulting directly and naturally in the ordinary course of events from the breach, but only loss which is more remote[1]

(iii) The Unfair Contract Terms Act

A General scope

The Unfair Contract Terms Act 1977[2] ("UCTA") applies generally to contracts governed by English law made on or after 1 February 1978,[3] subject to certain exceptions, of which the following may be relevant to Year 2000 problems:

- UCTA does not apply to International Sale of Goods Contracts.[4] These are defined in the Act in similar terms to the Hague Convention:

    - the possession or ownership of goods must pass *and*

    - the parties' places of business must be in different states *and*

        the goods must be carried from one state to another *or*

        the acts constituting offer and acceptance must be done in different states *or*

        the goods are delivered in different state to that where the acts constituting offer and acceptance take place

In the Thrombodirect example, the contract with Chipsrus for the supply of components would escape the operation of UCTA on this ground.

- Some of the provisions of UCTA[5] do not apply to contracts so far as they relate to the creation, transfer or termination of a right or interest in intellectual property.[6] In *The Salvage Association v CAP Financial Services,*[7] it was confirmed that this proviso only applies to clauses relating specifically to intellectual property rights, and did not cover other clauses of a contract simply because it contained provisions relating to intellectual property. Therefore this proviso is unlikely to affect Year 2000 issues.

---

[1] *Croudace Construction v Cawood's Concrete Products* [1978] 2 Lloyd's Rep 55.
[2] 11 *Halsbury's Statutes* (4th edn).
[3] Some control of exclusion and limitation clauses was introduced in statutes relating to the supply of goods prior to the Unfair Contract terms Act 1977. Other works should be consulted if this is relevant.
[4] UCTA, s 26, 11 *Halsbury's Statutes* (4th edn).
[5] UCTA, ss 2–4, 11 *Halsbury's Statutes* (4th edn).
[6] UCTA, s 1(2) and Sch 1, para 1(c), 11 *Halsbury's Statutes* (4th edn).
[7] [1995] FSR 654.

- Where English law is the governing law only by choice of the parties, the main provisions of UCTA do not apply.[1] However, the control of exclusion or limitation of liability for misrepresentation does apply in this situation.[2]

UCTA also applies where the contract is governed by a foreign law by virtue of a choice of law clause and:

- the choice of law clause appears to have been imposed wholly or mainly for the purpose of enabling the party imposing it to evade the operation of UCTA; *or*

- one of the parties dealt as a consumer and was habitually resident in the UK and the essential steps necessary for making the contract were taken in the UK.

Thus the contract between Anocomp and Thrombodirect may be subject to UCTA if it appears that Delaware law was chosen to evade UCTA, but not otherwise.

B Terms which are automatically invalid

In relation to some matters UCTA prohibits the exclusion or limitation of liability altogether. These matters are:

- Liability for death or personal injury resulting from negligence[3] (meaning the breach of any contractual duty to exercise skill and care, or any duty of care under the law of negligence or the Occupiers' Liability Act 1957[4]). Therefore, it would not be possible to exclude or limit liability to patients who suffer injury resulting from a failure of Thrombodirect equipment as a result of negligence in relation to Year 2000 issues.

- Liability for breach of the term of quiet possession implied by statute in contracts for the supply of goods.[5] As noted above, this term may be relevant if there is any objection based on intellectual property rights to the customer revising software to ensure Year 2000 compatibility.

- Liability to a person who dealt as a consumer for breach of the terms as to merchantable/satisfactory quality, fitness for purpose and correspondence with description and sample implied by statute in contracts for the supply of goods.[6] As noted above, the implied terms

---

[1] UCTA, s 27, 11 *Halsbury's Statutes* (4th edn).
[2] UCTA, s 8, 11 *Halsbury's Statutes* (4th edn).
[3] UCTA, s 2(1), 11 *Halsbury's Statutes* (4th edn).
[4] UCTA, s 1(1), 11 *Halsbury's Statutes* (4th edn).
[5] UCTA, ss 6(1), 7(3A), 11 *Halsbury's Statutes* (4th edn).
[6] UCTA, ss 6(2), 7(2), 11 *Halsbury's Statutes* (4th edn).

as to quality and fitness for purpose are particularly relevant and are likely to be breached by many Year 2000 defects.

A person deals as a consumer if:

- he neither makes the contract in the course of business nor holds himself out as doing so

- the other party makes the contract in the course of business *and*

- where the contract is for the supply of goods, they are of a type ordinarily supplied for private use or consumption.[1]

Supplies of goods to businesses for the private use of personnel of the businesses have held to be consumer sales for this purpose.[2] Thus the acquisition of games software by Thrombodirect plc for its directors and their families might well qualify under this provision, with the consequence that any exclusion or limitation of liability for breach of the implied terms of satisfactory quality and fitness for purpose would be invalid.

C Terms which are invalid unless they are reasonable

In relation to a wider range of matters, UCTA prohibits the exclusion or limitation of liability except to the extent that this is reasonable. These matters include:

- Liability for negligence (causing loss or damage other than death or personal injury).[3]

- Liability for breach of the terms as to merchantable/satisfactory quality or fitness for purpose implied by statute in contracts for the supply of goods (to persons not "dealing as consumers").[4] As discussed in section (5) above, it appears that the supply of software on a physical medium will be regarded as the supply of goods and hence subject to this provision. However, the supply of software by electronic transmission will not be regarded as the supply of goods, so that the exclusion or limitation of liability under similar terms which may be implied by common law will not be caught by this provision of UCTA, although it may of course be caught by other provisions, for example the provision applying to standard terms.

- Liability for misrepresentation prior to the contract.[5] It should be noted that this does not apply to misrepresentations made after the contract.

---

[1] UCTA, s 12, 11 *Halsbury's Statutes* (4th edn).
[2] *R&B Customs Brokers v UDT* [1988] 1 WLR 321; *Rasbora v JCL Marine* [1977] 1 Lloyd's Rep 645.
[3] UCTA, s 2(2), 11 *Halsbury's Statutes* (4th edn).
[4] UCTA, ss 6(3), 7(3), 11 *Halsbury's Statutes* (4th edn).
[5] UCTA, s 8, 11 *Halsbury's Statutes* (4th edn); Misrepresentation Act 1967, s 3, 29 *Halsbury's Statutes* (4th edn).

- Liability to

  a person dealing as a consumer *or*

  any person dealing on the standard terms of the person seeking to exclude or limit liability

  for

  breach of contract

  a contractual performance substantially different from what was reasonably expected or no performance at all in respect of the whole or any part of the contractual obligation.[1]

The application of s 3 of the Act to standard terms is of considerable significance since a large proportion of software is supplied on such terms. Moreover, a wide interpretation has been given to the phrase "standard terms". It includes terms which have not been used previously but which have been prepared in contemplation of use in future contracts.[2] Even where important matters were negotiated, it was held that terms which remained effectively untouched in the course of negotiation and incorporated into the final contract were "standard terms" and that the customer was "dealing" on them.[3]

D The requirement of reasonableness

(a) The basic test

The provisions of UCTA described above prohibit the exclusion or limitation of liability "except in so far as the contract term satisfies the requirement of reasonableness". The requirement of reasonableness is that the term was a fair and reasonable one to be included having regard to the circumstances which were or ought reasonably to have been known to the parties or in their contemplation at the time the contract was made.[4] Thus an exclusion of liability which turns out to be unreasonable in particular circumstances may still be valid if it was reasonable to include it at the time of the contract.

On the other hand, the Court of Appeal accepted in *Stewart Gill v Horatio Myer*[5] that the term as a whole must satisfy the requirement of reasonableness, although it appears that this point was not argued. Thus, if the term would exclude liability in circumstances where this would be unreasonable, the term as whole is invalid, even though its application in the instant case would be reasonable. It is thought that this interpretation is not justified by the wording of the Act, which uses the phrase "in so far as", and that it may be overturned in

---

[1] UCTA, s 3, 11 *Halsbury's Statutes* (4th edn).
[2] *Salvage Association v CAP Financial Services* [1995] FSR 654.
[3] *St Albans v ICL* [1997] FSR 251; *Salvage Association v CAP Financial Services* [1995] FSR 654.
[4] UCTA, s 11(1), 11 *Halsbury's Statutes* (4th edn).
[5] *Stewart Gill v Horatio Myer* [1992] QB 600.

the House of Lords.[1] On any view, it seems that it should be possible to sever provisions applying the traditional "blue pencil" test, and the test of "substantial severance" propounded by the House of Lords in the Greenham Common case[2] in relation to delegated legislation may perhaps find favour in this context. According to this approach, provisions covering matters which are separate in substance can be severed even if this cannot be done by merely striking through words in the text.

The onus lies on the party seeking to rely on the term to show that it satisfies the requirement of reasonableness.[3] Strictly speaking, if the view accepted by the Court of Appeal is correct, reasonableness must be shown in relation to all circumstances in which the term might apply; although it is thought that in practice a good case on the more relevant issues will prevail even if the evidence does not extend to peripheral matters. Great care must be taken in marshalling and presenting the case at any trial. The assessment by the trial judge will not be altered on appeal unless the Court of Appeal is satisfied that it was based on an erroneous principle or was plainly and obviously wrong.[4]

(b) Particular factors to be taken into account

The Act specifies that where the issue relates to liability for breach of the terms of merchantable/satisfactory quality and fitness for purpose implied by statute in contracts for the supply of goods, regard should be had in particular to the following matters:

- the strength of the bargaining positions or the parties, taking into account alternative means by which the customer's requirements could have been met;

- whether the customer received an inducement to agree to the term in question or had an opportunity to enter into a similar contract with others without this term;

- whether the customer knew or ought reasonably to have known of the existence and extent of the term;

- whether it was reasonable at the time of the contract to expect compliance with a condition where liability is excluded or limited if the condition is not complied with;

- whether the goods were manufactured, processed or adapted to the order of the customer.

---

[1] The point was left open by Lord Diplock in *George Mitchell v Finney Lock* [1983] 2 AC 803 in relation to the different wording of the Sale of Goods Act 1979, s 55(4), 39 *Halsbury's Statutes* (4th edn), restating the law applicable to contracts for the sale of goods made prior to the entry into force of the UCTA.

[2] *DPP v Hutchinson* [1992] 2 AC 783.

[3] UCTA, s 11(5), 11 *Halsbury's Statutes* (4th edn).

[4] *George Mitchell v Finney Lock* [1983] 2 AC 803; *St Albans v ICL* [1997] FSR 251.

Although these criteria are specified as applying only in relation to certain types of liability, at least the first three are evidently relevant generally to assessing whether an exclusion or limitation was reasonable.[1] It has in any event been held that the following matters should always be considered:[2]

- equality (or otherwise) of bargaining power;

- availability (or otherwise) of alternative sources;

- the difficulty of the task in relation to which liability is sought to be excluded;

- the practical consequences of the decision on reasonableness, including the ability of the respective parties to bear the loss, the availability to either party of insurance, and the possible desirability of spreading occasional losses among a large number of customers

Where liability is limited to a specified sum of money, the Act states that regard should be had in particular to the following matters:

- the resources which the party seeking to limit liability could expect to be available for meeting it;

- the availability of insurance.

Again, it seems that these criteria would also be relevant generally to exemption clauses and other limitations of liability.

(c) Application in practice

The courts have been prepared to strike down restrictive exclusion and limitation clauses even in commercial contracts between large organisations. In *St Albans v ICL*,[3] the defendant's terms had been reviewed together with other aspects of its tender by Coopers & Lybrand[4] on behalf of the plaintiff council and scored 18 out of 20, in contrast to 12 out of 20 for the main alternative, IBM. However, the courts concluded that the limitation of liability to £100,000 was not reasonable[5] given that:

- The Council was in a weak bargaining position, even though this was partly its own fault (or the fault of its advisers). All other suppliers capable of carrying out the project used largely the same conditions.

- The figure of £100,000 had not been justified and was small in relation to the potential risk and the actual loss.

---

[1] *The Flamar Pride* [1990] 1 Lloyd's Rep 434; *St Albans v ICL* [1997] FSR 251.
[2] *Smith v Bush* [1990] 1 AC 831; *St Albans v ICL* [1997] FSR 251; *Salvage Association v CAP Financial Services* [1995] FSR 654.
[3] [1997] FSR 251.
[4] This was prior to the appointment of one of the authors of the present work as head of IP and IT law at Coopers & Lybrand .
[5] Scott Baker J [1995] FSR 686, affirmed by the Court of Appeal [1997] FSR 251.

- ICL held product liability cover in an aggregate sum of £50 million worldwide.

- The practical consequences, that ICL was able to insure and pass on the cost of insurance, and that since it stood to make the profit it should also carry the risk. (This reasoning was slightly inconsistent, since if the matter was covered by insurance, ICL did not carry the risk.)

In *Salvage Association v CAP Financial Services*, [1] a limitation of liability to £25,000 for loss other than death, injury or physical damage was held not to satisfy the requirement of reasonableness, on the assumption that it applied even where the system had not been accepted by the customer. The decisive factor appears to have been the evidence that the supplier's management knew that £25,000 was far too low and had decided to revise it to £1 million. There was also evidence that the customer could not insure the project with a realistic premium, whereas the supplier was insured for £5 million with an excess of £500,000 and a premium of £457,644 (apparently considered realistic).

On the other hand, it appears that if not for the evidence that the £25,000 was known to be wrong, the judge might have been satisfied that CAP's limitation of liability met the requirement of reasonableness. He noted that exclusion and limitation clauses, particularly in relation to indirect and consequential loss, are an accepted feature of contracts for IS projects; that the parties were of equal bargaining power and the customer could have gone to competitors of the supplier; and that the contracts were negotiated with the assistance of professional advisers over a considerable period of time.

Furthermore, the judge considered that on a proper interpretation the limit of liability only applied where the system was deemed to be accepted following successful testing in accordance with defined criteria, and the position under UCTA was only considered in case this interpretation was incorrect. On this interpretation, the judge observed that the strict limits on the supplier's liability "do not appear entirely unreasonable", given that they would only apply once the system had been tested and accepted and the supplier would have continuing obligations under a maintenance and support agreement.

It has been observed in the House of Lords that in commercial matters where the parties are not of unequal bargaining power and risks are normally borne by insurance, the parties should be free to apportion the risks as they think fit.[2] However, the judge in the *Salvage Association* case commented that this observation is only applicable where insurance is available to both parties.[3]

In the light of these cases, the following guesses may be hazarded as to the likely position in IS project contracts:

- complete exclusion of the implied terms of satisfactory quality and fitness for purpose is unlikely to be considered reasonable;

[1] [1995] FSR 654.
[2] Per Lord Wilberforce in *Photo Production v Securicor Transport* [1980] AC 827.
[3] *Salvage Association v CAP Financial Services* [1995] FSR 654.

- limitation of liability to a figure significantly less than the insurance cover which the supplier could obtain is unlikely to be considered reasonable;

- limitation of liability to an amount commensurate with a prudent level of insurance cover maintained by the supplier is likely to be considered reasonable;

- significant limitation of liability, and possibly exclusion of the implied terms of satisfactory quality and fitness for purpose, following full acceptance testing may be considered reasonable, particularly if the supplier offers a satisfactory maintenance agreement;

- exclusion of liability for indirect or consequential loss may be considered reasonable, but such exclusion would not affect liability for loss resulting directly and naturally in the ordinary course of events from the breach.

(d) Terms officially approved

Finally there is an odd provision of UCTA[1] that a term is to be taken as satisfying the requirement of reasonableness if it is approved by a court, arbitrator, government department or public authority acting in the exercise of any statutory jurisdiction or function, other than a term of a contract to which the authority is itself a party. It would seem that a clause of a contract could effectively escape control under UCTA if it is an agreement which has been approved by a public authority for some quite different purpose, e.g. control of restrictive practices. However, it could perhaps be argued that this provision of UCTA only applies to terms which have been individually approved by the public authority. It is not known whether this provision has been invoked in any case.

E Measures of equivalent effect to exclusions and limitations of liability

The control of exclusion and limitation clauses cannot be evaded by provisions for indemnities,[2] guarantees,[3] secondary contracts,[4] or imposing restrictions or conditions in relation to enforcement and remedies.[5] This catches provisions which preclude the setting-off of liability where its exclusion or limitation is controlled by the substantive provisions of UCTA.[6] It would seem that it also catches provisions restricting complaints about defects not identified during acceptance testing or within a specified period less than the normal period of limitation. UCTA also applies to non-contractual notices excluding or limiting liability for negligence.[7]

---

[1] UCTA, s 29(2), 11 *Halsbury's Statutes* (4th edn).
[2] UCTA, s 4, 11 *Halsbury's Statutes* (4th edn).
[3] UCTA, s 5, 11 *Halsbury's Statutes* (4th edn).
[4] UCTA, s 10, 11 *Halsbury's Statutes* (4th edn).
[5] UCTA, s 13, 11 *Halsbury's Statutes* (4th edn).
[6] *Stewart Gill v Horatio Myer* [1992] QB 600.
[7] UCTA, s 2, 11 *Halsbury's Statutes* (4th edn).

(iv) The Unfair Terms in Consumer Contracts Regulations

The Unfair Terms in Consumer Contracts Regulations ("UTCCR")[1] implement EC Directive 93/13[2] with effect from 1 July 1995.[3] Although one hopes that goods or services supplied to consumers since July 1995 have been Year 2000 compliant, it is possible that this has not always been the case, and the regulations are therefore briefly reviewed below.

The Regulations apply to terms which have not been negotiated individually in contracts between a supplier of goods or services acting in the course of business[4] and a consumer,[5] being a natural person not acting in the course of business.[6] If such terms are unfair, they are not binding on the consumer.[7] A term is unfair if contrary to the requirement of good faith it causes a significant imbalance in the parties' rights and obligations under the contract to the detriment of the consumer[8] and regard is to be had[9] to:

- the strength of the bargaining positions of the parties;

- whether the consumer had any inducement to agree to the term;

- where the goods or services were supplied to special order;

- the extent to which the supplier has dealt fairly and equitably with the consumer.

A term is not unfair if it is in plain and intelligible language and defines the main subject-matter of the contract or concerns the adequacy of price.[10]

The Regulations contain an "indicative and non-exhaustive" list of terms which "may be regarded as unfair".[11] These include:

- excluding or limiting liability of the supplier in the event of death or personal injury of the consumer resulting from an act or omission of the supplier;

- inappropriately excluding or limiting the legal rights of the consumer vis-à-vis the supplier in the event of inadequate performance by the supplier of its contractual obligations.

---

[1] SI 1994/3159, 17 *Halsbury's Statutory Instruments*.
[2] OJ L95/29 of 21/4/93.
[3] UTCCR, reg 1, 17 *Halsbury's Statutory Instruments*.
[4] This includes a trade or profession and the activities of public bodies.
[5] UTCCR, reg 3, 17 *Halsbury's Statutory Instruments*.
[6] UTCCR, reg 2, 17 *Halsbury's Statutory Instruments*. A franchisee was held to be acting in the course of business, and not a consumer, in relations with the franchisor: Case C-269/95 *Benincasa v Dentalbit*, ECJ 3/7/97.
[7] UTCCR, reg 5, 17 *Halsbury's Statutory Instruments*.
[8] UTCCR, reg 4(1), 17 *Halsbury's Statutory Instruments*.
[9] UTCCR, reg 4(3) and Sch 2, 17 *Halsbury's Statutory Instruments*.
[10] UTCCR, reg 3(2), 17 *Halsbury's Statutory Instruments*.
[11] UTCCR, reg 4(4) and Sch 3, 17 *Halsbury's Statutory Instruments*.

A supplier is required to ensure that any written term is expressed in plain, intelligible language, and if there is any doubt the interpretation most favourable to the consumer shall prevail.

(8) REMEDIES FOR BREACH OF CONTRACT

(i) Introduction

One of the unique features of Year 2000 issues is that, in general, the damage resulting from use of a non-compliant system may not be suffered until after 31 December 1999. However, the cause of action in contract arises on breach, generally referable to the delivery of the 'defective' goods or services. The limitation period, within which a claim must normally be made if it is to have a prospect of success, is set by law as 6 years for most claims for breach of contract. The period may be over, or nearly over, by the time the damage is felt.

Certainty is not one of the features of Year 2000 issues and much of this discussion will necessarily be speculative. Recent cases involving defective software have concerned defects which came to light very shortly after delivery of the software. For the most part until fairly recently software and hardware procurements have not been made with any consideration of the change of millennium. Specifications did not include any mention of the effect of date changes; express Year 2000 warranties have not have been given by suppliers nor requested by purchasers. Systems which were tested have been accepted as conforming to specification without manifestation of the 'latent defect' ticking away. All these factors may have a serious consequences for claims for breach of contract.

(ii) Damages

A Types of damage/loss

The language surrounding the concept of damage is sometimes confusing. "Loss" and "damage" are used interchangeably. Loss may be subdivided into:

- direct loss - e.g. the diminution in value of the defective software itself;

- indirect loss - usually reserved for physical damage to property or personal injury, e.g. a hard disk crash caused by defective software, or the burning of a factory as a result of an unsuitable heating system as in *Harbutt's Plasticine v Wayne Tank and Pump*[1];

- consequential loss - this generally refers to indirect loss of profit, for example arising out of the use of the defective software.

[1] [1970] 1 QB 447.

This classification of loss does not answer the question whether it is too remote to be recoverable, discussed below. However, the different categories are frequently used in contractual provisions which attempt to limit liability, discussed above.

B Basis of damages

The basis of damages for breach of contract was stated in *Robinson v Harman*[1] by Parke B as follows:

'The rule of common law is that where a party sustains a loss by reason of a breach of contract he is, so far as money can do it, to be placed in the same situation with respect to damages as if the contract had been performed.'

Compensation is awarded to put the innocent party in the position in which he would have been if the contract had been performed. By contrast, in tort compensation is awarded to put the injured party in the position in which he would have been had the tort not been committed. There can be a significant difference in the amount of damages awarded. Where a statement is both a warranty and a representation and is incorrect, damages for breach of contract aim to put the innocent party in the position in which he would be if the statement had been true; whereas damages in tort for misrepresentation aim to put him in the position in which he would be if the statement had never been made.

In considering the nature of the losses which may be recoverable, there is a distinction to be made between the period running up to the millennium, where the focus is on achieving compliance, and the period following the millennium, where losses may arise from use of non-compliant systems. The current focus is on avoiding losses which may arise from use of non-compliant systems and claims may be made for the expenditure incurred. In the later period, there may be claims for losses resulting from operating non-compliant systems as well as remedial costs.

The compensation awarded for breach of a contractual obligation that a system be Year 2000 compliant would normally involve a sum necessary to make it compliant, including wasted expenditure, management time (if properly recorded) and cost of conversion. If it is not possible to make the system Year 2000 compliant, the claim may include the cost of an equivalent compliant system, assuming this is available.

However, where the cost of cure is out of proportion to the breach, the court may take a pragmatic approach. In *Ruxley Electronics v Forsyth*[2] a swimming pool was not built to the specified depth, although it could still be used for diving. The plaintiff had obtained the substantial benefit of the contract and was awarded £2,500 rather than the £21,000 necessary to rebuild the pool. Year

[1] (1848) 1 Exch 850 at 855.
[2] [1995] 3 All ER 268.

2000 compliance is not generally relative in the same way as the depth of a swimming pool; a system either is or is not compliant. However, one can envisage situations in which a system is or has been fixed to be compliant in all respects except that, e.g. it prints dates on invoices as in 1900 instead of 2000. In this case, it could be argued that the plaintiff has got the substantial benefit of the contract and the breach is minor. On the other hand, a plaintiff does not have to accept a solution which affects its reputation, and there could be more serious problems, e.g. the invoices may be sent electronically and not handled by a recipient's compliant system.

The approach to compensation discussed above is termed the "cost of cure" basis. An alternative is to assess damages on the basis of the difference in value between what was delivered and what should have been delivered. The latter is treated as the "prima facie" measure of damages for breach of warranty in the Sale of Goods Act 1979.[1] It is also more appropriate where the plaintiff has suffered consequential loss of profit so that compensation limited to the "cost of cure" would not be adequate. This is illustrated by *Cullinane v British Rema Manufacturing*,[2] where the defendant delivered a clay pulverising machine which was warranted to be able to process clay at six tons per hour. In fact it could only do so at two tons per hour. The court awarded damages based on the additional profits which the plaintiff would have made if the machine had complied with the warranty, rather than the cost of cure, assuming this was an available option. However, the plaintiff was refused additional compensation for wasted expenditure, since this would have involved double counting.

A further alternative is recovery of wasted expenditure. This may be appropriate where the plaintiff's potential gain from proper performance of the contract is speculative. Thus in *Anglia Television Ltd v Reed*,[3] the actor Oliver Reed repudiated a contract to star in a television production. The television company were awarded the wasted expenditure rather than the highly speculative profit they may have made from the completed production.

Where there are consequential losses from the operation of a non-compliant system, there is a further difficulty if the computer equipment was acquired by one of a group of companies for the use of all members of the group, as in the case of Thrombodirect. As discussed above, unless the procuring company can be treated as an agent for the other companies, only the procuring company has a contractual relationship with the suppliers. The question arises as to whether the procuring company can claim in respect of the damage suffered by other members of the group.

If the procuring company is a parent of the company suffering losses, the procuring company may be damaged in that the value of its shareholding in the suffering company may be diminished. This loss is in principle recoverable, but has to be proved by evidence.[4] Particularly where the companies are in different countries, it will not be presumed, in the absence of evidence, that £1 lost to the subsidiary will be £1 lost to the parent.

[1] S 53(3), 39 *Halsbury's Statutes* (4th edn).
[2] [1954] 1 QB 292.
[3] [1972] 160 QB .
[4] *Gerber v Lectra* [1997] RPC 443.

If the company suffering losses is not a subsidiary of the procuring company, recovery of the losses on the basis of breach of contract is more difficult, although an argument could be based on the principles considered in *Linden Gardens Trust v Lenesta Sludge Disposals*,[1] discussed above.

In all cases, the defendant's breach must be the cause of the plaintiff's loss. The 'but for' test is applied in contract as in tort, although (as will be seen) it is not the only criterion of the link between the loss and the breach. The question of causation may be a particularly thorny one in relation to Year 2000 issues, taking into account the complex relationship involving possibly a number of pieces of software, some of which may be bespoke, some bought off the shelf and some customised, running on a variety of hardware. The question of causation will be a matter of expert evidence as to what in fact caused the loss claimed. A breach by one party may be sufficient in its own right to have caused the loss, but in situations where there are concurrent or successive breaches by different parties, the 'but for' test cannot be applied too rigidly. So if two suppliers have been in breach then they may both be liable for the losses.

The standard of proof of loss will generally be the usual civil standard of 'balance of probability', not proof 'beyond a reasonable doubt'. However, where the loss is concerned with future or hypothetical events, such as loss of future profit, it may have to be proved with 'reasonable certainty'.

C Factors which may affect the damages awarded

Although the basic principle is that damages are awarded to put the innocent party in the same position as if the contract had been performed, this principle is subject to a number of qualifications and the following additional factors may affect the damages awarded:

> *Remoteness of the loss*
>
> The plaintiff will not be awarded those damages which are deemed to be too remote from the breach. Only losses which were or ought to have been in the contemplation of the parties will be awarded.
>
> *Intervening cause*
>
> There must be an unbroken chain of events between the breach and the loss. If there is an intervening event which could be said to be more the cause of the loss, the defendant will not be held liable.
>
> *The Plaintiff's 'duty' to mitigate loss*
>
> Whilst not strictly being a duty, the plaintiff should take reasonable steps to avoid or minimise the loss after the breach has occurred. The plaintiff may not recover for loss which it should have avoided, but may recover additional expenses incurred in taking reasonable steps to limit or avoid its loss.

---

[1] [1994] AC 85.

Contributory negligence

In tort, negligence of the plaintiff contributing to the loss is taken into account. However, it is questionable whether and in what circumstances this applies in contract claims.

Impecuniosity of the plaintiff

This issue is connected with the duty to mitigate and the issue of remoteness. The question is whether the plaintiff's lack of funds can be said to have increased the loss and therefore be taken into account to reduce any award of damages.

Liquidated damages / milestone payments

Contracts for development projects often contain provisions specifying sums to be paid by way of damages if the project or parts of it are not completed on time. If they amount to penalties, they are invalid, and the normal principles of compensatory damages apply. To avoid this difficulty, contracts may instead specify that payments are only made to contractors when specified milestones are reached and possibly provide incentives for early performance.

Betterment of the plaintiff as a result of the defendant's breach

The plaintiff may end up better off as result of action taken to remedy the breach, e.g. the provision of a new and up-to-date system. The question arises as to whether the damages should be reduced to take this into account.

Exclusion or limitation of liability clauses in the contract

This factor is fully discussed in section (7) above.

All of these factors, apart from the last, will be discussed below. There is often an overlap between them. For example, failure to take reasonable steps may be a failure to mitigate, but taking unreasonable steps may break the chain of causation. Unreasonable expenditure incurred could also be deemed to be a failure to mitigate. The distinction could be very important as damages may be reduced if there has been a failure to mitigate, but an intervening act may result in no damages being awarded at all.

D Remoteness

The series of cases which lay out the principles of remoteness start with *Hadley v Baxendale*,[1] where Alderson B stated:

> 'Where two parties have made a contract which one of them has broken, the damages which the other party ought to receive in respect of such breach of contact should be such as may fairly and reasonably be considered either arising naturally, i.e.,

[1] (1854) 9 Exch 34.

according to the usual course of things, from such breach of contract itself, or such as may reasonably be supposed to have been in the contemplation of both parties, at the time they made the contract, as the probable result of the breach of it.'

The case seemed to set out two categories of recoverable loss: those which flowed naturally from the breach and those within the reasonable contemplation of the parties at the time the contract was entered into. Normal losses fall into the first part, abnormal losses into the second *if* the defendant knew or ought to have known of the circumstances leading to them.

The facts were that a common carrier agreed to deliver a crank shaft which the owner of a mill had sent away for repair. Because of a delay in delivery the mill remained shut longer than it should have. The mill owners did not have a second one to use during the delay. The plaintiff claimed for loss of profit. The court held that the loss did not flow naturally from the breach as in the normal course of events mill owners had more than one crank shaft. If the defendants had been aware that the plaintiffs only had one shaft, the losses would have been in the reasonable contemplation of the parties.

In *Victoria Laundry v Newman Industries*[1] Asquith LJ discussed the concept of reasonable contemplation of losses. Reasonable contemplation is based on knowledge. Everyone is deemed to have knowledge of things that arise in 'the ordinary course of things' and this was the basis of the first part of the *Hadley v Baxendale* formulation. Compensation for additional losses outside the 'ordinary course of things' would be awarded only if the defendant had actual knowledge (and not merely imputed knowledge) of the special circumstances. The case involved the acquisition of a boiler by launderers and dyers who wanted to expand their business generally and in contemplation of some particularly profitable contracts. The engineers delivered it late. They had been told in correspondence that it was required urgently. The plaintiffs got damages for loss of profit from expanding the business but not for the 'highly lucrative' dying contracts.

In the *Heron II*[2] case the House of Lords considered what degree of probability of damage must be within the contemplation of the parties at the time when the contract was made for it to be recoverable. Phrases such as 'liable to result', 'not unlikely', 'a real danger' and 'a serious possibility' were used.

Unlike the cases just discussed, *H Parsons (Livestock) v Uttley Ingham*[3] involved not only loss of profits but also physical loss in the form of dead pigs. Lord Denning took the view that the principles set out in the cases discussed above applied to economic loss arising from breach of contract, and that where physical loss occurred the test of foresight established in the law of tort should apply. Scarman and Orr LJJ disagreed on this point, but thought that some illness to the pigs should have been contemplated and that death was an

[1] (1949) 2 KB 528.
[2] [1969] 1 AC 388.
[3] [1978] QB 791.

extension of illness. It was sufficient that the type of damage was within the reasonable contemplation of the parties; the extent of the damage need not be. All three judges agreed that the loss was not too remote to be recoverable.

The Sale of Goods Act 1979 specifies that the measure of damages for breach of warranty is the estimated loss directly and naturally resulting, in the ordinary course of events, from the warranty.[1] However, it is thought that this does not affect the application of principles established in the cases discussed above.

In the case of bespoke IS developments, the supplier will normally know a great deal about the operations of the customers and the nature of the losses which will ensue if there is a lack of Year 2000 compliance. Thus in *St Albans v ICL*[2] the contract was for the development of a system to handle poll tax collection and administration. ICL were held to be liable for losses arising from the incorrect calculation of tax levels.

By contrast, where a company acquires an off-the-shelf package, the supplier is less likely to be in a position to foresee all of the types of damage which the customer may suffer, unless the customer draws this to the attention of the supplier. Thus if a company acquires software because they not only wish to expand their business but also are contemplating entering into a particularly lucrative contract, this information should be transmitted to the supplier to avoid the loss in the event of a breach being deemed to be too remote.

Thrombodirect uses Debtpay 3.0 software package to manage its debts. If the package had been bought instead of "inherited", there might be a valid claim against the supplier for breach of the implied term of satisfactory quality if use of this package after 31 December 1999 leads to them being unable to recover money which is due. These losses would be recoverable as arising naturally from the use of the software.

Similarly, loss of profit arising out of the use of both the stock control and manufacturing control programs could also be recoverable as being in the contemplation of the parties at the time the contract was entered into. However, a court may hold that software acquired well before the millennium was not contemplated to be used beyond the millennium, and that resulting loss is therefore too remote. In the case of Thrombodirect, the fact that Medinvent is still being maintained may militate against such a finding.

E Intervening cause

Unreasonable conduct by the injured party after the breach may break the chain of causation between breach and damage. In *Lambert v Lewis*[3] a dealer supplied a defective trailer coupling to a farmer, who negligently continued to use it after it was obviously broken. An accident injured a third party. The farmer was found liable. He sued the dealer for a breach of contract, seeking to

[1] S 53(2), 39 *Halsbury's Statutes* (4th edn).
[2] [1997] FSR 251.
[3] [1982] AC 255.

recover an indemnity for damages he had paid to the injured third party. The House of Lords held that the farmer's negligence had broken the chain of causation. On the other hand, *Compania Naviera Maropan v Bowaters*[1] is authority for the proposition that reasonable acts of the plaintiff do not break the chain of causation.

Continued use of non-compliant hardware or software with knowledge of the defect may result in a similar finding to that in *Lambert v Lewis*. However, even without knowledge, continuous use of a non-compliant system may be held to amount to a failure to mitigate the loss affecting the user's right to damages.

F Mitigation

The responsibility to mitigate is a further factor which may go to restrict compensatory damages, and is likely to feature large in any claims arising in this area. The injured party should take reasonable steps to put himself in the position he would have been in if the contract had been performed and avoid a loss arising or at least minimise such loss. In *British Westinghouse Electric and Manufacturing v Underground Electric Rlys Co of London*,[2] Viscount Haldane LC stated that this principle

> '. . . imposes on the Plaintiff the duty of taking all reasonable steps to mitigate the loss consequent on the breach and debars him from claiming an part of the damage which is due to his neglect to take such steps.'

Thus inaction by the plaintiff may reduce or extinguish the loss. Adopting the ostrich position with regard to Year 2000 compliance may come to haunt plaintiffs when they attempt to sue for consequential loss. It may certainly be deemed to be unreasonable to refuse help from the party in breach or even to fail to request such help to remedy the defect.

Mitigation is closely tied up with remoteness of the loss and causation. It is deemed to be in the contemplation of the defendant that the plaintiff will try to mitigate the loss. Equally, unreasonable conduct of the plaintiff may break the chain of causation.

Whether the plaintiff has taken reasonable steps to mitigate his loss is a question of fact in each case. The burden of proof is on the defendant to prove that the plaintiff did not: *Payzu v Saunders*.[3] In some cases the duty to mitigate may mean that the customer should try to fix the defect in the non-compliant software or hardware and not to scrap it altogether. However, in other circumstances, it may be reasonable for the customer to start again. Thus in *Salvage Association v CAP*,[4] after giving the supplier a reasonable opportunity

[1] [1955] 2 QB 68.
[2] [1912] AC 673.
[3] [1919] 2 KB 581.
[4] [1995] FSR 654.

to remedy the breach, the plaintiff terminated the contract. Damages were awarded on the basis of the sums paid out to the defaulting supplier and wasted expenditure. The judge said:

> 'I am satisfied that SA's decision to abandon the CAP system altogether and start afresh was entirely reasonable ... CAP was not able to complete the system satisfactorily and there was no point in getting another software house to redesign and rebuild a discredited system. It was much more sensible to start afresh. The upshot was that the project to computerise SA's head office accounting with a system designed and developed by CAP had failed and SA's expenditure on that system had been wasted.'

If, on the other hand, it had been held that the plaintiff should have continued with CAP or brought in a third party to salvage the project, the sums paid to CAP would not have been recoverable as they should not have been wasted; but sums expended to complete the project could then have been recovered, except to the extent that they would have been expended in any event to complete the project.

A user faced with a number of alternatives in trying to mitigate the loss will not be prejudiced in having taken reasonable steps in the event that it turns out that a cheaper option was available: *Tito v Waddel (No 2)*.[1] Indeed, if the user, in trying to mitigate, actually increases the loss, even the additional loss may be recoverable. In *Esso Petroleum v Mardon*[2] the plaintiff was induced to enter into a tenancy of a petrol station by what turned out to be a misrepresentation. He was entitled to damages incurred when he entered into a fresh tenancy in an unsuccessful attempt to turn things round even after he was aware of the true facts.

G Impecuniosity

It seems that a plaintiff can recover for loss which it could not mitigate owing to its impecuniosity, although impecuniosity may be an intervening cause disentitling the plaintiff from recovering the resulting loss. In *The Liesbosch*[3] a dredger was sunk by the negligent navigation of the Edison. The plaintiff could not afford to buy a substitute dredger and hired one which increased the loss incurred. The court refused to allow damages for the loss over what would have been incurred by buying and adapting a substitute barge. The court seemed to distinguish between mitigation, where impecuniosity is not held against the plaintiff and an intervening cause as in this case. Although the case has not been overruled, the courts over the years have found reasons not to follow it. Lord Denning in *Perry v Sidney Phillips*[4] thought that *The Liesboch* should be confined to its special facts and should not be followed. However, the case is still a precedent of the House of Lords.

[1] [1977] Ch 106.
[2] [1976] QB 801.
[3] [1933] AC 449.
[4] [1982] 3 All ER 705.

Lack of resources may well be a factor when a company embarks on a Year 2000 compliance project. If the position is considered under the principles of mitigation, reasonable conduct in the circumstances, including the resources available, will not affect the ability to claim full compensation. However, if *The Liesboch* decision is applied, damages may not be recovered to the extent that actions which had to be taken because of lack of resources increased the loss.

H Contributory negligence

It is not clear whether the provisions for reduction of damages where there has been contributory negligence by the plaintiff apply to claims in contract. The Law Reform (Contributory Negligence) Act 1945[1] makes no express reference to breach of contract. Section 4 defines fault in s 1(1) as meaning

> '. . . negligence, breach of statutory duty or other act or omission which would give rise to a liability in tort, or would, apart form this Act, give rise to the defence of contributory negligence'.

In *Forsikringsaktieselskapet Vesta v Butcher*[2] the Court of Appeal approved the analysis by Hobhouse J at first instance. Contributory negligence could be raised "where the Defendant's liability in contract is the same as his liability in the tort of negligence independently of the existence of any contract." On the other hand, in *Barclays Bank v Fairclough*[3] the Court of Appeal held that contributory negligence was not available to limit damages where the contractual duty broken was one of strict liability.

If contributory negligence is not available to limit damages, this may paradoxically work against the plaintiff as damages become all or nothing. Instead of being able to apportion loss, the courts may be forced to award no damages on the ground that the chain of causation was broken or that the plaintiff failed to mitigate his loss. In *Schering Agrochemicals v Resibel*[4] the defendant admitted a breach of contract in supplying safety equipment that was not fit for the purpose. A fire broke out at the plaintiffs' factory which the safety alarm system failed to prevent. However, the plaintiffs were aware of an incident three weeks before the fire which should have led them to investigate the alarm system and uncover the defect. They were awarded no damages. The position might possibly have been different if the Court of Appeal had been able to apportion the blame and award reduced damages to the plaintiffs.

I Liquidated damages

If a contract contains a clause to the effect that a sum will be paid by way of damages in the event of a breach of contract this may be followed by the court when it comes to award damages. The damages agreed must be a genuine pre-

[1] 31 *Halsbury's Statutes* (4th edn).
[2] [1989] AC 582.
[3] [1995] 1 All ER 289.
[4] Unreported, 26 November 1992.

estimation of loss and not be held to be a penalty clause. It is not uncommon to find such clauses in IT contracts. In the leading case of *Dunlop v New Garage and Motor Co*[1] the House of Lords laid down some guiding rules:

- use of the word 'penalty' or 'liquidated damages' is not determinative;

- the issue depends on the circumstances at the time the agreement is made and not at the time of breach;

- a clause may be a penalty if it is extravagant and unconscionable in amount in comparison with the greatest loss that could conceivably be proved to have followed as a result of the breach;

- it is a presumption that the clause is a penalty if the same sum is payable on a number of breaches occurring where some may be serious and some trivial;

- it is no obstacle that the sum agreed is so agreed in circumstances where pre-estimation is almost an impossibility. In such a situation it may well be the case that the damages were agreed by the parties because of this difficulty

If the court decides that the clause is a penalty, damages are awarded on basic principles.

J Betterment of plaintiff

If, after the user has taken steps to remedy the defective system, he ends up with a system that is both compliant and has increased functionality, the question arises as to whether the court should disallow part of the costs incurred on account of the increased functionality. The plaintiff is not entitled to be put in a better position than he would have been in if the contract had been performed. In *British Westinghouse v Underground Electric*[2] the defendant supplied defective turbines. The plaintiff replaced them with ones that were more efficient and profitable. The benefit amounted to more than the loss and the court only awarded nominal damages. On the other hand, if the increased functionality is incidental to fixing Year 2000 defects and not of practical benefit to the plaintiff, the full costs may still be recoverable.

K Assessment of damages in a Year 2000 scenario

Assuming (and this a big assumption) that the plaintiff has got past all the barriers placed by the defendant by way of exclusion of liability, limitation of liability, and a possible limitation defence, how might a court go about assessing damages in practice?

---

[1] [1915] 1 AC 79.
[2] [1912] AC 673.

All companies are faced with a recognised modus operandi for finding out whether their computer systems, including hardware, software and embedded chips, will continue to function near and in the Year 2000.

Thus, in our example, Thrombodirect should investigate the effect of the various date changes throughout their operation. This will involve checking the mainframe, the various PCs, the software written in-house, Debtpay 3.0, Medinvent stock control software and the Manucont stock control system. They should carry out a legal audit of all the contracts involved to identify whether this indicates that the responsibility for doing remedial work may lie with Julian Associates (under the facilities management contract) or Anocomp (under the maintenance agreement).

Thrombodirect should contact all the relevant parties to gather information about the compliance or non-compliance of their products. The questions asked should be framed very carefully and the responses thoroughly reviewed. This may be the cause of some tension, as the suppliers may be sensitive as to their potential liability.

Thrombodirect should then decide on the steps needed to achieve compliance, taking into account discussions with the relevant parties, and analyse how the remedial steps will impact on the system as a whole. This may involve remedying some defects and replacing some parts of the defective system. The remedial work should then be carried out and the system tested for compliance. The question for Thrombodirect will be whether they can seek compensation from a third party for the cost of the compliance project.

In summary the above exercise will include:

- The technical audit of all the elements of the system to identify what work is required to achieve compliance. This exercise should identify which systems can be fixed and which will require to be replaced.

- A legal audit of the contracts, licences and relationships involved to assess whether responsibility to remedy the defects may lie elsewhere.

- An impact analysis of how the proposed remedial work will affect the system.

- Undertaking the work to make the system compliant. This may involve bringing in third party solution providers.

- Testing that the system is compliant and that the work undertaken has achieved the desired result, which may involve a cycle of further remedial work and testing until compliance is achieved.

- Discussions with third party suppliers to ensure that they are compliant, as this may impact on the company even if it achieves compliance.

The reality is that is that it is going to be a very complex picture. A number of suppliers have provided hardware and software, which may have been bespoke, off the shelf, or customised by the company or third parties. From whom the software was procured will have legal ramifications as far as liability is concerned. The contractual terms and conditions of the outsourcing or facilities management arrangements will impact on potential recovery.

The costs of system audit and impact analysis may well be irrecoverable, in that they are not caused by any breach of contract. However, any discussions between the parties should be taken into account. If the company failed to ask a supplier whether their product was compliant, this may mean that expenditure checking this was unnecessary and therefore not recoverable. On the other hand, if the supplier was asked and gave no response or an ambiguous or a false one, the costs of a technical audit may be more readily recovered, possibly as reasonable expenditure under the duty to mitigate. In any event, it seems unlikely that the cost of a legal audit will be recoverable.

Expenses reasonably incurred in making the system Year 2000 compliant and testing for compliance are more likely to be recoverable, on the basis of the ordinary principles discussed above. However, an important question in many cases will be whether the supplier should be given the opportunity to remedy the defect. This may depend on whether the user has reasonably lost confidence in the supplier, as happened in *Salvage Association v CAP*.[1] However, in other cases,[2] this may not be a reasonable course of action, and unnecessary expense engaging third parties may be irrecoverable.

(iii) Rights to terminate the contract and reject goods

Contracts frequently contain express terms specifying the circumstances in which the contract may be terminated, including in the event of breach. For example, it may specify that the contract is terminable if the breach is irremediable or is not remedied within a specified period. In the absence of such a provision,whether there is a right to terminate for breach depends on the nature of the term which is breached.

Terms are classified as conditions, warranties or innominate. Breach of a condition (however slight) normally entitles the injured party to terminate the contract as well as claiming damages. In the case of sale of goods, a breach of condition on the part of the seller also entitles the buyer to reject the goods. Breach of a warranty entitles the injured party to claim damages, but not to terminate the contract. Breach of an innominate term may or may not entitle the injured party to terminate depending on the circumstances If the breach goes to the root of the contract, it is treated as a breach of condition. If not, it is treated as a breach of warranty.

---

[1] [1995] FSR 654.
[2] See e.g. *Saphena Computing v Allied Collection Agencies* [1995] FSR 616.

Termination discharges the parties from further performance of the contract, but they remain liable for past breaches, including the breach which led to the termination.

Rights to terminate and to reject goods are lost if they are not exercised promptly or if the innocent party accepts the goods or affirms the contract with knowledge of the breach. By the time the Year 2000 latent defects are discovered, it is likely to be too late to reject goods supplied several years earlier. In many cases, the equipment will be deemed to have been accepted following completion of acceptance testing.

However, termination may be more relevant to ongoing maintenance contracts where the maintainer fails to make the system Year 2000 compliant. The user may have a difficult decision where it has little confidence in the maintainer's progress. If it purports to terminate too early, the user may itself be in breach of contract, as in the *Saphena* case. On the other hand, if it leaves it too late, it may have waived an entitlement to terminate. Although it was held in *Salvage Association v CAP Financial Services*[1] that the plaintiff was entitled to terminate after giving the defendant a number of chances to remedy the defects, there is no clear guidance as to how much time and opportunity has to be given before termination is justified.

(iv) Specific performance

The courts may order parties to perform contractual obligations specifically where damages would not be an adequate remedy. However, the courts are unwilling to order specific performance of obligations which require a high level of supervision or where it is not clear how they are to be carried out. In most cases involving Year 2000 it is thought that damages will provide an adequate remedy and that there would in any case be serious difficulties in making an order to fix software if it is not known whether and how it could be done. Specific performance is also refused if there has been significant delay.

However, there could be situations in which specific performance might be appropriate. For example:

- a supplier might be ordered to release the source code to enable the customer to rectify Year 2000 defects as a matter of urgency;[2]

- if a supplier has in fact prepared an upgraded version of the software eliminating Year 2000 defects, but demands a sum of money to which it is not entitled, the court might order the supplier to provide the upgrade to a person to whom the supplier is obliged to provide compliant software.

---

[1] [1995] FSR 654.
[2] Cf *Leisure Data v Bell* [1988] FSR 367.

(v) Limitation

Limitation may be the biggest obstacle facing potential plaintiffs who wish to sue in contract, for direct loss in the period leading to the millennium or for consequential losses arising after 31 December 1999 or any other technically problematic date, such as 9 September 1999.

The Limitation Act 1980 sets out various time periods within which claims should be brought in both contract and tort. The Act does not prevent a plaintiff from commencing an action outside of the time limits, but if he does the defendant may have a complete defence.

Limitation periods within which claims in tort can be brought may be more advantageous to a plaintiff. As there is the prospect of concurrent liability in contract and tort arising out of the same factual matrix, this will be a vital issue for Year 2000 loss claims. For a more detailed discussion of concurrent liability and limitation periods in tort see Chapter 6.

The time limit for actions on contracts which are not under seal is 6 years 'from the date on which the cause of action accrued'.[1] For contracts by deed the longer period of 12 years applies,[2] although it is unlikely that companies will have entered into contracts for IT supplies by way of deed.

It is obviously very important to know when the cause of action accrues in contract. In *Letang v Cooper*[3] the 'cause of action' was defined as the factual situation relied on by the plaintiff which, if proved, would give him entitlement to a remedy. The cause of action for breach of contract therefore accrues when the breach of contract took place, not when the plaintiff discovers this or suffers some damage. Where defective goods or services are supplied, this would normally be the date of delivery, although in a bespoke development, it may be the date when completion was due. Accordingly, where hardware or software was acquired more than 6 years ago, limitation may provide the potential defendant with a complete defence to a claim in contract, even though the effects of Year 2000 latent defects have yet to be felt. Where there is a danger of the limitation period expiring while a compliance exercise is under way, users should consider measures such as holding writs or stand still agreements: see Chapter 10.

By contrast, obligations in maintenance agreements to ensure Year 2000 compliance are likely to be continuing obligations, which continue to be breached until the system is made compliant. Limitation is unlikely to be a problem here.

Where the defendant has deliberately concealed facts relevant to the plaintiff's cause of action, the period of limitation does not start to run until the plaintiff discovers, or could with reasonable diligence have discovered the

---

[1] Limitation Act 1980, s 5, 24 *Halsbury's Statutes* (4th edn).
[2] *Ibid*, s 8(1).
[3] [1965] 1 QB 232.

concealment.[1] This may assist a user where the supplier has deliberately concealed facts or misled the user in relation to Year 2000 compliance. However, even in this situation, time may well have started to run in 1997, in that a reasonably diligent user should by then have carried out a full audit which would normally disclose Year 2000 defects.

---

[1] Limitation Act 1980, s 32, 24 Halsbury's Statutes (4th edn).

---

6 Torts

(1) INTRODUCTION

This chapter considers claims in tort - i.e. claims other than for breach of contract - arising out of Year 2000 problems. The more important potential bases for such claims are

- negligence

- misrepresentation

- the supply of unsafe goods contrary to the Consumer Protection Act

and these will be discussed in detail below.

In addition, failures resulting from lack of Year 2000 compliance may give rise to breaches of a wide variety of specific statutory provisions relating to the safety of equipment, products and working conditions. Those injured or damaged may or may not be entitled to claim compensation in respect of the breach, depending on the wording and scheme of the legislation in question. However, details of the particular statutes which may apply are outside the scope of this work.

Where there is liability in tort, it is common for several persons to be liable in tort and/or contract for the same damage. In such cases, a party which is liable may claim fair contributions from other parties which are liable. The entitlement to contribution gives rise to a separate cause of action which is discussed later in this chapter.

(2) TORT AND CONTRACT

Although most software and equipment likely to be affected by Year 2000 problems has been supplied under contracts, claims in tort may be important in practice for a number of reasons:

- As has been seen, the 6 year limitation period for breach of contract by the supply of non-compliant equipment normally runs from the date of supply. This may have expired by the time the damage is felt and consideration is given to the recovery of compensation. By contrast, in the case of tort, time generally runs from the date of damage and in the case of latent damage time runs from the date of knowledge of the facts constituting the cause of action.

- The contracting supplier may have ceased to exist following insolvency, restructuring etc., or may not be in a position to meet the claim (and claims of other parties), so that the only available claims are in tort against non-contracting parties.

- Depending on their wording, exclusion or limitation clauses in the contract of supply may possibly exclude or limit liability for breach of contract, but fail to exclude liability for tort.

Claims in tort can be made even though they arise out of relationships governed by contract. The House of Lords has confirmed that English law rejects the "temptation of elegance" to categorise relationships as governed either by contract of by non-contractual obligations.[1] However, the existence and terms of contracts may affect liabilities in tort in various ways:

- Liability in tort may be excluded or limited by contractual provision, as discussed in Chapter 5 above.

- The nature and terms of the contract may indicate whether responsibility for a particular matter (millennium compliance) is assumed by a particular party. As will be seen, assumption of responsibility is an important factor in determining whether a party owes a duty of care so as to be potentially liable in negligence.

- Entering into a contract relying on a misrepresentation by the other party may give rise to a claim for misrepresentation. On the other hand, depending on the circumstances, an "entire agreement" or "integration" clause in a contract may be regarded as establishing that it was not reasonable to have relied on the misrepresentation.

(3) APPLICABILITY OF ENGLISH LAW

English law clearly applies where both the act or omission and damage giving rise to the claim occurred entirely in England and Wales. However, where one or more of these factors occurred wholly or partly outside England and Wales - as in the case of the manufacture of non-compatible products abroad - the question arises as to which law or laws apply.

The English conflict of law rules governing this issue changed on 1 May 1996 when Part III of the Private International Law (Miscellaneous Provisions) Act 1995 entered into force. The common law rules apply in relation to acts or omissions prior to this date.[2] Under these rules an alleged tort committed outside the jurisdiction is normally actionable in English courts if, but only if, it is actionable under the laws of the place where it was committed *and* it would be actionable if committed in England.[3] This is commonly called the "double-actionability" requirement. However, the law of the place where the alleged tort

---

[1] *Henderson v Merrett* [1995] 2 AC 145.
[2] Private International Law (Miscellaneous Provisions) Act 1995, s 14(1), 45 *Halsbury's Statutes* (4th edn).
[3] *Boys v Chaplin* [1971] AC 56.

was committed may be exclusively applicable where this is more significantly related to the case as a whole or to a particular issue than the law of the forum.[1]

In the context of international trade it can be difficult to determine where the alleged tort was committed. There is no English authority which resolves this question in relation to the determination of the law applicable to tort. It is thought that some guidance may be obtained from decisions on jurisdiction, although the considerations are not the same and the decisions on jurisdiction are not wholly consistent in themselves.[2]

The more recent decisions under the English rules on jurisdiction have attempted to identify the place where the cause of action in substance arose, viewing the events as a whole. Thus where an employee of an English company was injured by an allegedly defective machine which had been made in Germany and supplied to the English company through the manufacturer's exclusive English agent, the Court of Appeal held that the manufacturer's alleged tort of supplying the machine without warning of its defect was committed in substance in England.[3] However, in an earlier case the Court of Appeal seems to have held that where a defective product was manufactured and put on the market in the US without warning as to the defect, the tort was committed in the US.[4] It has also been held that the tort of misrepresentation was committed in the jurisdiction where the communication was received and relied upon,[5] although an earlier case held that the tort was committed abroad where the communication was made abroad and acted upon in England.[6]

Decisions of the European Court of Justice under the Brussels Convention on Jurisdiction have held that the "harmful event" giving rise to a claim in tort takes place where either the wrongful act or the damage occurs.[7] However, for this purpose "damage" should not be equated with the financial consequences of damage.[8]

The 1995 Act abolishes the double-actionability rule[9] and lays down a general rule that the applicable law is that of the jurisdiction in which the events constituting the tort occur.[10] Where these occur in different countries, the applicable law is taken as the place where the damage to property or personal injury occur, if the cause of action is for damage to property, personal injury or death.[11] In other cases, the applicable law is taken as that of the country in which the most significant elements of the events consituting the tort occur.[12]

---

[1] *Red Sea Insurance v Bouygues* [1995] 1 AC 90.
[2] See the discussion in Dicey & Morris, *The Conflict of Laws*, Twelfh Edition, p 1509 et seq.
[3] *Castree v Squibb* [1980] 1 WLR 1248.
[4] *George Monroe v American Cyanamid* [1944] KB 432.
[5] *Diamond v Bank of London & Montreal* [1979] QB 333.
[6] *Cordova Land v Victor* [1966] 1 WLR 793.
[7] *Bier v Mines de Potasse d'Alsace* [1976] ECR 1735.
[8] *Dumez France v Hessische Landesbank* [1990] ECR I–49.
[9] Except in relation to defamation: s 13, 45 *Halsbury's Statutes* (4th edn).
[10] s 11(1), 45 *Halsbury's Statutes* (4th edn).
[11] s 11(2)(a),(b), 45 *Halsbury's Statutes* (4th edn).
[12] s 11(2)(c), 45 *Halsbury's Statutes* (4th edn).

However, the general rule is displaced if the law of another jurisdiction appears to be substantially more appropriate.[1]

In our example, Thrombodirect Manufacturing Limited may have claims against overseas suppliers, such as Chipsrus and Anocomp, and may be at the receiving end of claims from overseas customers and users of its products. To succeed in an action in the English courts in relation to acts or omissions before 1 May 1996, a claimant would in any case have to show that the acts or omissions gave rise to liability under English law. In addition, if the substance of the alleged tort took place in another country, it would be necessary to show that liability arises under the law of that country as well. Under the more recent authorities, it seems that torts based on the supply of products are likely to be considered to have been committed in the place to which the products were supplied. Thus Thrombodirect Manufacturing's claims would probably not be dependent on the law of Shenzen (in the case of Chipsrus) or Massachusetts (in the case of Anocomp). On the other hand, claims against Thrombodirect Manufacturing by French users of equipment sold through Thrombodirect SA might well require actionability under both French law and English law.

Where claims are based on acts or omissions after 1 May 1996, the (single) applicable law in relation to Thrombodirect Manufacturing's claims against its suppliers would probably be English law, and in relation to claims against Thrombodirect Manufacturing by (say) French users it would probably be French law. If the equipment was supplied before 1 May 1996, and French law is more favourable to the claimant than English, it may help the French user to contend that there was a wrongful failure to inform it of the danger after 1 May 1996, constituting a separate tort governed only by French law.

(4) NEGLIGENCE

(i) Introduction

The requirements of a valid claim for negligence are

- A duty of care owed to the claimant by the defendant in relation to the damage claimed

- Negligence of the defendant in breach of that duty of care

- Damage caused by the breach of the duty of care of a kind which is not too remote.

If these requirements are satisfied, liability is established subject to various defences, of which the most important are contractual exclusion or limitation of liability and limitation of actions. The requirements of the cause of action and the defence of limitation of actions will be discussed in the following sub-sections. Contractual exclusions and limitations have been considered in

---

[1] s 12, 45 *Halsbury's Statutes* (4th edn).

chapter 5. The section on damage will also consider factors affecting quantum, such as contributory negligence and mitigation.

Although mitigation of damages will thus be covered separately from the duty of care, the combined effect of these principles should be noted at the outset. On the one hand, a user of equipment containing computer programs should act prior to the millennium to avoid any damage which may be occasioned by non-compliance. On the other hand, the cost of achieving compliance is economic loss which is normally outside the scope of the duty of care except where there is a "special relationship" between the parties. This greatly reduces the circumstances in which there is a prospect of compensation for lack of compliance even if negligence can be established.

Where liability for negligence is established, the principle of vicarious liability and the provisions of the Employers' Liability (Defective Equipment) Act make employers liable for negligence of their employees and suppliers. These points will be discussed in section (v) below.

(ii) Duty of care

A General considerations

Recent decisions of the House of Lords[1] have sharply reversed an earlier trend of extension of the circumstances regarded as giving rise to a duty of care. This section will summarise the position according to the more recent decisions, but it should be borne in mind that a further shift in either direction cannot be ruled out.

The current position is that a duty of care to a claimant in relation to a type of damage will be recognised if, but only if:

- It was foreseeable that the claimant would suffer that type of damage as a result of the negligent act or omission

- The claimant is sufficiently proximate to the defendant

- It is fair, just and reasonable to impose liability

The third criterion involves considerations of policy and the recent cases emphasise that a major factor in the courts' evaluation is whether a duty of care has previously been recognised in a similar situation. The currently prevailing view is that any further development of the law by the courts should be incremental and by analogy with established categories, rather than by reference to more general considerations.[2] Therefore consideration of potential

---

[1] *Peabody v Lindsay Parkinson* [1985] AC 210; *Leigh and Sillavan v Aliakmon* [1986] 785; *Yuen Kun Yeu v AG of Hong Kong* [1988] AC 175; *Caparo v Dickman* [1990] 2 AC 605; *Murphy v Brentwood* [1991] 1 AC 398; *Henderson v Merrett* [1995] 2 AC 145; *White v Jones* [1995] 2 AC 207; *Spring v Guardian Assurance* [1995] 2 AC 296; *Marc Rich v Bishop Rock Marine* [1996] 1 AC 211.

[2] *Sutherland v Heyman* (1985) 157 CLR 424 per Brennan LJ, cited with approval in *Yuen Kun Yeu v AG of Hong Kong* [1988] AC 175 and *Murphy v Brentwood* [1991] 1 AC 398.

claims for negligence arising out of Year 2000 problems should be based primarily on whether the circumstances come within any of the established categories where duties of care have been recognised or rejected.

In particular, duties of care have been recognised in the following situations:

- The supply of a product where no intermediate examination is contemplated and a defect foreseeably causes personal injury or damage to other property of the user.

- Incorrect statements or advice by a person professing special skill or knowledge cause economic loss to a person to whom the maker or giver has assumed responsibility for their accuracy.

These categories will now be considered in turn, followed by a discussion of other situations where Year 2000 problems may arise.

B Supply of products causing personal injury or damage to other property

Where products are supplied in the expectation that they will be used *without intermediate examination*, the supplier owes a duty of care to avoid defects which will foreseeably result in injury or damage to *other* property of users.[1] Two issues of particular importance to millennium liability are

- whether the duty of care is excluded by the opportunity of checking compliance (intermediate examination)

- the limitation of the duty of care to damage to other property or personal injury.

(a) Opportunity of checking compliance

The relevance of this issue will vary according to the circumstances:

- Year 2000 defects are embedded in integrated circuits and checking for compliance remains impracticable. If this continues to be the case, it is thought that in this situation the duty of care would be unaffected.

- Checking for Year 2000 compliance or other defects was not contemplated when the product was supplied, but may reasonably be expected of the user now. Although this does not fit precisely the formulation in *Donoghue v Stevenson*, it is thought that this would negate the duty of care. Even if it does not negate the duty of care, it would be relevant to whether damages should be reduced on the grounds of contributory negligence or failure to mitigate, discussed below.

[1] *Donoghue v Stevenson* [1932] AC 562; *Grant v Australian Knitting Mills* [1936] AC 85; *Farr v Butters* [1932] 2 KB 621; *Murphy v Brentwood* [1991] AC 398 at 464, 475, 492.

- Checking for defects (for example, acceptance testing) was contemplated when the product was supplied; the potential Year 2000 problem was not tested by the user at the time but may reasonably be expected of the user now. This is a stronger case for excluding the duty of care.

- Checking for Year 2000 compliance was not contemplated when the product was supplied, but may now reasonably be expected of the person to whom the product was supplied (e.g. the Millshire Trust, in the case of dialysis machines supplied by Thrombodirect), although not by the ultimate user (the patient) who is injured. It is a difficult question whether Thrombodirect owes a duty of care to the patient in these circumstances.

- The user took reasonable steps to check and secure Year 2000 compliance, but was unsuccessful. The duty of care would not be excluded in this situation.[1] It would seem that the position should be the same if the user did not take reasonable steps, but even if it had, they would not have been successful.

(b) Limitation to personal injury or damage to other property of the user

The duty is to take care to avoid personal injury (including death) and damage to other property. It is well established that it extends to economic loss resulting from personal injury (e.g. medical expenses and loss of earnings) and it appears to extend also to economic loss resulting from damage to other property (e.g. loss of profits due to the other property being unavailable for use).[2] However, the duty of care does not extend to the diminution of value of the product supplied, or the cost of rectifying the defect or of replacing the product supplied, or any other economic loss[3] (e.g. loss of profits due to the product supplied being unavailable for use).

On this basis, a supplier of a non-compliant product would not be liable in negligence for the costs of making it compliant or for loss resulting from it not being used because it is unsafe. On the other hand, if the non-compliant product is used and damages other equipment, data or software, the supplier could be liable for the cost of repairing or restoring the other equipment, data or software and the economic loss attributable to the damage to the other equipment, data or software e.g. due to its unavailability for use pending repair/restoration. (This is subject to issues such as intermediate examination, mitigation and contributory negligence.)

However, the distinction drawn between economic loss resulting from damage to other property (recoverable) and other economic loss (irrecoverable)

---

[1] See *Nitrigin Eireann Teoranta v Inco Alloys* [1992] 1 WLR 498.
[2] *British Celanese v Hunt* [1969] 1 WLR 959; *SCM v Whittal* [1971] 1 QB 337; *Spartan Steel v Martin* [1973] QB 27; *Greater Nottingham Coop v Cementation Piling and Foundations* [1989] QB 71; *Nitrigin Eireann Teoranta v Inco Alloys* [1992] 1 WLR 498.
[3] *D&F Estates v Church Commissioners* [1989] AC 177; *Murphy v Brentwood* [1991] AC 398.

may be difficult to maintain where the property damage is slight or intangible (as in the case of damage to data or (other) software). Moreover, the recoverability of economic loss resulting from damage to other property has not been confirmed by the House of Lords and most of the cases supporting it concern negligent works causing damage to neighbouring property rather than the supply of defective products. It is quite possible that the recoverability of such economic loss may be cut back by future decisions of the House of Lords.

A further difficulty arises where the defect is in part of a larger structure, for example in one integrated circuit of a device or one program on a computer system. Lord Bridge appeared to consider that damage to the rest of a structure is recoverable if it is positively inflicted by the malfunction of a defective part but not if it is due merely to a failure of a defective part to fulfil its function.[1] If this distinction is applied, difficult issues may arise as to whether a lack of millennium compliance is a malfunction or merely a failure to function, and whether resulting damage to interfacing software, data or hardware is positively inflicted thereby.

Finally, it appears that this duty of care is owed only to persons having a proprietary interest in the property damaged, and not (for example) to persons who have a contractual right to use it or to acquire it in the future.[2] Thus in the Thrombodirect example, if non-compliant *Manucont* software corrupts other software belonging to Systems, Plc will not be able to recover its loss from being unable to use that other software by a claim in negligence against *Manucont*.

C Incorrect statements or advice causing economic loss

Where a person professing special skill or knowledge assumes responsibility to another person for the accuracy of a statement or advice based on that skill or knowledge, knowing that the other person will rely on it, the person making the statement or giving the advice owes a duty of care to the other person to avoid inaccuracy which would cause foreseeable economic loss to that person.[3]

In this situation, there is a "special relationship" between the claimant and defendant, over and above the mere fact that damage to the claimant is foreseeable if the defendant is negligent, and the claimant may recover economic loss which is generally not allowed in the law of negligence.

The "special relationship" may in particular be one which is akin to contract but where there is no contract. Thus in the Thrombodirect example, B&W Agon will owe a duty of care to Systems to give accurate advice regarding Year 2000 compliance, even if there is no contract because the terms have not been

---

[1] *Murphy v Brentwood* [1991] AC 398 at 478.

[2] *Leigh and Sillavan v Aliakmon* [1986] AC 785.

[3] *Hedley Byrne v Heller* [1964] AC 465; *Mutual Life v Evatt* [1971] AC 793; *Smith v Bush* [1990] 1 AC 831; *Caparo v Dickman* [1990] 2 AC 605; *James McNaughton v Hicks Anderson* [1991] 2 QB 113; *Henderson v Merrett* [1995] 2 AC 145; *White v Jones* [1995] 2 AC 207; *Spring v Guardian Assurance* [1995] 2 AC 296; *Marc Rich v Bishop Rock Marine* [1996] 1 AC 211; *Machin v Adams,* CA 7.5.97.

settled. Systems and Wytook probably owe duties of care to all the companies in the group since they have assumed responsibility for the IT systems and millennium compliance.

Auditors generally assume responsibility to the company and existing shareholders but not to potential investors, unless they provide information or advice to such investors which they know will be relied upon in connection with a specific transaction.[1] Thus if Anomerge negligently fail to advise Thrombodirect that its accounts are materially inaccurate because of Year 2000 problems, they could be liable to Thrombodirect and its existing shareholders, but not to potential investors such as the Gregorian Trust, unless they provide information specifically in connection with the proposed placement which they know will be relied upon by subscribers.

A sub-contractor does not normally assume responsibility for the quality of its work to the ultimate customer; its duties are governed by its relationship with the contractor which engaged him.[2] Thus where the main contractor of an IT project has gone out of business, the customer is unlikely to be able to claim for economic loss against sub-contractors responsible for non-compliant software. However, in particular circumstances, there may be a special relationship between the ultimate customer and a nominated sub-contractor giving rise to a duty of care.[3]

D Other situations

It is not clear whether or in what circumstances a supplier of services will be regarded as having a duty of care to avoid foreseeable personal injury or damage to property where there is no "special relationship". Contractors carrying out building operations have been considered to owe a duty of care to avoid damaging property on neighbouring land,[4] and an architect was held liable to a workman injured by the collapse of a wall which he negligently advised could be left standing.[5] It has also been observed that there will normally be a duty of care to avoid direct physical damage which is foreseeable.[6] On the other hand, in *Marc Rich v Bishop Rock Marine*,[7] it was held that a marine classification society did not owe a duty of care to the

---

[1] *Caparo v Dickman* [1990] 2 AC 605; *James McNaughton v Hicks Anderson* [1991] 2 QB 113; *Morgan Crucible v Hill Samuel* [1991] Ch 295; *Galoo v Bright Graham Murray* [1994] 1 WLR 1360; *Possfund v Diamond* [1996] 1 WLR 1351 (held to be arguable that reporting accountants liable to subscribers).
[2] *Simaan v Pilkington* [1988] QB 758; *Henderson v Merrett* [1995] 2 AC 145.
[3] *Junior Books v Veitchi* [1983] 1 AC 520 has been explained on this basis, although it has also been described as a case turning on special facts and of no general assistance: see *D&F Estates v Church Commissioners* [1989] AC 177 at 202, 215; *Murphy v Brentwood* [1991] 1 AC 398 at 466, 481; *Henderson v Merrett* [1995] 2 AC 145; *Nitrigin v Inco Alloys* [1992] 1 WLR 498 at 505.
[4] *SCM v Whittal* [1971] 1 QB 337; *Spartan Steel v Martin* [1973] QB 27; *Greater Nottingham Coop v Cementation Piling and Foundations* [1989] QB 71.
[5] *Clay v Crump* [1964] 1 QB 533, cited with approval in *Marc Rich v Bishop Rock Marine* [1996] 1 AC 211 at 237.
[6] *Murphy v Brentwood* [1991] 1 AC 398, 486–7 per Lord Oliver; distinguished in *Marc Rich v Bishop Rock Marine* [1996] 1 AC 211.
[7] [1996] 1 AC 211.

owners of cargo lost with a ship which they negligently certified as seaworthy. Significant considerations were that the society was not primarily responsible for the decision to sail and that the regime already provided by the Hague rules should not be disturbed.

It is suggested that where the service creates or enhances a tangible product (as in the case of the supply of software without transfer of a physical support) the situation could be regarded as analogous to the supply of goods and governed by the principles set out in *Donoghue v Stevenson*. This approach would be consistent with that adopted in relation to contractual implied terms in *St Albans v ICL*.[1]

On the other hand, in the current climate, it is possible that a person providing a pure service, such as a Year 2000 technical audit, does not owe any duty of care to persons with whom there is no "special relationship" who may suffer damage to property or injury, for example from using medical equipment whose non-compliance should have been detected in the audit.

(iii) Negligence

The basic criterion of negligence was set out by Alderson B:[2]

> "Negligence is the omission to do something which a reasonable man, guided upon those considerations which ordinarily regulate the conduct of human affairs, would do: or something which a prudent and reasonable man would not do."

However, in the case of persons professing to have a special skill, such as the design of computer systems and the creation of software, the test is the standard of the ordinary skilled person exercising and professing to have that skill.[3]

Matters to be taken into account include the magnitude of the risk[4] and the cost and practicality of overcoming the risk.[5] Accordance with common practice is strong evidence of reasonable care, but not conclusive;[6] negligence may be found where there is no logical basis for the practice.[7] Subsequent experience indicating that greater precautions should have been taken does not establish negligence, because it is easy to be wise after the event.[8]

Whether it was negligent to fail to provide for the transition to the Year 2000 will no doubt be controversial. It appears to have been a common practice and at one time may have been justified by the considerations of cost and practicality discussed in chapter 3. On the other hand, there came a time when

[1] [1997] FSR 251.
[2] *Blyth v Birmingham Waterworks* (1856) 11 Ex 781.
[3] *Bolam v Friern Hospital* [1957] 1 WLR 582, *Bolitho v City and Hackney*, HL 13.11.97.
[4] *Glasgow Corp v Muir* [1943] AC 448.
[5] *The Wagon Mound (No 2)* [1967] 1 AC 617.
[6] *General Cleaning Co v Christmas* [1953] AC 180; *Cavanagh v Ulster Weaving* [1960] AC 145.
[7] *Bolitho v City and Hackney*, HL 13.11.97.
[8] *The Wagon Mound (No 1)* [1961] AC 388 at 424.

it ceased to be justified, and it could be argued that after this time it was negligent

- for those advising on the specification of IT requirements to fail to specify Year 2000 compliance

- for those designing and creating software to fail to provide Year 2000 compliance

- possibly, when the problem became well known, for those preparing or advising on IT contracts and professing special skill in this area, to fail to protect their clients in relation to Year 2000 risks.

In view of the overwhelming publicity which has now been given to the problem, it would seem that the continued use of older software without taking reasonable steps to check for and remedy non-compliance would normally be negligent.

(iv) Damage

Damage caused by the negligence which is not too remote is an essential requirement of the cause of action for negligence and this has implications for limitation periods as discussed below. Significant issues also commonly arise in relation to the quantification of such damage.

The basic principle is that the defendant is liable for all damage caused by the breach of the duty of care if it is of a kind which is reasonably foreseeable.[1] On the other hand, damage does not count if it is outside the ambit of the duty of care (e.g. economic loss in the absence of a "special relationship" as discussed above) or if it is of a *kind* which was not reasonably foreseeable (hence too remote).

The implications of this test of remoteness depend on the generality of classification of damage. It appears that the classes are broad. Personal injury, whether psychiatric or physical, is all of a kind for this purpose,[2] and death of livestock was regarded as the same kind of damage as their illness.[3]

In principle, the damages awarded should, so far as possible, put the claimant in the position in which it would have been if it had not sustained such damage. If damage of a particular kind is foreseeable, the defendant is liable for the full extent even though the extent was not foreseeable.[4] In the case of personal injury and death which money cannot restore, an arbitrary tariff of financial compensation is applied.

A number of factors may affect the amount of damages. Some of these can be regarded as incidents of the basic principles identified above, while others

---

[1] *The Wagon Mound (No 1)* [1961] AC 388; *The Wagon Mound (No 2)* [1967] 1 AC 617.
[2] *Page v Smith* [1996] 1 AC 155.
[3] *Parsons v Uttley Ingham* [1978] QB 791.
[4] *Hughes v Lord Advocate* [1963] AC 837.

are qualifications. Most of them apply similarly to claims for breach of contract, have already been discussed in Chapter 5 and need only be noted here.

- Causation must be established and may be negatived by an intervening cause.[1] The claimant's lack of resources to avoid or mitigate damage may possibly constitute an intervening cause breaking the chain of causation.

- The claimant should take reasonable steps to mitigate damage and will not be able to claim in respect of damage which it should have avoided (or did avoid). On the other hand, the claimant will be able to claim additional expense incurred in mitigating damage if it is within the ambit of the duty of care.[2] However, since such expense is economic loss, it is unlikely to be recoverable unless the defendant has assumed responsibility to the claimant for ensuring Year 2000 compliance so as to create a "special relationship" akin to contract.

- Contractual provisions for liquidated damages or limitations of liability may affect the damages which may be awarded.

- Betterment of the claimant may be taken into account.

- Where the claimant's damage is partly due to its own negligence, breach of statutory duty or other fault, the damages must be reduced to such extent as the Court thinks just and equitable having regard to the claimant's share in the responsibility for the damage.[3] Failure to take steps to ensure compliance and continued operation of non-compliant equipment may well be regarded as contributory negligence, resulting in a reduction of damages if they are not excluded altogether on the ground of failure to mitigate.

(v) Liability of employers

An employer is vicariously liable for the negligence of its employees in the course of their employment. Whether a person is an employee or an independent contractor depends on a number of factors. The extent of control exercised by the "employer" is important.[4] The name given to the relationship by the parties and their tax arrangements are not conclusive. It is common for computer programmers to operate through companies ostensibly engaged as independent contractors. However, it is possible that the Courts will see through such arrangements where the programmer is in reality an employee.

The course of employment includes acts which the employee is employed to do and acts incidental to these.[5] Doing negligently a task which the employee is employed to do carefully is within the course of employment.

[1] See also *Galoo v Bright Graham Murray* [1994] 1 WLR 1360.
[2] See *Murphy v Brentwood* [1991] 1 AC 398.
[3] Law Reform (Contributory Negligence) Act 1945, ss 1, 4, 31 *Halsbury's Statutes* (4th edn).
[4] *Lee Ting Sang v Chung Chi-Keung* [1990] 2 AC 374.
[5] *Staton v NCB* [1957] 1 WLR 893.

The Employers' Liability (Defective Equipment) Act 1969[1] provides that where an employee sustains personal injury because of a defect in equipment provided by his employer for the purposes of business, and the defect is attributable to the fault of a third party, the injury is deemed to be also attributable to the fault of the employer.

(vi) Limitation periods

Claims for negligence are barred if legal proceedings are not commenced within the periods specified by the Limitation Act 1980. The basic period for tort is 6 years from the date on which the cause of action accrued.[2] A cause of action for negligence accrues when the damage occurs, not when the negligent act was committed. For this reason alone, a claim for negligence may be made when the period of limitation for breach of contract (typically 6 years from the date of supply of defective products) has already expired.

The basic period for negligence can be extended in cases of latent damage. The claimant may bring proceedings for negligence within the period of 3 years from when it had the knowledge required to bring an action.[3] For this purpose the knowledge required to bring an action is knowledge of

- facts about the damage as would lead a reasonable person to consider it sufficiently serious to justify proceedings against a defendant who did not dispute liability and was able to satisfy a judgment

- the fact that the damage was attributable to the alleged negligence

- the identity of the defendant

- if the defendant is alleged to be liable for the negligence of another person, the identity of that person and the facts supporting an action against the defendant.[4]

Knowledge includes knowledge which the claimant might reasonably be expected to acquire from facts observable or ascertainable by him, including facts ascertainable with the help of expert advice which it is reasonable for him to seek, unless he took all reasonable steps to obtain and act on such advice.[5]

On the other hand, there is an overriding period of limitation for negligence actions of 15 years from the date of the negligence.[6]

Special rules apply in relation to personal injuries. The basic period in such actions is 3 years from the date of accrual of the cause of action or the date of knowledge[7] (defined in a somewhat similar way to the above[8]). However, this

[1] 16 *Halsbury's Statutes* (4th edn)
[2] s 2, 24 *Halsbury's Statutes* (4th edn).
[3] s 14A, 24 *Halsbury's Statutes* (4th edn).
[4] s 14A(6)–(9), 24 *Halsbury's Statutes* (4th edn).
[5] s 14A(10), 24 *Halsbury's Statutes* (4th edn).
[6] s 14B, 24 *Halsbury's Statutes* (4th edn).
[7] s 11(4), 24 *Halsbury's Statutes* (4th edn).
[8] s 14, 24 *Halsbury's Statutes* (4th edn).

period may be extended if it appears to the Court that it would be equitable to allow the action to proceed.[1]

Where the defendant has deliberately concealed facts relevant to the claimant's right of action, the basic periods of limitation run from the date when the claimant discovered or could with reasonable diligence have discovered the concealment.[2]

(5) MISREPRESENTATION

(i) Introduction

A negligent misrepresentation may give rise to liability under the tort of negligence discussed above. However, there is a separate cause of action for misrepresentation which may be established even though the requirements of the tort of negligence are not met. This independent cause of action is discussed in this section.

Prior to the Misrepresentation Act 1967,[3] a fraudulent or reckless misrepresentation was required to found a claim for damages under the tort of misrepresentation.[4] However, by section 2 of the 1967 Act, where a party has suffered loss as a result of entering into a contract after a misrepresentation has been made to it by another party to the contract, the first party is entitled to claim damages as if the misrepresentation had been made fraudulently, unless the other party proves that it believed and had reasonable grounds to believe that the statement was true up to the time the contract was made.

As a result of this Act, it is often easier to establish liability under the independent tort of misrepresentation than under the tort of negligence, since

- under the tort of misrepresentation the burden of proof lies on the defendant to show that it had reasonable grounds to believe that the representation was true; whereas under the tort of negligence the burden of proof lies on the claimant to show that the representation was made negligently

- to be regarded as innocent under the tort of misrepresentation, the defendant must believe and have reasonable grounds to believe that the statement was true up to the time the contract is made; whereas under the tort of negligence, the primary question is whether the misrepresentation was made negligently, although liability could be based on a negligent failure to correct an earlier misrepresentation which was not negligent when made.

---

[1] s 33, 24 *Halsbury's Statutes* (4th edn).
[2] s 32, 24 *Halsbury's Statutes* (4th edn).
[3] 29 *Halsbury's Statutes* (4th edn).
[4] *Derry v Peek* (1889) 14 App Cas 337.

The availability of damages under the tort of misrepresentation is also more favourable to the claimant.

The requirements of the cause of action for misrepresentation are:

- Misrepresentation

- Reliance on the misrepresentation

- Damage flowing from the misrepresentation

These will be discussed in turn in the following sections.

Misrepresentation also gives rise to a right to rescind a contract entered into in reliance on it in circumstances where it is possible to restore the status quo ante. However, this will not normally be relevant in the context of Year 2000 problems.

(ii) Misrepresentation and reliance

The misrepresentation must be as to a fact which is incorrect. A statement of intention (e.g. that a system will be compliant) is not a misrepresentation merely because it is not fulfilled.[1] However, it can be a misrepresentation if no such intention is in fact held.[2] A mere statement of opinion which proves to be unfounded is not regarded as a misrepresentation,[3] but it may imply a misrepresentation that the maker has reasonable grounds for making it, if these are lacking.[4] More generally, a misrepresentation may be implicit; for example, a description of premises as "offices" was held to imply a representation as to the availability of planning consents.[5] Similarly, it might be considered that a description as to the functionality of software implies that it is capable of maintaining this functionality without further modification over a reasonable period of time.

The claimant must rely on the misrepresentation. There is no cause of action if the claimant was not in fact influenced by it, for example where the claimant relies on its own examination. Where the representation is fraudulent, the reliance can be any act which results in prejudice to the claimant. However, for an innocent misrepresentation to give rise to a cause of action under section 2(1) of the Misrepresentation Act, the claimant must have entered into a contract in reliance upon it.

[1] *Brown v Raphael* [1958] Ch 636.
[2] *Edgington v Fitzmaurice* (1885) Ch D 459.
[3] *Bisset v Wilkinson* [1927] AC 177; *Hummingbird Motors v Hobbs* [1986] RTR 276.
[4] *Esso v Mardon* [1976] QB 801.
[5] *Laurence v Lexcourt Holdings* [1978] 1 WLR 1128.

(iii) Damage

The claimant is entitled to damages for misrepresentation to put it in the position in which it would have been if the misrepresentation had not been made.[1] The claimant is not entitled to be put in the position in which it would have been if the representation had been true, unless the representation has become a term of contract and it is able to claim for breach of warranty. It may be difficult to establish what would have happened if a misrepresentation as to Year 2000 compliance had not been made. In many cases the party to which the representation was made might have overlooked the point altogether and entered into the contract all the same.

The claimant is entitled to damages for any loss which flows from the misrepresentation. There is no restriction to foreseeable loss[2] and no reduction for contributory negligence.[3]

(iv) Exclusion and limitation of liability for misrepresentation

The exclusion or limitation of liability for misrepresentation prior to a contract is subject to control under the Unfair Contract Terms Act.[4]

(v) Limitation periods

The basic limitation period is 6 years from the accrual of the cause of action. In a claim under s 2(1) of the Misrepresentation Act it would seem that the cause of action normally accrues when the contract is entered into in reliance on the misrepresentation.[5] However, where a material fact is deliberately concealed by the defendant, the period of 6 years runs from the date when the claimant discovered or should have discovered the concealment.[6]

(6) BREACH OF CONSUMER PROTECTION ACT

Part I of the Consumer Protection Act 1987[7] imposes liability where a defect in a product causes personal injury or damage to other property. It implements the EC Product Liability Directive 85/374 and so far as possible should be interpreted in accordance with that Directive.

Liability is imposed on

---

[1] *Doyle v Olby* [1969] 2 QB 158.
[2] *Doyle v Olby* [1969] 2 QB 158; *Royscott Trust v Rogerson* [1991] 2 QB 297.
[3] *Alliance & Leicester v Edgestop* [1994] 1 All ER 38.
[4] 11 *Halsbury's Statutes* (4th edn).
[5] Limitation Act 1980, s 2, 24 *Halsbury's Statutes* (4th edn).
[6] Ibid, s 32, 24 *Halsbury's Statutes* (4th edn).
[7] 39 *Halsbury's Statutes* (4th edn).

- the producer

- any person who holds himself out as the producer by putting his name or mark on the product

- any person who imports the product into the EU

- any other person who has supplied the product and does not identify any of the foregoing persons on request.[1]

"Product" is defined in the Act as "any goods or electricity"[2] and in the Directive as "all movables", subject to certain exceptions, and including electricity. It is thought that software supplied on a physical medium would be regarded as a product. It is not clear whether the same would apply to software supplied in other ways.[3]

There is a "defect" in a product if the safety of the product (with regard to damage to property or personal injury) is not such as persons generally are entitled to expect.[4] Thus there would be no breach of the Act unless the non-compliant software was liable to cause personal injury or damage other property. There is room for dispute as to whether damage to data would qualify as damage to property for this purpose. In addition, it is a defence to show that the defect did not exist in the product when it was supplied (or generated in the case of electricity).[5] It could be argued that a non-compliant product does not become "unsafe" until the end of the end of 1999, and therefore was not defective when supplied at an earlier date.

Liability is in principle strict (i.e. irrespective of fault), although it is a defence to show that the state of scientific and technical knowledge at the time was not such that the producer might be expected to have discovered the defect.[6] It is arguable that this would apply to lack of millennium compliance at a time when the implications were not widely appreciated.

There is in any case no liability for damage to the product itself,[7] or for damage to property not intended for private use[8] or for damage to property not exceeding £275.[9]

The basic period of limitation is 3 years from accrual of the cause of action or from the date of knowledge[10] (defined in a generally similar way as in relation to latent defects and personal injury[11]) with an overriding period of 10 years from the supply.

---

[1] Consumer Protection Act 1987, s 2(1), 39 *Halsbury's Statutes* (4th edn).
[2] Ibid, s 1(?), 39 *Halsbury's Statutes* (4th edn).
[3] Cf the distinction drawn in *StAlbans v ICL* [1995] FSR 686.
[4] Consumer Protection Act 1987, s 3, 39 *Halsbury's Statutes* (4th edn).
[5] Consumer Protection Act 1987, s 4, 39 *Halsbury's Statutes* (4th edn).
[6] Consumer Protection Act 1987, s 4(1)(e), 39 *Halsbury's Statutes* (4th edn).
[7] Consumer Protection Act 1987, s 5(2), 39 *Halsbury's Statutes* (4th edn).
[8] Consumer Protection Act 1987, s 5(3), 39 *Halsbury's Statutes* (4th edn).
[9] Consumer Protection Act 1987, s 5(4), 39 *Halsbury's Statutes* (4th edn).
[10] Limitation Act, s 11A., 24 *Halsbury's Statutes* (4th edn).
[11] Ibid, s 14(1A), 24 *Halsbury's Statutes* (4th edn).

(7) CONTRIBUTION

Where two or more persons are each liable to another person in respect of the same damage, each may claim a contribution from the other.[1] A person who makes or agrees to make a payment in bona fide settlement of a claim is treated as if he is liable for the damage claimed.[2] The amount of the contribution recoverable from another person is such as the Court finds just and equitable having regard to the extent of that person's responsibility for the damage.[3]

The limitation period for a contribution claim is 2 years from the date the right accrued, namely the date of settlement or compromise.[4] Thus a patient might bring a claim in 2004 against the Ennium Hospital for negligent operation of non-compliant equipment, within the period of 3 years from 2002 when he discovers that he has a cause of action. Woolf permitting, the claim might be compromised by the hospital 3 years later in 2007. The hospital would then have until 2009 to claim a contribution from Thrombodirect.

(8) OTHER LIABILITIES

The possibility that modifying or decompiling software to achieve Year 2000 compliance may infringe copyright is discussed in Chapter 7. The fiduciary and other duties of company directors are discussed in Chapter 8.

---

[1] Civil Liability (Contribution) Act 1978, s 1(1), 13 *Halsbury's Statutes* (4th edn).
[2] Ibid, s 1(4), 13 *Halsbury's Statutes* (4th edn).
[3] Ibid, s 2(1), 13 *Halsbury's Statutes* (4th edn).
[4] Limitation Act 1980, s 10, 24 *Halsbury's Statutes* (4th edn).

7 Escrow, copyright and data protection

(1) ESCROW

Escrow is an ancient legal term meaning money, goods or a written document, held by a third party pending fulfilment of some condition. In the IT context, the item held is software source code. Ideally, the third party or "escrow agent" should be independent and impartial.

An escrow arrangement is a way of dealing with a conflict inherent in almost every software licensing situation. The licensee is concerned lest the owner of the source code becomes unable or unwilling to maintain the software and would like the comfort of having a copy of the source code at its disposal should it need to bring in a third party to support the software. However, the source code owner is loathe to let anybody gets its hands on what is, probably, its most valuable asset.

Typically, there are three parties to an escrow agreement. The main agreement is between the source code owner and the escrow agent. This sets out the terms of business between those two parties and, additionally, the terms under which the source code may be released by the escrow agent to a licensee of the software program. The third party is normally a licensee of the software program who becomes a party to the escrow agreement by signing a schedule to that agreement and paying a "confirmation fee" to the escrow agent. This schedule will contain the terms on which the source code may be used by the licensee should it be released to him. Once a software supplier has deposited the source code to a software program in escrow, it may offer each licensee the option to become a party to the escrow agreement. Hence, escrow agreements often become "multi-licensee".

An escrow agreement can include any triggering event providing it is definable and legal. This could cover the failure of the supplier's business and/or the failure of the supplier to maintain the software program in accordance with a maintenance agreement in place with the licensee. It could also include the failure of the product to meet certain specific Year 2000 criteria.

There may of course be differences of opinion between source code owners and software licensees as to whether the software in question is or is not compliant and an escrow agreement should contain provision for determining whether the escrow is to be released and to whom in the event of a dispute. In the absence of such a provision, the agreement has to be interpreted as any other contract in accordance with the principles discussed in Chapter 5.

The leading escrow agent in the United Kingdom is the National Computing Centre ("NCC") in Manchester. Excerpts from the NCC's summary "Millennium Safety Net - Minimise Your Risk", are set out in Appendix 2. The

NCC wording for its Year 2000 source code release trigger is set out in the Model Clause Appendix.

(2) COPYRIGHT

(i) General

Modifying a computer program without the consent of the owner of the copyright in it is, in principle, an infringement of that copyright[1]. Therefore a person fixing a Year 2000 defect could infringe copyright if it does not own the copyright in the software or have a licence from the copyright owner. In many cases, contracts for IS projects contain express provisions relating to copyright in the software and specifications, covering which party will own the copyrights and whether the customer will be entitled to modify the software. However, even where there are express provisions, they may not cater for all contingencies; for example they may provide a non-assignable licence to the customer which cannot be used by its successor in business.

Where there are no express terms, there will sometimes be an implication that the copyright is to belong to the party which commissioned and paid for it[2]. However, in many cases such a term will not be implied[3]. Where software is designed for use by a party and ownership of copyright is retained by the supplier or others, there will often be an implied licence that the customer will be entitled to take such steps as may be necessary to use it and keep it operational[4]. However, even this may not be the case, for example where arrangements are made for continuing maintenance and support by the supplier[5]. It was held in the *Saphena* case that there was an implied term of the agreement terminating the contract between the customer and the supplier that the customer would be entitled to correct bugs[6]. However, in other circumstances the position could be different.

Clearly it is necessary to examine the contractual position in each case to determine whether a customer is entitled to fix Year 2000 problems by "self-help". However, there are various statutory provisions and general legal principles which may be relevant.

---

[1] Copyright Designs and Patents Act 1988, s 21(3)(ab), 11 *Halsbury's Statutes* (4th edn).
[2] See e.g. *Richardson v Flanders* [1993] FSR 497.
[3] See e.g. *Saphena Computing v Allied Collection Agencies* [1995] FSR 616.
[4] Cf the licence to repair goods recognised in e.g. *Solar Thomson v Barton* [1977] RPC 537.
[5] As apparently would have been the case in *Saphena Computing v Allied Collection Agencies* [1995] FSR 616.
[6] *Ibid* at 638-640.

(ii) Acts necessary for lawful use

Under s 50C of the Copyright Designs and Patents Act 1988[1] ("CDPA"), it is not an infringement for a "lawful user" of a program to copy or adapt it where this is necessary for its lawful use, including in particular error correction, and is not prohibited under a term or condition of an agreement regulating the circumstances under which its use is lawful. As discussed in Chapter 5 above, the wording of this provision differs from the corresponding provisions of EEC Directive 91/250 which it is supposed to implement. For the reasons explained earlier, it is thought that s 50C would be interpreted in accordance with the Directive. The Directive provides that a lawful *acquirer* of software is entitled to do acts necessary for the use of a program *in accordance with its intended purpose* unless prohibited by *specific contractual provisions* [emphasis supplied].

Fixing Year 2000 defects would normally be necessary for the use of software in accordance with its intended purpose. Therefore in the absence of specific contractual provisions to the contrary, it seems that the lawful acquirer of software is entitled by virtue of this provision to amend it to make it Year 2000 compliant. It is also thought that the protection of this provision would extend to investigations to check Year 2000 compliance and identify what may need to be amended. On the other hand, unlawful acquirers (such as Thrombodirect in the case of the *Debtpay* package taken by Wytook from Hardman & Co when they ceased to trade) are not able to rely on this provision.

(iii) Decompiling

Section 50B of CDPA specifically provides that the lawful user of a program may decompile it to create an interoperable program and this entitlement may not be excluded by agreement[2]. Again, this provision is supposed to implement EC Directive 91/250 which refers to the entitlement of the lawful acquirer. This provision may be applicable where new programs are created to fix Year 2000 defects, for example by bypassing problem steps in the existing software.

Section 56 of CDPA provides that where

- a copy of a work in electronic form (such as program) has been purchased on terms which allow the purchaser to copy or adapt it in connection with its use (whether expressly or impliedly or by virtue of any rule of law),

- there are no express terms governing its transfer or the rights and obligations of a transferee, and

- the copy is transferred to another person

---

[1] 11 *Halsbury's Statutes* (4th edn).
[2] CDPA, s 296A, 11 *Halsbury's Statutes* (4th edn).

the transferee may do the things which the purchaser was entitled to do, and the purchaser ceases to be entitled to do them.

"Purchaser" and "transferee" are not defined for the purpose of this provision. It is not clear whether the "purchaser" must acquire ownership under a contract of sale and whether the transferee must become the owner of the copy or whether acquisition of possession brings the provision into play. However, it is thought that this provision confirms the effect of s 50C as discussed above, but similarly does not help in circumstances such as those relating to the *Debtpay* package in the example.

(iv) Implied right to repair

As mentioned above, a right to repair an article is generally implied in a contract of sale, and rectifying Year 2000 incompatibility is in the nature of a repair of a computer system. However, this implied licence only extends to the purchaser of the goods, and not to a third party which may devise a fix for commonly used software. Furthermore, the implied licence may be excluded by express terms, subject to the control of the Unfair Contract Terms Act 1977[1], discussed above.

In *British Leyland v Armstrong*[2] the House of Lords held that a manufacturer of motor cars was not entitled to use its copyrights to prevent or charge royalties on the manufacture of spare parts to be used for repairs in derogation of the rights of ownership granted to purchasers. It can be argued that this principle should apply equally to fixes of Year 2000 defects. However, in *Canon v Green*[3] the Privy Council held that *British Leyland v Armstrong* turned on very special facts and should not be extended. In addition, it could be said that the balance of rights between authors and acquirers of computer programs has been addressed by legislation in the form of the EEC Directive and ss 50A–50C of CDPA, and should not be re-adjusted by the Courts. It is therefore now difficult to predict whether the Courts will regard the solution of Year 2000 problems as a special case where policy considerations justify a departure from the strict enforcement of copyright.

(3) DATA PROTECTION

(i) Principles of data protection and Year 2000

The data protection legislation currently in force in the UK is the Data Protection Act 1984.[4] However, it is shortly to be replaced by new legislation giving effect to EC Directive 95/46.

---

[1] 11 *Halsbury's Statutes* (4th edn).
[2] [1986] RPC 279.
[3] [1997] FSR 817.
[4] 6 *Halsbury's Statutes* (4th edn).

The fulcrum of both the 1984 Act and the new legislation is the eight principles of data protection derived from the European Data Protection Convention of 1981.

If a computer system holding personal data cannot cope with the change to 2000, there is an obvious risk of contravention of the fifth principle, that personal data shall be accurate and, where necessary, kept up-to-date.

If the processing of the data is date-dependent, there is also a risk of contravention of the first principle, which requires (inter alia) that personal data shall be processed fairly. For example, ages may be calculated incorrectly, as explained in chapter 3, and individuals may be unfairly disadvantaged as a result.

The eighth principle requires (inter alia) appropriate security measures to be taken against accidental loss or destruction of personal data. This may be infringed where individual records are deleted (for example, following an incorrect age calculation) or where there is catastrophic failure of a system.

The consequences for individuals may vary from minimal to very serious. Under the 1984 Act the Data Protection Registrar has power to issue enforcement and deregistration notices. Failure to comply with an enforcement notice or continuing to hold data to be processed after deregistration is subject to criminal sanctions. In addition, individuals can bring civil proceedings for rectification of inaccurate data and compensation for damage suffered as a result of inaccuracy. Enforcement procedures are likely to be strengthened in the new legislation.

(ii) Registration

The 1984 Act establishes a system of registration of data users and computer bureaux providing services to data users. In the case of a data user, the registration must describe the data held and the purposes for which it is held or used. It is illegal to use data or provide computer services to data users services without being registered or outside the scope of the registration.

It is now common practice for IT users to engage the services of external service providers to render part or the whole of their operations Year 2000 compliant. This often involves the service provider having access to data which is covered by the 1984 Act. In such circumstances, the IT user should ensure that its registration covers the provision of the data to a third party such as the solution provider. In addition, the activities of the solution provider itself may necessitate its registration under the Act.

(iii) Export of data

As illustrated in the Thrombodirect example, companies may seek assistance in solving Year 2000 problems from overseas. Where this involves the export of databases, the provisions of the legislation controlling the export of personal data are likely to apply.

Under the 1984 Act, a data user may register an intention to export data world-wide. Although the Registrar has power to prevent export of data by use of a Transfer Prohibition Notice, it is understood that this power has only been exercised once.

The approach of the new Act will be that data must not be exported unless the jurisdiction to which the data is to be sent has an adequate level of protection or protection is afforded by contractual provision. The aim is that within the EU there will be free exchange of data as all member countries will implement the Directive and therefore have the necessary level of protection.

Potential problems will arise in relation to exports of data to countries outside the EU. It is contemplated that there will be a "black list" of jurisdictions, where the level of protection is deemed inadequate. The assessment of adequacy will be based on two requirements: substantive law guaranteeing an adequate level of protection; and the existence of a data protection registrar or equivalent functionary. The alternative of securing protection by contractual provision may well be important in practice.

8 Company directors' duties in the context of the system of corporate governance[1]

(1) INTRODUCTION

It has already been observed in Chapter 4 that company directors have a responsibility to ensure that the appropriate enquiries and investigations are made to ascertain and then deal with the business risks arising from the millennium problem. The risks include the impact of difficulties experienced by customers and suppliers as well as the group's own products failing to cope.

The difficult area of law governing directors' duties will be explained in this chapter and related to the millennium problem and its practical resolution. The consequences of failing to resolve the problem will be considered for all the players in the corporate governance system. The directors' duties in relation to the company's financial statements specifically will not be further elaborated in this chapter as this matter has been covered in Chapter 4.

The following diagram illustrates the British corporate governance system specifying the stakeholders. The system is evolving and this is reflected in the developing jurisprudence discussed below.

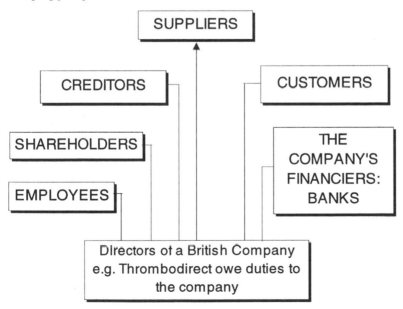

[1] On the system of Corporate Governance see generally S Sheikh and WM Rees (eds), *Corporate Governance & Corporate Control* (Cavendish, 1995); N. Maw *et al*, *Maw on Corporate Governance* (1994); *The Cadbury Report on the Financial Aspects of Corporate Governance System* (1992).

Directors owe duties to the company itself but are also legally required to take full account of the interests of shareholders, employees and creditors. Generally the interests of the shareholders will take precedence. However, there are judicial dicta suggesting that the directors need to consider the *continuing body* of shareholders rather than just the present shareholders.[1] It should moreover be noted that the categories may overlap: directors may also be shareholders and/or employees, and employees may also be shareholders.

The main duties imposed by law on company directors by virtue of their position are

- fiduciary duties to act in the best interests of the company

- common law duties to exercise care, skill and diligence

- a statutory duty to consider employees

- statutory and possibly other duties to creditors.

These duties are discussed in turn in sections (2)–(5) of this chapter. Additional duties may of course be imposed by contract, for example a contract of employment of an executive director, and such duties will be based on the express and implied terms of the contract in accordance with the principles set out in Chapter 5 above. It should also be appreciated that under English law directors are not absolved from liability to other persons on the ground that the liability results from their conduct as directors of a company.[2] Thus a director can be liable to persons other than the company for his negligence or misrepresentation when acting for the company in accordance with the principles discussed in Chapter 6 above.

Apart from being called to account at company meetings, directors in breach of duties owed to the company are in principle liable to pay damages to the company in accordance with ordinary principles. However, in some circumstances directors may be relieved from liability under s 727 of the Companies Act 1985,[3] or by insurance, or by ratification by the shareholders; and these possibilities are discussed in sections (6)–(8) of this chapter.

The position of non-executive directors is analysed in section (9) and considerations relevant to the dismissal of executive directors are raised in section (10).

Although the company may in principle dismiss and/or bring proceedings against a director for breach of duty, particular difficulties arise where the shareholders do not agree as to the course of action. Sections (11)–(12) consider the principle of majority rule, the circumstances in which the courts may intervene at the behest of minority shareholders and the removal of entrenched directors.

---

[1] See note 4 below; The Royal Society of Arts, *Tomorrow's Company* (RSA, 1995); and P. Goldenberg, *Shareholders v Stakeholders: the Bogus Question* (1998) 19 *The Company Lawyer* (forthcoming).
[2] *Evans v Spritebrand* [1985] FSR
[3] 8 *Halsbury's Statutes* (4th edn).

The possibilities of disqualification and criminal liability arising from serious neglect to ensure Year 2000 compliance are considered in sections (13) and (14). Section (15) reviews some of the implications in relation to the Thrombodirect example. Finally, section (16) covers the Bill introduced in Parliament by David Atkinson MP to require companies to carry out millennium assessments.

(2) DIRECTORS' FIDUCIARY DUTY

(i) Scope

The directors' fiduciary duties are owed to the company *alone*[1] by *each* director *individually*. Subject to limited exceptions, *no* fiduciary duties are owed to individual (including majority) shareholders as such. Historically, a director owed no fiduciary duties either to a prospective buyer of shares in the company or to future shareholders. Yet there are dicta suggesting that it is now the directors' task to balance the present shareholders' short-term interests with the long term interest of future shareholders.[2]

The legal duty placed on directors is for them to act *bona fide* in what *they*, not a court, consider is in the *best* interests of the company[3]. Thus, the test to be applied is primarily *subjective*. It is extremely difficult to show that the directors have broken their duty of good faith to the company. However, breach of this duty may be established where it is shown that directors knew of the likely *serious* consequences of their inaction for the company, but still failed to act.

The listing of the breaches of directors' fiduciary duties from the case law—namely as misappropriation of company property, exercising powers granted for one purpose in order to achieve another, putting oneself into a situation where duty and interest conflict, and fettering discretion—has tended to be used as a statement of the duties themselves. This can lead to the fallacy that, if the directors' behaviour does not fall under one of the above headings, as in the case of failure to take action on Year 2000 compliance, then it cannot be a breach of fiduciary duty. However, it is suggested that the categories of breaches of fiduciary duty are not closed in this way. In each case the question should be whether the conduct is bona fide in the best interests of the company.

Where the directors act in *their own* (i.e. selfish) interests and not in the company's interests, they can be in breach of their fiduciary duties, even if they act without any conscious dishonesty;[4] the latter is not required for there to be such a breach of a director's fiduciary duties.

---

[1] The leading authority for this is *Percival v Wright* [1902] 2 Ch. 421.
[2] Note the dicta of Megarry J in *Gaiman v National Association for Mental Health* [1971] Ch 317, 330; and of Lord Cullen in *Dawson International plc v Coats Patons plc* [1988] 4 BCC 305, 313. See also the Inspector's Report into the 2nd Savoy Hotel Investigation of 1954.
[3] See Lord Greene MR in *Re Smith and Fawcett* [1942] Ch 304, CA.
[4] See eg. *Re W & M Roith Ltd.* [1967] 1 WLR 432.

Historically the courts have been reluctant to intervene in this general context[1]. However, the learned editors of *Palmer's Company Law*[2] have suggested that currently the courts *will* intervene, where asked, if a *reasonable* director could not have concluded that a particular course of action was in the company's interests.[3] The same considerations must apply where little or no action is taken.

Where the company is one of a group the directors must continue to act in that company's interests and not look only at the group's overall interests, though the group's interests may be relevant to what is in the company's interests.[4]

A further question is whether the course of conduct or decision can be condoned or excused by a majority in the shareholders' general meeting. It is highly arguable that the duty to act *bona fide* in the interests of the company is an overriding duty. Indeed, as Professor Janet Dine has indicated,[5] the courts have come very close to unequivocally acknowledging its overriding quality. It is suggested that Professor Dine is right to conclude that "It is difficult to accept the ratification (excusing) of something which is the breach of a fundamental duty."[6]

(ii) Provisions exempting directors

The Companies Act 1985, s 310[7] generally declares void "any provision, whether contained in a company's articles or in any context with the company or otherwise, for exempting any officer of the company . . . from, or indemnifying him against, any liability which by virtue of any rule of law would otherwise attach to him in respect of any negligence, default, breach of duty or breach of trust of which he may be guilty in relation to the company." This ensures, *inter alia*, that "the unthinkable" cannot happen, namely that a company's directors validly arrogate to themselves any rights (say, in the Articles of Association) to act in bad faith against the company's interests.

The precise wording of the company's Articles may well be important in a millennium case where action is taken against the directors. For the courts have certainly permitted companies' Articles either to redefine or remove what would otherwise be prohibitions or disabilities[8]. In *Movitex v Bulfield and Ors*[9], for example, Vinelott J found that the company's Articles had not exempted the directors from a duty contrary to what is now s 310, but had relieved the

---

[1] See now *Popely v Plananite Ltd.* [1997] 1 BCLC 8.
[2] See *Palmer's Company Law*, para 8.508.
[3] See, for example, *Shuttleworth v Cox Bros & Co (Maidenhead) Ltd.* [1927] 2 KB 9,18, Banke LJ, CA; *Re A Company, ex parte Burr* [1922] BCLC 724, 731; and *Heron International Ltd v Lord Grade* [1983] BCLC 244, CA.
[4] See Farrar's *Company Law* (Butterworths 3rd ed) p 385.
[5] See her *Criminal Law in The Company Context* (Dartmouth, 1995), Chapter 2.
[6] *Ibid*, p 28. See further section (8) of this chapter.
[7] I.e. subject to s 310(3), which is also discussed in section 8 below.
[8] See further Dine *Criminal Law in The Company Context* (Dartmouth, 1995).
[9] [1988] BCLC, 104, Ch D..

director from a prohibition or disability under which he would normally be placed. Thus, this company was able to agree in advance that certain sorts of behaviour would not be regarded *automatically* as a breach of the fundamental duty to act in good faith in the interests of the company. Professor Dine concludes that Vinelott J's "separation of the fundamental duty to the company and the disadvantages and disabilities imposed by equity gives the court enormous flexibility to define the content of the fundamental duty to the company."

(3) DIRECTORS' COMMON LAW DUTY OF CARE, SKILL AND DILIGENCE

(i) Introduction

In contrast to the position concerning fiduciary duties, a director may owe duties of care in relation to his conduct as a director to persons other than the company, including, in certain circumstances, shareholders. The classes of persons to whom a director owes a duty of care are determined in accordance with the general principles discussed in Chapter 6 above. The discussion in this chapter primarily addresses the content of the duty of care owed to the company, which may also be relevant in considering the duties owed to others.

(ii) The *locus classicus* and the development of the law

Historically it has been appropriate to contrast directors' relatively light duties of care, skill and diligence at common law in relation to required levels of competence with their heavier duties of loyalty and good faith in relation to required honesty and avoiding conflicts of interest.

The old judicial views on care, skill and diligence were reflected in a whole host of nineteenth century cases. One such case was *Re Cardiff Savings Bank*[1] where the Marquis of Bute, having been appointed President of the Bank when 6 months old and then only attending one board meeting in his 38-year life, was held not liable for an alleged breach of duty. It is submitted that this is very likely not to be considered good law today. Despite Stirling J's strong dicta[2] in that case, non-attendance at board meetings can no longer be used effectively as a defence to a breach of duty[3]. Passive, non-attending directors of a company afflicted by millennium problems are most unlikely to escape legal liability on the grounds of passivity and non-attendance. It defies logic and fairness to give greater protection to a director who does not try at all to fulfil his duties than to one who tries hard but fails to meet the requisite standard of care, skill and diligence.

---

[1] [1892] 2 Ch 100.
[2] *Ibid*, at p. 109.
[3] See now *Dorchester Finance Co. Ltd. v Stebbings* [1989] BCLC 498.

The *locus classicus* on directors' common law duties of care and skill is to be found in *Re City Equitable Fire Assurance Co.*[1] where Romer J effectively summarised the position in three key propositions:[2]

- Directors need not show a greater degree of skill than may reasonably be expected of a person of their knowledge and experience.

- Directors need not give continuous attention to the affairs of their company: their duties, which are intermittent in nature, must be performed at periodical board meetings, and at meetings of any board committee on which they are placed; directors are not bound to attend all such meetings, but should whenever reasonably able to do so.

- Directors can delegate their duties to company officials in whom they have trust.

However, the position today is more complex. In determining whether a director has been negligent today, a court would wish to take account particularly of the ordinary course of management and practice of director(s), the whole character of their company business, the constitution of the company, the number of directors, the extent of the experience and knowledge of the director(s), and the circumstances of the case[3].

Regarding Romer J's first proposition, it is now clear that a director is not expected to be an expert unless appointed as such.

In relation to his second proposition, giving diligent attention to the company is now essential for a director. He is expected to have knowledge of those facts which it is his/her duty to be aware of *qua* director.

Romer J's third proposition, that "In respect of all duties that, having regard to the exigencies of business, and the articles of association, may be left to some other official, a director is, in the absence of grounds for suspicion, justified in trusting that official to perform such duties honestly"[4] is, it is suggested, still good law. There is earlier House of Lords authority on the point: *Dovey* v *Cory*,[5] where the matter was delegated to a plainly inappropriate official and the director was liable. Thus, the clear advice to directors is to ensure that, if they delegate responsibilities to an employee in relation to the millennium problem, then they *must choose* an *appropriate employee* for the task(s).

---

[1] [1925] Ch 407. The case went to appeal, but the propositions of Romer J were not doubted and have always been treated as authoritative.
[2] See further *Palmer's Company Law* at paras 8.408 *et seq.*
[3] See further *Palmer's Company Law*, para 8.411.
[4] [1925] Ch 407, at 429.
[5] [1901] AC 477.

(iii) **The more modern approach**

The start of the more modern approach to the common law duties can be traced to *Dorchester Finance Co. Ltd. and anor* v *Stebbing and ors*[1], decided in 1977 but much delayed in being fully reported. In that case, Foster J suggested that Romer J's statement in *Re City Equitable*[2] that "a director need not exhibit in the performance of his duties a greater degree of skill than may reasonably be expected from a person of his knowledge and experience", should *only* apply to the exercise of *skill*. This duty of *skill* thus should be distinguished from his duty of *diligence*, which required "such care as an ordinary man might be expected to take on his own behalf." The latter is an *objective* test and is plainly intended to be set at a pretty high level on the reasonable assumption that the ordinary man would be diligent in looking after his own affairs.

There is now significant evidence that the winds of change are blowing through the Chancery Division of the High Court, in relation to requiring directors to comply with their common law duties of care, skill and diligence[3]. The judges appear to be beginning to throw off the shackles of long-standing caution by becoming more proactive and gaining some inspiration from the Insolvency Act 1986, especially s 214(4),[4] to update these common law duties even where a company is not in liquidation: see, for example, *Norman* v *Theodore Goddard*[5], where the judge, Hoffman J., was "willing to assume" that s 214 represented the common law position.

It would appear that the Company Directors Disqualification Act 1986[6] ("CDDA"), which extended the courts' powers to disqualify individual directors from such office, has also influenced the judiciary to take a more interventionist approach to assessing the appropriate level of care, skill and diligence required of directors at common law[7].

The interesting question is how far the now more proactive judicial attitude is likely to go by the critical Year 2000 and just beyond.

(iv) **The landmark decision of *Re D'Jan of London Ltd*[8]**

This decision marks a change in judicial approach to considering how a company director must fulfil the common law duties of care, skill and diligence, in addition to acting in his company's best interests. Hoffman LJ (sitting at first instance) stated that the triple common law duty should be both

[1] [1989] BCLC 498, at especially 501–502.

[2] [1925] Ch 407, at 427.

[3] See e.g. P. Davies (ed) *Gower's Company Law* (Sweet & Maxwell, 1997 edn, pp 640 *et seq*).

[4] 4 *Halsbury's Statutes* (4th edn).

[5] [1991] BCLC 1028, Ch D.

[6] 8 *Halsbury's Statutes* (4th edn), discussed in section 14 below.

[7] See also further K Wardman, *Directors, Their Duty to Exercise Care and Skill: Do the Provisions of the Company Directors Disqualification Act 1986 Provide a Basis for the Establishment of a More Objective Standard?* (1994) 15 *Business Law Review*, 71.

[8] [1993] BCC 645, Ch D, Hoffman LJ.

updated and upgraded so as to apply all the time: "In my view the duty of care owed by a director at common law is accurately stated in s 214(4) of the Insolvency Act 1986." It is the conduct of "a reasonably diligent person having both the general knowledge, skill and experience that may reasonably be expected of a person carrying out the same functions as are carried out by that director in relation to the company and the general knowledge that that director has." Thus, the director was held to be negligent on the basis of the application of an objective test for signing, without reading, an insurance proposal form.

Importantly, Hoffman LJ here and in *Norman v Theodore Goddard* suggested that *both* the duties of care and skill should be subject to an objective test. Indeed, as the learned editor of *Gower's Company Law*[1], Professor Paul Davies, points out: "the line between an (objective) duty of diligence and a (subjective) duty to exercise skill is not always easy to draw, nor in principle should such a line be drawn." Professor Davies also rightly emphasises (at p 643) that whereas directors generally may be *en route* "to becoming subject to a uniform and objective duty of care, what the discharge of that duty requires in particular cases will not be uniform."

For precisely *what* is to be required of each director will depend on the functions given to him[2], the type of executive director or non-executive director that he is, and the type and size of the company.

(v) Factors determining what is required of directors

Where the directors delegate responsibility for millenium compliance and the employee to whom the task has been delegated is himself plainly negligent, one question will be: did the directors act in sufficient time in relation to what the employee did or did not do in relation to the millennium issue? English courts may follow developments in the Commonwealth, especially in this sphere as well as more generally in relation to directors' duties.[3] In particular, Australian judges have to date been more exacting in relation to directors' delegation of responsibility to their management personnel. English directors would therefore be well advised in both large and smaller companies to ensure that they are always in a position to monitor day-to-day management and so be able to ascertain quickly when matters are going wrong. This consideration plainly applies strongly in relation to the millennium problem.

[1] P. Davies (ed) *Gower's Company Law* (Sweet & Maxwell, 1997 edn), at p 642.
[2] The Insolvency Act 1986 formulation explicitly acknowledges this: see particularly the wording of s 214(5).
[3] See further the Hon Justice Ipp, *The Diligent Director*, (1997) 18 *The Company Lawyer* 162.

(4) DIRECTORS' DUTY TO CONSIDER THE COMPANY'S EMPLOYEES

The Companies Act 1985, s 309,[1] requires directors to pay regard in performing their functions to the interests of their company's employees in addition to those of the shareholders. This duty is owed just to the company, not to employees or members/shareholders as such. It could possibly be raised in the context of the failure to deal with the millennium problem. The duty is enforceable in the same manner as are fiduciary duties owed to the company. A shareholder can bring an action, despite the *Foss* v *Harbottle*[2] rule.

(5) DIRECTORS' DUTY TO THE COMPANY'S CREDITORS

Directors need to be aware of their potential legal liability for wrongful trading under the Insolvency Act 1986, s 214.[3] This will arise where a company has gone, or is about to go, into insolvent liquidation (and for our present purposes in the context of a financial disaster arising from the millennium problem); *and* the director(s) failed at that time to appreciate that there was no prospect of the company avoiding going into liquidation, so that the company continued to trade, failing to minimise the loss to creditors. An objective standard, as noted above, is applied under s 214. Under s 214(5), if he/they fail to carry out any functions that have been entrusted to them, judgment is applied as if he/they had fulfilled them. So a failure to act, including non-attendance at board meetings, for example, can render the director liable for wrongful trading. There may well even be circumstances relating to an insolvency situation where directors may have to give priority to creditors' interests over those of their shareholders. Again these considerations need to be particularly borne in mind where the millennium problem has caused the company grave financial problems.

There are judicial dicta suggesting that directors owe no duty to creditors apart from under the Insolvency Act 1986, ss 99 and 213–214[4]. To the contrary are dicta of Lord Diplock in *Lonrho* v *Shell*[5], of the Court of Appeal in *Liquidator of West Mercia Safetywear Ltd* v *Dodd and anor*[6] and of Lord Templeman in *Winkworth* v *Edward Baron Development Co Ltd & ors*[7]. It is submitted that these latter dicta are to be preferred. On the other hand, in determining whether directors have failed to comply with any general duty to creditors, it has to be borne in mind that the directors may have to balance the interests of creditors against those of other stakeholders. Thus in *Re Welfab*

---

[1] 8 *Halsbury's Statutes* (4th edn).
[2] (1843) 2 Hare 461.
[3] 4 *Halsbury's Statutes* (4th edn).
[4] See eg. Dillon LJ in the *Multinational Gas & Petrochemical* case [1983] 3 WLR 431, 442.
[5] [1980] 1 WLR 627.
[6] [1988] 4 BCC 30.
[7] [1987] 1 All ER 114, 118.

Engineers[1] Hoffman J held that directors were entitled to take into account the
desirability of saving the business as well as the interests of creditors.

(6) RELIEF AGAINST LIABILITY

Under the Companies Act 1985, s 727[2] the court can at its discretion give relief
against liability for *inter alia* negligence, default or breach of duty, *provided*
that, in the court's view, the director has behaved *reasonably and honestly* and
that he should be excused, having regard to all the circumstances. Section 727
is unavailable in relation to third party claims against a director.[3]

(7) INSURANCE AGAINST LIABILITY

A company can obtain an insurance policy on behalf of any of its directors (and
officers) ("D & O" insurance) which would cover the director should personal
liability be incurred while acting for the company. It was not until the
Companies Act 1989, s 137(1) amended s 310(3) of the Companies Act 1985[4]
that it became totally clear that this sort of insurance was permissible, although
it had been available on the market for some half a century.

The amendment to s 310, coupled with an increasing appreciation of
directors' potential liabilities, has led to a substantial increase in insurance
policies being taken out for both executive directors and NEDs during the
1990s. Yet the insurance policies available generally do not, and indeed cannot,
provide total comfort to directors. Certain claims are excepted. Any losses in
relation to directors' criminal liability cannot be covered simply as a matter of
public policy. Policies frequently specify that no claim can be brought where a
director has been dishonest or where environmental liability is raised. Whether
a director is covered for Year 2000 computer-related liabilities depends upon
the policy's precise wording. In any event, even with a protecting policy in
place, the director may not avoid litigation with its associated time costs,
stresses and potentially unfavourable publicity and damage to reputations.[5]

---

[1] [1990] BCLC 833, Ch D.
[2] 8 *Halsbury's Statutes* (4th edn).
[3] See *Customs & Excise Commissioners v Hedon Alpha Ltd* [1981] QB 818, CA.
[4] 8 *Halsbury's Statutes* (4th edn).
[5] See further S Turnbull and V Edwards *Companies Act 1989: Directors' and Officers' Liability
Insurance* (1990) 134 Solicitors Journal 768; and C Baxter *Demystifying D & O Insurance* (1995)
15 Oxford Journal of Legal Studies 537.

(8) RATIFICATION BY SHAREHOLDERS OF DIRECTORS' BREACHES OF DUTY

(i) Introduction

The courts have recognised for many years that a straight majority of the shareholders at a general meeting can release directors from certain types of breach of their fiduciary duties as long as the company is still a going concern. This is based on a general principle that a fiduciary duty may be released by the persons to whom it is owed if full disclosure of the relevant facts is made.

Judicial dicta suggesting that shareholder ratification via a resolution in general meeting can absolve a director in breach of a duty to the company from personal liability are exemplified by *Regal (Hastings) Ltd v Gulliver*.[1] There the directors, according to Lord Russell, " . . . could, had they wished, have protected themselves by a resolution (either antecedent or subsequent) of the Regal shareholders in general meeting. In default of such approval liability to account must remain . . . ".[2] However, there has been argument[3] as to whether there exists any reported English case in which a court has applied this so called Regal principle in favour of a director. Professor Cheffins recently concluded: "Because of the paucity of cases, judges have not had much of an opportunity to come to terms with the complexity and subtlety of the legal doctrines associated with ratification and the fraud on the minority exception. Consequently it should not be surprising that there is confusion surrounding this area of the law."[4]

The rule in *Foss v Harbottle*, discussed below, should also be borne in mind here. Even if a director is not released from liability, there may be no practical consequences if he cannot be sued. The courts have also suggested[5] that they would give effect to a shareholders' resolution expressly specifying that a minority shareholder could not litigate on behalf of their company.

(ii) Shareholders' exercise of voting rights

There is substantial case law authority which supports the idea that shareholders can vote as they wish and have no duty to take account of the interests of the company or of the other shareholders. For example, Jessel MR in *Pender v Lushington*[6] stated that a shareholder "may be actuated in giving his vote by interests entirely adverse to the interests of the company as a whole. He

---

[1] [1942] 1 All ER 378, HL.
[2] *Ibid*, at. p 389.
[3] See further RSC Partridge *Ratification & the Release of Directors from Personal Liability* (1987) 46 *Cambridge Law Journal* 122, especially at 137–8 and 143–47; and GR Sullivan, *Restating the Scope of the Derivative Action* (1985) 44 *Cambridge Law Journal* 236, especially at 247–50.
[4] Cheffins *Company Law* (Clarendon Press, 1997), p 335.
[5] See *Pavlides v Jensen* [1956] Ch 565, Ch D; and *Smith v Croft(No 2)* [1988] Ch 114, Knox J, Ch D.
[6] [1877] 6 Ch D 70.

may think it more for his particular interest that a certain course may be taken
which may be in the opinion of others very adverse to the interests of the
company as a whole, but he cannot be restrained from giving his vote in what
way he pleases because he is influenced by that motive". It appears that a
wrongdoer director can vote as a shareholder to ratify his/her own misconduct
on the *Pender* line of authorities. For example, Sir R Baggallay in *N W
Transportation Co Ltd & Beatty v Beatty*[1] stated: "every shareholder has a
perfect right to vote upon any such question, although he may have a personal
interest in the subject matter opposed to, or different from, the general or
particular interests of the company".[2]

(iii) The shareholder ratification issue in perspective

While the above statement of Jessel MR in 1877 is widely considered to be the
locus classicus on the subject, the legal position today is a little more complex.
It is widely accepted that if there is fraud or illegality involved, the company in
general meeting *cannot* ratify it. This consideration may potentially be relevant
in a case in relation to the millennium issue. A director, furthermore, who
ratifies his wrongdoing may generate grounds for a Companies Act 1985, s 459
petition.

To identify the precise limits on shareholders' power to ratify breaches of
fiduciary duties is a difficult issue. Indeed virtually a generation ago one
commentator[3] suggested that the question of which breaches of duty are
ratifiable, and which are not, is "the most difficult in company law." There is an
important argument for our present purposes that a breach of directors' duties
to act *bona fide* in the company's interests cannot be ratified by an ordinary
shareholders' resolution. In *Neptune (Vehicle Washing Equipment) Ltd. v
Fitzgerald*[4], Lightman J suggested that the Articles must expressly allow an
interested director to vote *qua* shareholder in order for this to be permissible.
However, earlier the Court of Appeal in *Bamford v Bamford*[5] operated on the
basis that such ratification was permissible. The current orthodox position in
English law is authoritatively summarised in *Gower's Company Law*[6]: "a wide
range of breaches of duty by directors may be ratified, whether arising out of
lack of bona fide . . . or negligence, provided no dishonesty or expropriation of
corporate property is involved".

However, in relation to negligence, there is a conflict of authorities. In
Pavlides v Jensen,[7] directors' negligence was held to be ratifiable, whereas in
Daniels v Daniels,[8] the court's implicit view was that it was not.[9] Furthermore,

---

[1] (1887) 12 App Cas 589, 593, PC.
[2] See also *Burland v Earle* [1902] AC 83, PC.
[3] SM Beck in 1973.
[4] [1995] 3 All ER 811, 814, Ch D; see also *Hogg* v *Cramphorn* [1967] Ch D.
[5] [1972] Ch. 212.
[6] 1997 edn, p 648.
[7] [1956] Ch 565.
[8] [1978] Ch 406.

whether *gross* negligence inflicting loss on *creditors* is ratifiable was considered by Cumming-Bruce and Templeman LJJ in *Re Horsley & Wright Ltd*[1] as non-ratifiable, at least where the directors utilise their own votes to absolve themselves. Yet the Court of Appeal later doubted the width of these dicta in *Multinational Gas & Petrochemical Co v Multinational Gas & Petrochemical Services Ltd.*[2] It should also be noted that in certain circumstances negligence in the company's management can warrant a Companies Act 1985, s 459 petition by a minority shareholder(s).

(9) THE POSITION OF NON-EXECUTIVE DIRECTORS

(i) Definition

Frequently the words "non-executive director" ("NED"), "independent director" and "outside director" are used interchangeably and loosely. However, this is incorrect as each is properly distinguishable from the other, although the categories can overlap. There are occasions when it is vital to use each expression correctly. For example, the Cadbury Committee on the Financial Aspects of Corporate Governance recommended[3] that a listed company should have three NEDs of whom two should be "independent", and Stock Exchange Rules now require the board's remuneration committee in such a company to consist *only* of outside directors.

Put simply, a NED is a company director who sits on the board without holding executive responsibilities, i.e. is outside the day-to-day management team. An outside director is a director on the board who is not employed full-time by that company. It has to be recognised that the NED is the phrase commonly utilised generically in the UK, whereas general US usage favours "outside director" often to describe the same person. The independent director, which is the narrowest of the three categories, sits on the board and may have shares in the company, but otherwise is not connected with the company (via a business or indeed any other relationship); the idea being that he is to be a *genuinely* independent mind on the board.

Thus, a company's accountant and/or solicitor from private professional practice who sit on the board would be *both* NEDs and outside directors, but not technically independent directors because of their professional business relationship with the company. This same categorisation would apply to an ex-executive board member who has recently retired from that position and become a NED.

In the following discussion, the term "NED" is used in the generic sense described above, except where otherwise indicated.

---

[9] See further, for example, M. Sterling (1987) 50 *Modern Law Review* 468; and Lord Wedderburn, (1984) 47 *Modern Law Review* 87.
[1] [1982] Ch 442, 455–456, CA.
[2] [1983] Ch 258. See further *Farrar's Company Law* at Chapters 25, 27.
[3] See *The Cadbury Report on the Financial Aspects of Corporate Governance System* (1992), p 22.

(ii) The NED's duties and potential liabilities

At present in English law, *all* directors, whether executive, NED, independent or outside, owe the *same* legal duties. Each is basically equally responsible for decisions reached by the whole board of directors, although the judiciary can, of course, build into their judgment in any particular case some allowances for differences in knowledge and experience between directors. Thus, an IT specialist NED, appointed to the board for his IT experience, who fails to face up to the millennium problem and/or to give the board the appropriate advice, is likely to be held in breach of his common law duties if there are serious problems which could have been averted. It was, for example, confirmed in *Dorchester Finance Co. Ltd v Stebbing*[1] that executive directors and NEDs *both* owed the *same* duties of care, skill and diligence.

Yet we await to see whether English (and Welsh) judges will soon acknowledge the increasingly widely recognised reality, that executive and NEDs fulfil distinctly different roles, and take this into account fully and explicitly. It is submitted that this legal development could easily occur in a millennium case. The Australian judiciary has already at least partially shown the way.[2]

We need, therefore, to consider briefly the usual functions of a NED today in a public company. Firstly, the NED will be monitoring and reviewing the executives' performance so as to be able to have a grip on whether they are fulfilling their legal duties and meeting the regulatory requirements as well as the appropriate ethical standards. So, in short, the NED is, or at least should be, regularly asking: is the company being run in the interests of the shareholders? Any potential or actual millennium problem within the company has to be addressed by the NED in relation to fulfilling this first role, as it may well be too in relation to the role discussed next. Secondly, the NED helps the executives to fulfil their functions. This will involve the NED offering advice (which, as we have already noted, may be specialist) and developing/utilising connections within other relevant organisations.

NEDs need to be fully aware today that any view that they may have held historically, that they were operating in a pretty risk-free environment legally, would be profoundly mistaken. They are nowadays operating in a more litigious, faster moving corporate culture and are inevitably facing legal risks, which are no more appropriately and strongly exemplified than by the millennium problem. As Henry LJ noted in *Re Grayan Building Services Ltd*[3], the "statutory climate is stricter than it ever has been."[4]

---

[1] [1989] BCLC 498.
[2] See notably the Supreme Court of New South Wales (NSW) decision of *AWA Ltd. v Daniels* (1992) 7 ACSR 759, although it should be appreciated that no particular distinction was drawn between executive and NEDs on appeal, although the judgment was upheld: (1995) 16 ACSR 607, 664.
[3] [1995] 3 WLR 1, 15.
[4] See generally on NEDs, Professor Brian Cheffins, *Company Law* (Clarendon Press, 1997), pp .96–108.

(iii) Practical pressures on NEDs

Unquestionably NEDs need to assert themselves to ensure that the millennium problem is firmly tackled wherever it could arise in relation to their company. Doubts have been expressed about the effectiveness of NEDs in influencing corporate affairs with pejorative nicknames being used to describe them[1]. Now, post the Cadbury Report, almost 50 per cent of the average board of a public listed company consists of NEDs, and this percentage is growing.[2] This should facilitate co-operation and even alliances between NEDs on boards. This consideration should help to reduce significantly the likelihood of NEDs being "toothless watchdogs" in relation to millennium computer compliance issues. NEDs very much trade (for future board appointments) on their reputations and track records as having been successful within companies, so that fear of a negative press on the millennium issue would be another factor which may well galvanise them into action to make sure their companies deal with this issue properly. NEDs of sizeable companies simply cannot afford to lose the confidence of institutional investors.

There have been a number of well documented examples of NEDs being centrally involved in the removal and replacement of leading directors, including chief executives and/or chairmen of plcs when matters "go wrong" in their companies (eg. the resignation of BP's Chief Executive in 1992 and the departure of Maurice Saatchi from Saatchi & Saatchi plc in 1995). Where executive directors responsible for handling millennium compliance issues fail to perform, NEDs may well need to assert themselves before it becomes too late to avoid disaster.

Should a company hit major financial difficulties through millennium non-compliance, it may lead to resignations of both some NEDs and some executive directors. Such self-sacrificing acts have symbolic importance and can prevent the need for litigation, which may be lengthy and very costly in more than purely financial terms.

(10) DISMISSAL OF EXECUTIVE DIRECTORS

The provisions of the director's service contract would be relevant as to whether the company would proceed to dismiss him/her summarily for *gross* misconduct. Executive directors of sizeable companies are very often employees so that the Employment Rights Act 1996[3] and its unfair dismissal provisions would be *prima facie* relevant to them, especially if they have two years' continuous employment with the company. An investigation and hearing

---

[1] See e.g. C Boyd, *Ethics and Corporate Governance* . . . (1996) 15 *Journal of Business Ethics* 167, 174; and Ross Perot's use of the words "board stiffs" and "pet rocks" to describe outside directors in the US, both cited by Professor Cheffins, *ibid.* at p 105.

[2] See e.g. the survey evidence cited in (1995) 3 *Corporate Governance: An International Review* at 72–3, 208, 215 especially.

[3] 16 *Halsbury's Statutes* (4th edn).

should take place, both as a matter of good employment practice and as a defensive mechanism for the company, before any director were to be summarily dismissed for gross misconduct. One issue would be whether gross misconduct was defined in the director's service contract. It would be helpful to the company if it were, and if it effectively covered the director's behaviour complained of in relation to the millennium problem. It would also be desirable for a company disciplinary code and procedure to apply to the director and be scrupulously followed.

The directors' service contract or the Companies' Articles of Association may provide that a director *must* resign where the majority of the board call upon her/him to do so. This neat "solution" avoids the need for any technical legal difficulties over a dismissal because there will simply not be one. This is subject, of course, to the proviso that there is no *constructive* dismissal (at common law, a wrongful dismissal, and under statute, an unfair dismissal), i.e. that there was no repudiation of the director's contract by the company (a fundamental breach *going to the root of the* contract) justifying the director in walking out at that time. This provision could be particularly useful where one director is plainly responsible for dealing with the millennium issue and fails in his task on the company's behalf. It leaves aside the separate question of potential liability of the director for damages as having been negligent in relation to the handling of the millennium problem.

(11) THE PRINCIPLE OF MAJORITY RULE

(i) The current position

Foss v Harbottle established the principle that the decision to enforce the company's rights against wrongdoing directors by suing them should normally be taken by the majority of shareholders in general meeting. The limited exceptions to the so called 'rule' in *Foss v Harbottle* have given rise to a complex and restrictive group of criteria for deciding when an individual shareholder can sue to enforce the company's rights against wrongdoing directors.

The remedy most commonly used by minority shareholders particularly in the smaller private company context is the personal remedy for unfairly prejudicial conduct under the Companies Act 1985, ss 459–461.

The Court of Appeal laid down guidelines in *Re Saul D Harrison & Sons plc*[1] as to when conduct might be "unfairly prejudicial". The principles set out in *Ebrahimi v Westbourne Galleries Ltd*[2] are also important in relation to the application of s 459, although it was a winding-up case.

---

[1] [1995] 1 BCLC 14.
[2] [1973] AC 360, HL.

In accordance with these principles, the courts will be prepared to go beyond any contractual documentation to ascertain whether any underlying understandings and/or expectations exist which provide a basis for relief under s 459. Furthermore, a petitioner under s 459 may succeed where the respondents have not been in breach of the company's Articles of Association or of any relevant statutory provisions, *provided that* the petitioner can prove that the conduct, which is the basis of the complaint, has had a sufficiently serious effect upon him to amount to "unfair prejudice". On the other hand, the judiciary have preferred to leave the players within the company to determine what obligations and rights exist *inter se*, although s 459's wording would appear to permit courts to grant relief on the basis of unfair prejudice irrespective of what the parties had actually agreed expressly. Warner J in *Re JE Cade & Son Ltd*[1] emphasised the court's "very wide discretion" in applying "the jurisdiction conferred on it by s 459 and 461 . . . but it does not sit under a palm tree . . . ".[2] Earlier, Hoffman J in *Postgate & Denby (Agencies) Ltd*[3] noted "s 459 enables the court to give effect to the terms and understandings on which the members of the company became associated *but not to rewrite them*".

The applicant under s 459 does *not* have to show that those controlling the company tried to harm him, or acted in bad faith or unethically or intended to act in an otherwise discriminatory way.[4] The decision in *Re Macro (Ipswich) Ltd*[5] is a good example of directors' negligent conduct substantiating a s 459 action where there was serious mismanagement, involving specific problematic acts which had gone unremedied *and* had a prejudicial financial impact.

However, the current orthodox view is that s 459 may not be used in respect of negligence as such: it really requires *serious* mismanagement in general[6]. Failure to make satisfactory progress on millenium compliance would be unlikely to justify the intervention of the court on this basis except, perhaps, in a serious case. The Law Commission also considered that under the present law a derivative action based on negligence can only be brought if the majority profited by the negligence. This consideration would *currently* appear to be a serious constraint in relation to the derivative action being utilised in the context of the millennium generating serious problems for a particular company and its shareholders.

(ii) Possible reform

The rule in *Foss v Harbottle*[7] has been subject to severe criticism over the years by many legal commentators.[8] It is now the subject of the Law Commission's

---

[1] [1992] BCLC 213, Ch D.
[2] *Ibid*, at p 227.
[3] [1987] BCLC 8,14, Ch D.
[4] See *Re Sam Weller & Sons Ltd* [1989] BCC 466, Ch D.
[5] [1994] 2 BCLC 354, Ch D.
[6] See Law Commission Report, para 6.38.
[7] (1843) 2 Hare 461. See the classic analysis by Wedderburn [1957] Cambridge Law Journal 194.
[8] See, for example, *Gower's Company Law* (1997 edn) p 659.

Report "Shareholder Remedies"[1], following on from the earlier Consultation
Paper[2] on this subject. The Commission prepared, *inter alia*, a new draft
Companies (Members' Proceedings) Bill with full explanatory notes, a new
draft rule 50 on Derivative Claims to go into new Draft Civil Procedure Rules,
a draft regulation 119 (on exit rights), plus a number of reforms to the
Companies Act 1985[3] and Insolvency Act 1986[4]. These could be in place by the
Year 2000 or soon after.

The Law Commission described the exceptions to the rule in *Foss v
Harbottle* as "rigid, old fashioned and unclear".[5] The Report[6] recommends a
new derivative procedure to be available, *inter alia,* if the cause of action arises
as a result of an actual or threatened act or omission including negligence,
default or breach of duty by the director(s); it will be against the director
(including a "shadow" director), or another person, or both. Only current
members should be allowed to bring a derivative action in the Commission's
view.[7]

The remedy under ss 459–461 was found to be costly, cumbersome and
inefficient with cases reaching trial often taking weeks rather than days.
Enormous costs can build up which exceed the sum of money in dispute.[8] The
Law Commission therefore proposed new primary legislation in relation to the
unfair prejudice remedy. Also since "prevention is better than cure", the
Commission has recommended (potentially most importantly in relation to a
millennium problem being satisfactorily resolved within a company) a new
Article to be added to the Standard Table A, i.e. the statutory model form of a
Company's Articles of Association, which provides a basic dispute-resolution
mechanism. This should in the future encourage shareholders to have pre-
agreed avenues to resolve disputes without resort to litigation. This will need a
statutory instrument for its implementation. In the meantime companies are free
to amend their Articles to incorporate such a new Article by following the
required procedure for amending the Articles.

The Commission's overall proposals fit neatly with the reforms for the civil
justice system proposed by Lord Woolf in July 1996.[9] Thus, for example, ADR
should be facilitated in this sphere. All these considerations are highly relevant
as to what *will* be appropriate actions to take in the Year 2000.

The Law Commission[10] recommends incidentally no reform of s 14
concerning a shareholder's enforceable rights under the company's
constitution.

---

[1] Report No 246 of October 1997.
[2] Consultation Paper No 142.
[3] 8 *Halsbury's Statutes* (4th edn).
[4] 4 *Halsbury's Statutes* (4th edn).
[5] See Consultation Paper No 142, at paras 1.6 and 14.1–14.4.
[6] *Ibid*, at para 6.49.
[7] *Ibid*, at para 6.50.
[8] See *Re Elgindata Ltd.* [1991] BCLC 950: costs of the 43 day hearing amounted to £320,000 with
the shares being finally valued at *just* £24,600.
[9] *Access To Justice* HMSO, 1996.
[10] See ibid, para 7.12 especially.

(12) REMOVAL OF DIRECTORS BY SHAREHOLDERS

The shareholders of a company have the right at any time to remove one or more of the directors (or even all of them) by ordinary resolution in a general meeting of the shareholders: see further Companies Act 1985, s 303.[1] Section 303(1) states: "A company may, by ordinary resolution remove a director before the expiration of his period of office, notwithstanding anything in its articles or in any agreement between it and him."

Section 303(1) does not, however, provide shareholders with an untrammelled right. Indeed the apparently considerable power provided to shareholders by s 303(1) can readily be reduced in a number of different ways. The directors may (long) previously have taken considerable steps to entrench themselves.

They may, for example, have made it an extremely expensive business to remove them by provisions in their service contracts for substantial "golden handshakes" in the event of dismissal or even "golden handcuffs". This may have been justified by the directors on the basis of a need for a "poison pill" to exist in order to repel hostile take-over bids.

The directors may also have persuaded the company to adopt Articles of Association which provide for weighted voting at any general meeting where a resolution is proposed for the removal from office of any director, as occurred in *Bushell v Faith*,[2] where the brother's three votes prevented his removal by his two sisters. In the case of public listed companies, such weighted voting would not be allowed. However, directors in private companies can still take advantage of *Bushell v Faith* type clauses to protect their own interests.

The directors have a number of other cards in their hands which they can utilise for their own benefit and to the potential detriment of critical shareholders. Apart from the matters which the directors are obliged to disclose to shareholders, the board of directors is in control of the flow of information to shareholders. Directors are aware of the old adage that "information is power". The directors are always able to put the most favourable gloss to themselves on any information that they are either required to give or choose to provide to shareholders. Directors also enjoy the power to solicit proxy votes from shareholders for which the company itself pays.[3]

A major restriction on shareholder power will occur where the directors hold effectively a majority of the shares. This can be less than 50 per cent of the shares in practice. In relation to a large public company it is commonly recognised that approximately 30 per cent of the shares held by the directors would be sufficient to give them effective control of the company because of the apathy factor applying to numbers of shareholders. Yet if the latter were to assert themselves, aroused by a seriously threatened collapse of the company

[1] 8 *Halsbury's Statutes* (4th edn).
[2] [1970] AC 1099, HL.
[3] *Peel v North Western Railway Co* [1907] 1 Ch. 5.

owing to a failure by the board of directors to address the Year 2000 computer compliance issue, the effective control figure would rise to nearer 50 per cent. Undoubtedly where the shareholder capital investment or dividend is threatened, shareholders are more likely to assert themselves.

Where the shareholders wishing to take action against the offending and/or negligent directors are minority shareholders, this will almost certainly necessitate them giving serious consideration to utilising the courts. This is most likely to involve them either using the statutory action under the Companies Act 1985, s 459[1] or seeking to use the problematic derivative action, with the attendant disadvantages discussed in section 11 above.

(13) DISQUALIFICATION

Before finding a company director to be unfit to be such under the Company Directors Disqualification Act 1986, s 6[2] ("CDDA"), the court needs to be satisfied that the director has been guilty of one (or more) serious failure(s), whether through incompetence or deliberately, to perform those duties of a director which are attendant upon the privilege of trading through companies with limited liability where the company has become insolvent. A court will make a disqualification order of between 2 and 15 years if it is is so satisfied. Peter Gibson J made it clear in *Re Bath Glass Ltd*[3] that any conduct of the director, whether as a director of the insolvent company or of other companies, *may* be relevant. This is even if it does not fall within a specific provision of the Companies legislation.

Until the 1991 landmark Court of Appeal decision of *Re Sevenoaks Stationers (Retail) Ltd*[4] the judicial line had tended to be that ordinary commercial misjudgement was not *per se* sufficient to justify disqualification and that normally the evidence needed to show a lack of commercial probity. It should also be appreciated that from the legislation's inception the courts have considered that disqualification is certainly appropriate where the evidence shows an extreme case of *gross* negligence or one of extreme incompetence.[5] Yet in the *Re Sevenoaks Stationers* case[6] the Court of Appeal stated that it was not required that a director should have shown total incompetence in order to be disqualified, effectively disapproving the somewhat cautious approach that the Chancery Division of the High Court had previously been taking. The Chancery judges have since tended to follow the bolder *Sevenoaks* line.

These judicial developments, and the likely legal consequences for directors, should now be understood by those directors failing to deal with the millennium issue, particularly where they should have appreciated that their

---

[1] 8 *Halsbury's Statutes* (4th edn).
[2] 8 *Halsbury's Statutes* (4th edn).
[3] [1988] 4 BCC 130,133.
[4] [1991] BCLC 325.
[5] See further *Re Lo-Line Electric Motors Ltd* [1988] 2 All ER 692, 696.
[6] See especially the dicta at pp 330 and 337 of the judgment.

company would be unable to avoid liquidation and so would be facing legal proceedings for wrongful trading too.

(14) CRIMINAL LIABILITY

(i) The nature and extent of the problem

Leading experts have suggested that the Year 2000 problem could cause danger to human life and thus impliedly could even result in deaths.[1] The major area for concern lies with software in embedded systems used to control various machinery and equipment.[2] These problems could affect nuclear power stations, critical temperatures on process lines, medical equipment, lifts, traffic lights and train signals. For example, many infusion pumps in intravenous drips contain an embedded chip which registers when the last periodical recalibration occurred and compares it with the current date. With the arrival of the millennium, such pumps would stop because the date calculation would indicate the last recalibration had occurred almost a hundred years ago unless they are properly modified.

(ii) EC Regulations in relation to criminal and civil liability

The Management of Health and Safety at Work Regulations 1992[3] require an employer to assess the scale and nature of any risk to occupational health in order to take the appropriate preventative and protective steps. Evidence that assessments have been done and recommendations fully complied with would be highly useful in defending any proceedings arising out of Year 2000 hazards.

The 1992 Regulations implemented in the UK many of the provisions of the EC Framework Directive (EC Directive 89/391) as well as some provisions of other related directives. The Regulations to implement individual directives made under the Framework Directive appear to be of strict liability. This is significant in relation to the embedded chips issue and millennium-compliance. Regulation 5(1) of the Provision and Use of Work Equipment Regulations 1992[4], for example, specifies that: "Every employer shall ensure that work equipment is so constituted or adapted as to be suitable for the purpose for which it is used or provided." Then reg 5(4) goes on to specify: "...suitable means suitable in any respect which it is reasonably foreseeable will affect the health or safety of any person."

---

[1] See particularly Julia Vowler, *How lethal is the millennium bug?* (1997) *Computer Weekly*, 6 November issue, pp 21–22.
[2] The degree of concern becomes greater in the light of the PA Consulting Report *Defusing the Millennium Bomb* (December 1997) which found that 44 per cent of organisations in their survey had not included embedded systems in their audits.
[3] SI 1992/2051, 9 *Halsbury's Statutory Instruments*.
[4] SI 1992/2932, 9 *Halsbury's Statutory Instruments*

The employer may be able to plead one of the general defences to civil
liability, or a defence provided by the particular statutory provision, where
there is potential criminal liability, *provided* that this has been permitted by the
relevant statute.[1] Some, but not all, of the newer regulations permit the
defendant employer in criminal proceedings to avoid liability where it can be
established that due diligence has been exercised. A reasonable practicability
defence may be available in *criminal* proceedings.[2]

(iii) The Health and Safety at Work Act 1974

The Health and Safety at Work etc 1974[3] ("HSWA") contains provisions with
the force of criminal law. Section 3(1) states that "It shall be the duty of every
employer to conduct his undertaking in such a way as to ensure, so far as is
reasonably practicable, that *persons not in his employment* who may be affected
thereby are not thereby exposed to risks to their health and safety". This is the
provision which has so far generated the most prosecutions. Under s 2(1) the
employer's duty is "to ensure, so far as is reasonably practicable, the health,
safety and welfare at work *of all his employees*". Section 4 requires that "each
person who has, to any extent, control of premises" must "take such measures
as it is reasonable for a person in his position to take to ensure, so far as is
reasonably practicable, that the premises . . . are safe".

In *Mailer v Austin Rover Group plc*,[4] Lord Jauncy stated: "ss 2 and 3
impose duties in relation to safety on a single person, whether an individual or a
corporation, who is in a position to exercise control over the matters to which
the duties extend. An employer can control the conditions of work of his
employees and the manner in which he conducts his undertaking". Lord
Jauncey also suggested[5] that "The ambit of s 4 is far wider then that of ss 2 and
3. It applies to anyone who is in occupation of non-domestic premises and who
. . . makes the premises available on a temporary basis for others to carry out
work in . . . " Lord Goff[6] described the defendant's duty as "an absolute duty".

The House of Lords examined the scope of the general duties in ss 2 to 8 of
the HSWA for a second time in *R v Associated Octel Co Ltd*[7], underlining the
highly onerous statutory obligations imposed on employers.

In *R v British Steel*[8] the Court of Appeal upheld the conviction of British
Steel for breach of its s 3(1) duty, with its derisory sentence of a fine of £100,
following the death of an independent contractor. British Steel had been
providing the equipment and supervision so that organisational failure was at
issue. Steyn LJ reaffirmed that s 3(1) imposes *absolute* liability in the absence

---

[1] See further the Health and Safety at Work etc Act 1974, s 47C3, 19 *Halsbury's Statutes* (4th edn).
[2] See further the Health and Safety at Work etc Act 1974, s 40, 19 *Halsbury's Statutes* (4th edn).
[3] 16, 19 *Halsbury's Statutes* (4th edn). See generally Professor Brenda Barrett (1997) 26 Industrial
Law Journal 149.
[4] [1989] 2 All ER 1087 at 1097, HL.
[5] At p 1098.
[6] At p 1090.
[7] [1996] 1 WLR 1543.
[8] [1995] 1 NCR 310, CA.

of a defence of reasonable practicability, adding[1] that "it would drive a juggernaut through the legislative scheme if corporate employers could avoid criminal liability where the potentially harmful act is committed by someone who is not the directing mind of the company".[2]

The Court of Appeal has most recently taken a similar approach in *R v Gateway Foodmarkets Ltd*[3] in relation to s 2(1). As Ann Ridley and Louise Dunford have recently noted,[4] "the effect . . . is to render a company vicariously liable for the acts and omissions of all its employees and, in most cases, those of its independent contractors".

(iv) Manslaughter

There has to date only been one corporate manslaughter conviction in England: *R v Kite and ors* (1996). This arose out of the Lyme Bay canoe deaths. The Managing Director was sentenced to three years' imprisonment, which was reduced by a year on appeal to the Court of Appeal.[5] The company was fined £60,000. There was very considerable evidence of *gross* negligence.

Ognall J had correctly directed the jury in his summing-up at the *Kite* trial: "what must be proved against the company is precisely what must be proved against Mr. Kite. A company can only act by, and be criminally responsible through, its officers or those in a position of real responsibility in conducting the company's affairs. It is usually put in this way, "is it proved that some person or persons who were the controlling minds of the company were themselves in this case guilty of manslaughter?" If the answer to that question is a sure "yes", then the company is likewise guilty".[6]

Since OLL Ltd was really a small company of the quasi-partnership type, significantly the identification of the mental state (*mens rea*) and the actions (*actus reus*) of the Managing Director with those of OLL Ltd proved possible.

The question is immediately raised of whether this would be possible with a large company (whether plc or private limited company). Would the structure of its management be too diffuse and/or complex to permit the prosecutor to attribute the act(s) or omission(s) to a director or other senior managerial figure within such a company ? While the answer would depend on the strength of the evidence and the full facts of the particular case. Ridley and Dunford[7] consider that "a large company would almost certainly escape liability".

---

[1] At p 313.
[2] See further I Mackey *Corporate Liability for the Health & Safety of Others* (1996) 146 New Law Journal 441.
[3] [1997] 1 RIR 189.
[4] In *Corporate Killing—Legislating for Unlawful Death?* (1997) 26 Industrial Law Journal 99 at 105–106.
[5] See *The Times*, 9 February 1997.
[6] Trial Transcript, p 18.
[7] Ridley and Dunford *Corporate Killing—Legislating for Unlawful Death?* (1997) 26 Industrial Law Journal 99 at p 107.

The difficult question of attribution has recently been the subject of attention from the Judicial Committee of the Privy Council, and Lord Hoffman in particular, in *Meridian Global Funds Management Asia Ltd v The Securities Commission*.[1] While it was a financial services case and thus apparently a long way from the issue of corporate manslaughter, Lord Hoffman's judgment, as Professor Celia Wells has rightly noted[2] "parallels the thinking of the Law Commission about the appropriate form of attribution to apply to corporate manslaughter".[3]

In *Meridian* the issue of whether securities legislation had been breached particularly depended upon whether the company had knowledge of the activities of its investment managers. Lord Hoffman effectively indicated that the so-called "directing mind" model may not always be appropriate in relation to attributing knowledge, or indeed other *mens rea* to a company. Indeed two other cases, *R v British Steel* and *In re Supply of Ready Mixed Concrete No 2*[4] in addition to *Meridian*, "show a shift in the courts' approach from the "directing mind" test involving the identification of a person within the company towards a test involving the attribution of a person's conduct to the company and permitting a more "organisational" approach, which recognises the reality of corporate decision-making".[5]

A practical question for our purposes is thus whether the judiciary would be willing to apply the *Meridian* approach to the sort of serious *common law* offence that manslaughter is, given that the three above cited cases all concern *statute* based law. Lord Hoffman stated:[6] " . . . their Lordships would wish to guard themselves against being understood to mean that wherever a servant of a company has authority to do an act on its behalf, knowledge of that act will for all purposes be attributed to the company. It is a question of construction in each case as to whether the particular rule requires that the knowledge that an act has been done, or the state of mind with which it was done, should be attributed to the company . . . ".

It should be emphasised that, post-*Meridian,* corporate manslaughter, a common law offence, needs proof of *gross* negligence by a *natural* person who is also *responsible for* the *death resulting.*

(v) The short term future

The Law Commission in its Report "Legislating the Criminal Code: Involuntary Manslaughter"[7] has proposed a new statutory offence of corporate

---

[1] [1995] 3 All ER 918.
[2] In *The Corporate Manslaughter Proposals: Pragmatism, Paradox and Peninsularity* [1996] Criminal Law Review 545 at 547.
[3] See further below for analysis of the potential practical implications in relation to criminal law liability for the purposes of the Law Commission's proposals.
[4] [1995] AC 456.
[5] Ridley and Dunford *Corporate Killing—Legislating for Unlawful Death?* (1997) 26 Industrial Law Journal 99 at p 107.
[6] [1995] 3 All ER 918, at 928.
[7] No 237 of March 1996.

killing. In 1994 it had produced a Consultation Paper[1] "Involuntary Manslaughter", which had considered the law of manslaughter at large. Its 1996 Report reflected considerably changed thinking on the Commission's part after a consultation process.

The Commission concluded that the approach of *R v British Steel* "would go far too wide" in a couple of respects:[2] namely: it would "virtually make the corporation strictly liable for the acts and omissions of any employee which resulted in death"; and it would become criminally liable without regard to the breach in question.[3] The Commission proposes that the ingredients of the offence of killing by gross carelessness should be applied to companies in a form adapted to the corporate context which does not involve the principle of identification.[4] The requirement that the risk of death or serious injury would have been obvious to the company or to a reasonable person in the defendant's position (since a company plainly cannot be placed in the same position as a human) would not therefore be applied here.

It will remain necessary for the prosecution to show that the conduct of the company was far below the standard that could reasonably be expected of it in all the circumstances. The judge in his summing-up will need to give guidance to the jury in its demanding task of balancing particularly the likelihood of harm and the cost of eliminating the risk of serious injury or death in relation to the company deciding whether or not to institute one or more safety measures.

The Law Commission proposes that the causation requirement will need to be adapted to the context for an accused company. The following questions would be relevant. What was the sort of conduct which led to the death? Was the perpetrator's conduct caused by the management failure? The Commission proposes that the focus should be on how the company undertakes its business on the assumption that prophylactic action can be taken organisationally against negligent or otherwise defective conduct. In relation to sanctions/remedies[5] the proposal is now for fines and remedial orders such as the court regards as appropriate in the light of the representations made.

It can be expected that the implementation of these proposals would lead to more successful prosecutions. One important factor here is the withdrawal of the need for identification within the definition of the offence. In the context of disasters arising from the Year 2000, it would be easier to obtain convictions in cases warranting prosecution of companies for corporate killing. Yet in practice *very much* would depend on the judgment of the jury in a trial: indeed the Commission explicitly recognises that conviction "relies on an unusual degree" on this factor.[6]

[1] Consultation Paper No 135.
[2] See Legislating the Criminal Code, Report No. 237 of March 1996, para 7.26.
[3] See *ibid*, para 7.27.
[4] See *ibid*, para 7.36.
[5] See *ibid*, paras 8.71–8.76.
[6] See Report, para 8.65.

A particular weakness, which has been well highlighted by Ridley and Dunford,[1] in the Commission's Report is that there is no consideration of the division of responsibility between the HSE/HSC and CPS nor of the role of the Police. Clearly these vital issues will need to be resolved before the Commission's proposals become law.

Two recent articles in The Times,[2] by Stephanie Trotter and by Gareth Watkins, raise the question of whether directors will *also* be commonly prosecuted and convicted where their companies are successfully convicted of the proposed new corporate killing offence. In a substantial correction[3] to the originally published article, Ms. Trotter opines that the emphasis can be expected to be on convicting companies themselves rather than on pursuing individual directors. Mr. Watkins, took the same view in relation to *large* companies held responsible for killing contractors, customers, employees or members of the public. But he rightly expresses concern that there may turn out to be an imbalance in treatment in applying the new law "because it will still remain easier to secure individual convictions against directors of small businesses" so that "directors of smaller companies will face greater punishment than the bosses of big business".

The new offence could easily become law before the end of 1999 so that it would be applicable in millennium cases which cause death. It seems that the Law Commission's proposals are being actively considered by Government and a Consultation Paper is expected to follow in 1998. A Government Bill could be introduced before the end of 1998 and become law in 1999.

(15) SOME COMMENTS ON THE CASE STUDY: IS TIME TICKING AWAY FOR THROMBODIRECT?

The Thrombodirect Group is potentially facing serious millennium problems given the nature of its manufacture and supply of medical equipment, including particularly time-controlled drug-delivery mechanisms.

The directors (apart from Mr. Wytook), are extremely ill-advised to take the view that the fears about the inability of computer systems to cope with the change of millennium are mostly the result of media hype. The NEDs hold *prima facie* the same legal liabilities as the executive directors. Mr. Wytook and the other directors will be facing various legal liabilities if they fail to avoid millennium problems. This looks a very serious possibility because Mr. Wytook does not have sufficient time to vet the operation of the software used by the group himself; and has not established a proper legal underpinning to the informal consultancy argument with B&W Agon Ltd, which is the company Mr. Wytook is expecting to help in the extensive operation. Furthermore, it appears that he has not carried out any due diligence inquiry as to B&W

[1] Ridley and Dunford *Corporate Killing—Legislating for Unlawful Death?* (1997) 26 Industrial Law Journal 99 at p 112.
[2] Stephanie Trotter *Safety must always come first*; Gareth Watkins *Small-firm bosses may suffer*, both *The Times*, 11 November 1997, p 45.
[3] *The Times*, 18 November 1997.

Agon's arrangements for sub-contracting through an informal arrangement with an agency in New Delhi. Since the Thrombodirect group heavily depends on IT for its operations, this is a very high risk strategy, which a court could find to be a reckless and negligent course of conduct by Mr. Wytook, in breach of his common law duties as a director.

Mr. Wytook should be advising his fellow directors that their complacency and ignorance are seriously misplaced. He should be putting this advice in writing and ensuring his advice is minuted at board meetings for his own legal protection. Mr. Wytook ought to be seeking to persuade his fellow board members that the companies and group as a whole should be investing sufficiently in the vetting operations to ensure a satisfactory and timely outcome. In addition to being out of a job, he could easily be a defendant in more than one set of legal proceedings.

(16) THE COMPANIES (MILLENNIUM COMPUTER COMPLIANCE) BILL 1997

(i) The context and need for the Bill

David Atkinson, MP, introduced this Bill into the House of Commons in early 1997 as a Private Member's Bill under the Ten Minute Rule Bill Procedure. Its basic objective is to require companies to conduct an audit, later changed in the course of its proceeding through the House to *an assessment*, of the capability of their computer systems to deal with calendar dates after 31 December 1999 and to report both on those assessments and on the consequential actions that their directors propose to take.

The Bill has had support from many quarters of the House, being formally brought in during February 1997 by, *inter alia*, Paul Channon, Sir John Cope and John Townend on the Conservative side, Richard Caborn and Tam Dalyell on the Labour side, Sir Russell Johnston of the Liberal Democrats, Dafydd Wigley of Plaid Cymru and the Rev Martin Smyth of the Unionists in Northern Ireland. It was, however, opposed by the Conservative Government on the ground that the proposed new legislation would impose greater burdens on business at a period when the Government was seeking to reduce such responsibilities and regulation of business.

Members of the Commons Standing Committee on this Bill were inevitably sympathetic to its objectives as they were chosen by its sponsor. Ian Taylor, then the Conservative Government's Information Technology Minister at the DTI, naturally took his Government's line but nevertheless put up amendments to the Bill as it proceeded. It went through its Commons Committee stage and then reached Report stage in late February 1997 but the General Election then intervened soon afterwards.

Mr Atkinson obtained approval in July 1997 for the Bill to be considered afresh in the new Parliamentary Session. However, there is little chance of its becoming law in 1998 unless the new Labour Government were to become very supportive of it and find time for it to be considered within its current busy Parliamentary timetable.

Perhaps the Bill's real value is as an awareness-creating vehicle for the Year 2000 computer compliance issue in a context of complacency and/or apathy. During 1997, for example, various national newspapers discussed the Bill to a greater or lesser degree. The more specialist IT press has also covered the Bill.

During 1996 David Atkinson MP had tabled Parliamentary Questions to each Government Department to which he received a range of responses. He then followed this up with a contribution to an adjournment debate in the Commons. The previous Information Technology Minister, Ian Taylor, at least partly in response announced the establishment of Task Force 2000 to be led by Robin Guernier and sponsored by the DTI in order to promote awareness of the computer compliance issue.

Mr Atkinson consulted the Top 100 FTSE Companies and in the light of their advice made certain amendments at Committee stage to his Bill. 80 per cent of those FTSE companies apparently wanted to see the Bill enacted.

(ii) The provisions of the Bill

It is a modest Bill containing just a couple of substantive provisions. Clause 1(3) seeks to amend the Companies Act 1985 by inserting a new section, namely s 719A (1) and (2): Section 719A(1) would specify:

> "It shall be the duty of every company in each financial year ending before 31st December 1997 to assess the capability of every computer system operated by the company and essential to the continued trading of the company and programmed to manipulate calendar dates to deal accurately with dates later than 31st December 1999 ("a millennium computer assessment")".

Section 719A(2) would state:

> "In this section, "computer" and "computer system" shall be construed to include any means of processing instructions capable, when incorporated into a machine-readable medium, of causing a machine having information-processing capabilities to indicate, perform or achieve a particular function, task and result and will further include (without limitation to the foregoing) a semiconductor chip embedded within a machine".

The second substantive proposed amendment to the 1985 Act is in Sch 7 (matters to be dealt with in directors' report), where the following would be inserted:

"Part VII
MILLENNIUM COMPUTER ASSESSMENT

13. — (1) This part of this schedule applies to a report by the directors of a company for a financial year ending in 1998 or 1999 (a "relevant year").

(2) The Report shall with respect to a relevant year state —

(a) the outcome of the millennium computer assessment required under section 719A above; and

(b) the proposals of the directors (if any are necessary) to make reasonable efforts to ensure that every computer system operated by the company and essential to the continued trading of the company and which is programmed to manipulate calendar dates will be able to deal accurately with dates later than 31st December 1999."

The Bill does not create any specific new remedies, sanctions or penalties for directions failing to meet its provisions. The ordinary existing remedies would apply where the company's directors' Annual Report to shareholders for financial years ending 1998 and 1999 failed to meet the proposed requirements of the new Sch 7, Part VII, para 13. The directors could also be held to account at the AGM by the shareholders for any failures. Furthermore any breaches could be reported to the DTI for it to consider appropriate action.

9 Due diligence

(1) INTRODUCTION

The Year 2000 problem represents a potential serious discontinuity in the business affairs of any company, affecting both its ability to trade effectively and the value of its underlying assets. Acquisitions made before 1 January 2000 must therefore have due regard to the likely implications, which may range from machinery, such as lifts, malfunctioning to the business as a whole being unable to trade or being crippled by overwhelming liabilities arising from defective goods or services supplied to a third.

The following fundamental questions should be raised by anyone contemplating the partial or total acquisition of a company or business ("the Target"):

- is there a problem for the Target?
- what is that problem?
- how will the Target's business be affected?
- how easily can it be remedied?
- is the Target aware of the problem and doing anything about it?
- is what the Target is doing appropriate?
- what are the remedial costs?
- how much less would the Target be worth in the event of remedial actions being unsuccessful?
- can the problem be transferred to someone else?

These concerns highlight the vital importance of due diligence in corporate transactions with respect to the Year 2000 problem.

(2) MEANING OF DUE DILIGENCE

In the context of commercial transactions, the term "due diligence" includes any investigation into the acquisition of a company or assets in a commercial context, risk analysis in financing or general pre-contractual enquiries.

Table 1: Different applications for due diligence

Type of person	Meaning
A buyer or seller of a company or business or assets	The investigation of the assets and liabilities of a company or business for the purposes of buying or selling it or its assets
A potential joint venture partner	The investigation of the assets being transferred to the joint venture vehicle and potential joint venture partners
A lender providing finance	The assessment of the viability of the project and the status of the borrower
A state body being privatised	The investigation of the assets and liabilities of the state enterprise for the purposes of privatisation
A company listing on a recognised Stock Exchange	The process of verifying information when preparing the listing prospectus
Entering into a contract	An analysis of the ability of the other contracting party or parties to perform

The common threads to each of these situations are:

- assets are being transferred from one party to another or obligations are being created
- risks exist that may affect the future value of those assets or obligations
- the parties need to apportion those risks between them

Accordingly, due diligence is applicable in varying degrees to a multitude of circumstances including asset swap transactions and creation of obligations.

This chapter covers due diligence for all forms of transactions but concentrates on the sale and purchase of a company or business and joint venture situations where the highest levels of due diligence are required. Due diligence processes for these transactions can be adapted for use in other commercial transactions. Accordingly, references to a buyer, should, where the context requires, be construed as including references to a joint venture party, lender or contracting party and references to a seller should be construed, similarly, to include a joint venture party, borrower or contracting party.

The scope and intensity of the exercise will depend on the size and importance of the transaction and, also, the human resources available to each of the parties.

(3) EXTENT OF THE PROBLEM AND SCOPE OF DUE DILIGENCE

When entering into a corporate transaction, the buyer will be concerned that:

- the value of the assets of the Target are not reduced as a result of the Year 2000 issue

- the Year 2000 issue will not expose the Target to unforeseen liabilities or commitments

Each of these is considered in turn below. However, it is worthwhile considering first the potential extent of the problem.

The Year 2000 problem does not just affect computer software, but can affect any equipment with embedded computer chips. Due to the proliferation of chips in industrial and office equipment, every piece of plant and equipment operated by a business must be considered as a prospect for failure after 31 December 1999.

Given the limited time typically available in a due diligence exercise, the buyer's strategy must therefore be one of selective analysis, focusing on the critical business systems operated by the Target and those of any key business partners.

(4) VALUE OF THE TARGET

(i) In general

The smooth operation of the Target may be affected by the Year 2000 issue:

- in relation to the performance of its own plant and equipment,

- indirectly impacting on the Target through its relationship with third party organisations with a Year 2000 problem.

(ii) Impact on Target's own plant and equipment

An obvious area of vulnerability is the Target's own plant and equipment, including of course its IT systems. The buyer should understand the full nature of the Target's plant and equipment. The key questions are:

- what parts of the Target's plant and equipment might be affected by a Year 2000 problem?

- has any analysis or testing been done to ascertain whether there is a problem?

- which critical business systems will be affected? Might this cause the Target to breach any obligations to third parties such as delivery of goods or services or payments to third parties including financiers?

- can liability for the Year 2000 compliance problem be transferred to a third party other than the seller, including:

    —suppliers of hardware;

    —assignors of intellectual property or software licences;

—licensors of software;

—suppliers of services, such as facilities managers, outsourcers, and maintenance suppliers?

- If so, what is the reliability of that entitlement and the covenant of the person liable? Might such an entity escape liability by terminating the current agreement, if any? Is there any contractual or tortious entitlement of the Target or seller that needs to be passed to the buyer?

Some of the specific questions the buyer should be asking are referred to in Table 2.

Table 2: The Target's IT system and Year 2000

• What plant and equipment, including software is the Target operating? An inventory should be prepared, highlighting that which contains embedded chips
• Who owns the plant and equipment?
• If owned by the Target, who supplied it?
• Was the licence or intellectual property in the software assigned to the Target by a third party? Were the assets purchased as part of a larger acquisition, with warranties attached?
• Is the equipment leased or subject to a hire purchase arrangement?
• Who procured the plant and equipment? If a third party, did their obligations include ensuring it was Year 2000 compliant?
• In respect of each piece of plant and equipment, who supplied the chip? Is the chip Year 2000 compliant?
• In the case of software, was the Target involved in developing it so as to shift some of the responsibility from the supplier?
• Are any IT or other services to be supplied by the seller after closing? If so, who will be responsible for Year 2000 compliance?
• If IT or other services are outsourced or managed by a facilities manager, what are the obligations of that supplier with regard to Year 2000 compliance?
• Who is responsible for any maintenance and is there any responsibility on them for Year 2000 compliance?
• Are there any other service providers who might be responsible for creating or repairing a Year 2000 problem?
• Does the Target's insurance protect it against business interruption and other losses as a result of a Year 2000 problem?
• If work has been done on Year 2000 compliance, was an external solution provider involved? If so, are they known as being credible? What warranties (and limits on them) did they provide for the quality of their work? What is the reliability of their covenant?
• Could any third party obligations to the Target in respect of Year 2000 compliance be adversely affected by the proposed transaction?

Where the buyer's enquiries reveal a potential Year 2000 problem which is of sufficient size, consideration will need be given to the best way of managing the cost involved in repairing the problem and, in certain cases, the viability of the acquisition itself. The "win win" situation for the buyer and seller is for an external party to be responsible for the problem. If existing contractual obligations are unclear with a supplier, it may be desirable for the seller to endeavour to negotiate a binding obligation with the supplier prior to closing.

(iii) Impact of third party organisations on the Target

The buyer should also consider which other organisations have a relationship with the Target close enough to impact upon it in the event that the third party has a Year 2000 problem. These may include those listed in Table 3.

Table 3 Third party organisations which may impact on the Target

Type of third party	Examples of problems
Suppliers	Failing to deliver goods or services due to Year 2000 problems.
	Breakdown of operational relationship based on IT interface.
	Inability to process financial and other records accurately.
Customers	Breakdown of operational relationship based on IT interface.
	Inability to process financial and other records accurately.
	Inability to service customer orders.
Franchisors, franchisees, agents, distributors, licensors, licensees	Breakdown of operational relationship based on IT interface.
	Inability to process financial and other records accurately.
Other group companies	Breakdown of operational relationship based on IT interface.
	Inability to process financial and other records accurately.

The general questions that the buyer should be asking in each case are:

- Might a Year 2000 problem in any one of these organisations have an adverse effect on the operation of the Target?

- If so, what might the impact be?

- If the impact is serious, what steps have been or can reasonably be taken to manage the problem?

- If no steps have been taken, should any analysis of the size of the problem be done before closing?

- Can the buyer transfer the cost of the problem onto someone else e.g. the third party, the seller or an insurer? If a third party, what is the reliability of their covenant?

Particular care should be taken where the Target manufactures or assembles plant or equipment. Have its suppliers been Year 2000 compliant in the past when supplying the Target? Are they now? If not, will this have an impact on the Target's production and potential liabilities? One can imagine a situation where a key supplier is not Year 2000 compliant, causing the Target's entire production facility to grind to a halt.

(5) LIABILITIES

(i) Introduction

The buyer should also consider whether the operation of the Target (whether past, present or future) might pose significant risks, liabilities or commitments. This will primarily apply where the buyer is purchasing the shares in the Target rather than its assets, as contractual liabilities do not usually pass to the buyer in an asset sale.

The key question here is whether the activities of the Target might expose it to claims from third parties if it has a Year 2000 problem. This area can be divided into two:

- product liability;
- incidental liability

(ii) Product liability

The buyer's key concern will be whether any of the Target's products or services might expose it to liability for a Year 2000 problem. This will include past products or services. Consideration should be given to 'bundled' products supplied, where another party's software operates the Target's product but both items have been supplied by the Target. Might the Target be liable for a Year 2000 problem arising from that software?

Product liability will also apply to any organisations for which the Target may have been liable in the past or the future, such as where the Target has sold a business and provided warranties for any problems arising in the future. Consideration should also be given to any organisations for which the Target may be liable under contractual arrangements with the customer or under product liability legislation. This area has added poignancy due to the potential criminal penalties on the managers and directors appointed by the buyer, as well as the organisation.

As mentioned earlier, all services and products provided currently and over an appropriate past period should be considered as to whether they expose the Target to liability. Some lateral thinking should be injected into this analysis. Could a failure of a component or system reliant upon goods or services supplied by the Target lead the customer to incur liability itself, which is then laid at the door of the Target? An example might be a component supplied by the Target which forms part of the steering system of oil tankers, which fails causing the tanker to crash.

If there is a potential problem, the Target's liability under its terms of supply and any statutory and general law provisions should be considered. The problem will then need to be quantified. Can the liability be transferred to another party, such as any supplier or other party involved in the design, manufacture or supply of the product or service, or an insurer?

Obviously, this issue will be of greater concern where the Target is involved in the IT industry or the supply of equipment containing embedded chips.

(iii) Incidental liability

The buyer should also consider the impact of the Target's operations, both past and present, on third parties and any liability that might arise from that. These will include those parties referred to in Table 3.

(6) LEGAL PROTECTION

(i) Inquiries, responses and warranties

In considering the various questions and issues referred to above, the buyer should seek the views of the Target as well as use its own intelligence. Whilst the Target management will know the business of the Target far better than the buyer will, the Target may not have addressed the Year 2000 problem in any depth, and analysis by the buyer may be more incisive.

When doing its due diligence, the buyer should endeavour to structure the process so as to maximise the amount of legally binding representations being provided by the seller. There are two ways in which this is usually done:

- where the seller has agreed to warrant the accuracy of written responses provided to written enquiries by the buyer's lawyers, by putting careful written enquiries through its lawyers;

- by framing warranties in the Sale Agreement which cover the situation.

However, the above types of warranty are unlikely fully to protect the buyer, as they are usually limited as to amount and time. They can also be difficult to collect on, being subject to dispute and the potential insolvency of the sellers although the buyer's position can be bolstered by requiring some of the purchase price to be deferred. Nor do they protect against criminal penalties. Accordingly, the buyer should also consider additional forms of protection as referred to below.

Where the buyer becomes aware that there is a Year 2000 problem prior to closing, its knowledge may vitiate a claim in respect of any representation by the seller under the responses or a warranty from the seller that there is no problem. In such case, the buyer should negotiate some form of indemnity or compromise from the seller to compensate for the problem. Where possible, the problem should be remedied in advance of closing to reduce the risks to either side. In some cases it is necessary to restructure the transaction.

(ii) Remedying the problem

In a limited number of circumstances, the seller may be able to transfer the risk of a Year 2000 problem onto a third party ahead of closing, particularly if the problem reduces the value of an asset. For instance, the seller may be able to arrange for documentation to be completed whereby a supplier confirms its responsibility for Year 2000 compliance. However, any contractual documentation with a third party which assumes liability for the problem should be carefully considered to ensure that it will not be vitiated by the acquisition. This will particularly apply if the transaction is an asset sale. Contracts are often personal to the parties originally contracting, and may not be assignable.

(iii) Indemnities

The buyer may want the seller to undertake to indemnify it for losses arising in the future as a result of the problem. The weaknesses regarding indemnities are the same as those discussed above regarding warranties, namely limitation as to quantum and time, and uncertainty of collection.

(iv) Compromise on terms

The buyer may also seek some form of compensation in the terms of the transaction to account for the problem. In this case, the buyer usually assumes the future risk and receives its compensation now.

(v) Insurance

Where the Target has insurance protection in place covering risk to its own assets and business or its liability to third parties, the buyer should consider whether the benefit of that cover will pass to the buyer on closing. What are the terms, conditions and limitations of that cover? If cover is to pass to the buyer, the buyer should seek a warranty from the seller that all requirements of the insurance have been complied with.

The buyer should also consider whether its own insurance may cover the Target, particularly where it has a group policy in place. However, careful analysis of the policies should be undertaken to ensure that cover will be effective and adequate.

(vi) Deferring the transaction

As most Year 2000 problems will manifest themselves either in the run up to 1 January 2000 or very soon thereafter, the buyer may decide to defer the transaction accordingly and wait to see whether any problems arise.

(vii) Restructuring the transaction

Where the buyer has identified potential serious liabilities, particularly those which are difficult to quantify, it may be better to structure the transaction so that the buyer is acquiring the assets of the Target rather than the shares in it. In this way, the liabilities generated before closing will largely remain with the Target company and will not be passed to the buyer.

(viii) Walking away

Where the liabilities are potentially high, and the Target cannot be acquired by way of asset sale, the buyer may be forced to make the difficult decision to walk away from the transaction.

(7) CONCLUSION

The importance of due diligence cannot be overstated, particularly when the well known case of Ferranti International is considered. There, one of the greatest names in British corporate history was forced to call in the receivers after have been weighed down by more than £140 million of debt following its acquisition in 1989 of a US company, International Signal & Control.

Because of the potentially serious issues arising from the Year 2000 problem, buyers will need to have particularly regard to due diligence in this area.

10 Litigation and Dispute Resolution

(1) INTRODUCTION

The procedural aspects of Year 2000 litigation may appear unimportant to the prospective litigant, at least until the litigation itself begins. Thereafter, procedural issues will loom larger, as these can radically tilt the playing field in one direction or the other, and possibly even lead to a rapid "technical" victory or defeat. This chapter deals in outline with aspects of the machinery of dispute resolution which ought to be in the mind of anyone faced with the prospect of Year 2000 litigation. Of course, in such a position, there is absolutely no substitute for proper legal advice, taken as early as possible.

This chapter deals exclusively with actions for damages, not for injunctions, declarations or other equitable remedies. Although it is difficult at this remove to foresee exactly what forms the legal response to the Year 2000 situation will take, it seems likely that the vast majority of Year 2000 claims will be for money compensation alone. It is unlikely that a plaintiff will wish a defendant to alter his future behaviour, which is the object of an application for an injunction, and it is likely that damages will be regarded as an adequate remedy in the vast majority of cases.[1]

It should be remembered that settlement and the use of alternative dispute resolution ("ADR") are alternatives to litigation. As well as the potential saving of costs, they can result in solutions which continue a working relationship between the parties which cannot be provided by litigation. ADR is discussed in section (9) below.

(2) THE STAGES OF LITIGATION

(i) Which tribunal?

Assuming that the case is to be heard within the jurisdiction of England and Wales, the possible venues for Year 2000 litigation are the High Court, the County Court or arbitration. Under current rules, the County Court may be used for actions where the total damages claimed, including interest, is less than £50,000, and must be used for those worth less than £25,000. The likely complexity of a issues involved is also taken into account. A dispute may go to arbitration either because it is covered by an arbitration clause, or because the disputing parties agree to submit the matter to arbitration. There are, of course,

---

[1] *London and Blackwall Ry. Co. v Cross* (1886) 31 Ch D 354, 369, and see, in general, 24 *Halsbury's Laws*, para 826.

no limits as to the sums which may be involved. Arbitration is covered in section 8 of this chapter.

The procedural rules of the High Court and the County Court are generally similar. The text below will cover the position under the Rules of the Supreme Court[1] ("RSC") which apply to the High Court.[2] However, readers should note that some important changes to the procedures in all courts in England and Wales are likely as a result of the Woolf Report, which is discussed in section 10 of this chapter.

(ii) Time limits

The text below mentions certain standard time-limits which apply to the service and validity of procedural documents. Although these are prima facie mandatory, it is possible for them to be extended, either by agreement with the other side and/or by application to the court under RSC, Ord 3, r 5.

(iii) The letter before action

It is traditional, although not mandatory, to give one's opponent a "final warning" that proceedings will be commenced unless he complies with one's wishes within a certain time. The drafting of a letter before action is usually done with the aid of legal advice.

(iv) The writ

The issue of a writ by the court, in terms requested by the plaintiff, formally begins the action.[3] The writ states the cause of action of the plaintiff, and the relief sought. The writ may also have endorsed on it the statement of claim, which is a summary of the facts said to give rise to the cause of action. In complex actions, the statement of claim is usually served separately.

The writ must be served within four months of the date of its issue, otherwise it becomes invalid, although the plaintiff can apply for extension of the four month period if service is proving difficult.[4] Separate rules, including a six-month period of validity, apply to service of writs outside England and Wales.[5]

---

[1] SI 1965/1776. All Rules of the Supreme Court may be found in 5 *Halsbury's Statutory Instruments*.
[2] The Rules of the Supreme Court are made up of Orders ("Ord") and Rules ("r").
[3] See, in general, RSC, Ord 5.
[4] Ord 6, r 8.
[5] See, in general, Ord 11.

(v) Acknowledgement of service

Once the writ has been served on the defendant, he must acknowledge service and state whether he intends to defend the action within fourteen days. Failure to acknowledge service allows the plaintiff to seek judgment in default, that is without hearing from the defendant, where the action is for damages or certain other remedies.[1]

(vi) Statement of claim

The statement of claim is a pleading, that is a document setting out, in a concise form, the material facts on which the plaintiff relies. Other pleadings are the defence, and reply, if any. The statement of claim must be served on the defendant within fourteen days of receipt of the acknowledgement of service form, although a longer period can be either ordered by the Court or agreed by the parties if necessary.[2]

(vii) Defence

The defence is the defendant's pleading in response to the statement of claim. It sets out the defendant's version of events, usually disputing elements of the facts asserted by the plaintiff, or pleading other matters which are alleged to disentitle the plaintiff from the remedy claimed. Any allegation in the statement of claim which is not traversed in the defence is deemed to be admitted[3], so it is important that the defence either denies or states that it does not admit any fact asserted in the statement of claim which the defendant disputes or is not sure of. Further, the defence must specifically plead any positive case of the defendant which might otherwise take the plaintiff by surprise, e.g. limitation, performance, illegality etc.[4] The defence must usually be served within fourteen days of the service of the statement of claim.[5]

(viii) Counterclaim

If the defendant has a cross-claim against the plaintiff for which he has not yet begun proceedings, he may plead it in the action begun by the plaintiff in mitigation or extinction of the plaintiff's claim and/or as a separate claim in itself. The counterclaim is treated as a claim against the plaintiff, so that he must serve a defence to it, and the various procedural rules discussed in this chapter in relation to the main action apply equally to the counterclaim.[6]

[1] Ord 13, rr 1–5.
[2] Ord 3, r 5.
[3] Ord 18, r 13(1).
[4] Ord 18, r 8.
[5] Ord18, r 2.
[6] Ord 18, r 18.

(ix) Reply

If new factual matters are raised by the defence the plaintiff may serve a reply to it, which may also include a defence to any counterclaim. The reply should be limited to the matters raised in the defence and should be served within fourteen days of the service of the defence.[1] It is also possible for further pleadings (rejoinders, surrejoinders etc) clarifying the issues between the parties to be served with the leave of the court[2], although this is very rare.

(x) Clarifying the matters pleaded

If any part of a pleading is unclear, or a party wishes to "draw out" an opponent as to the factual basis of his claim or defence, or have his opponent admit certain facts so as to save costs at trial, then a request for further and better particulars of a pleading[3], or interrogatories[4] (questions as to specific issues) or a notice to admit certain facts[5] may be served.

(xi) Discovery

In High Court writ actions, discovery usually occurs without the making of an order, fourteen days after the close of pleadings.[6] Each side discloses lists of those documents which are relevant to the case and are within the possession, custody or power of that party.[7] Once lists are disclosed, each party must allow the other side to inspect and take copies of the documents listed except those protected by legal privilege.[8] In practice, photocopies of documents are often requested and provided instead of the physical inspection of the originals.

"Documents" in this context also refers to non-paper methods of information storage which can be read by means of a machine, such as computer databases and word-processing files.[9]

It is essential that every relevant and qualifying document is disclosed. Failure to disclose an "unhelpful" document is viewed extremely seriously by the court. Ord 24, r 16 allows the court to deal with a failure to comply with an order for discovery by making such order as it sees fit, including dismissing a claim, striking out a defence and entering judgment. Parties receiving documents on discovery may only use them for the purpose of the litigation and

---

[1] Ord 18, r 3.
[2] Ord 18, r 4.
[3] Ord 18, r 12.
[4] Ord 26.
[5] Ord 27, r 2.
[6] Ord 24, r 2.
[7] Ord 24, r 1.
[8] Ord 24, r 9.
[9] *Derby & Co v Weldon (No 9)* [1991] 1 WLR 652; *Alliance & Leicester BS v Ghahremani* [1992] 32 RVR 198.

not for any ulterior purpose[1], unless it has been read or referred to in open court.[2]

(xii) Directions

Usually one month after the close of pleadings, the plaintiff must take out a summons for directions.[3] Directions hearings are to allow the court and the parties to prepare for the trial of the action. Matters considered include whether the action should be transferred to a County Court or the Official Referee's Court, the number and types of experts who can be called, the dates on which witness statements and expert reports will be exchanged and the service of any interrogatories or further and better particulars of a pleading. In default of the plaintiff taking out a summons for directions, the defendant may do so, or apply for the action to be dismissed.[4] In theory, all procedural matters should be covered by the summons for directions, but in practice there are often separate applications in relation to procedural disputes as they arise.

(xiii) Pre-Trial review

Under the County Court Rules, where there are often automatic directions for the conduct of the litigation, the court may make an order that a pre-trial review ("PTR") should be held instead of ordering automatic directions.[5] In the County Court, the PTR has a similar function to the directions hearing in that the District Judge will consider the course of proceedings and make the appropriate directions, including directions for the date of trial.

In the High Court, it is becoming more common for the court to conduct PTRs in lengthy or complex cases. In the Chancery Division, PTRs are required for cases which are listed to take more than ten days.[6] In the Commercial Court, those conducting the action are required to consider whether a PTR would be useful in addition to the directions hearing.[7]

(xiv) Trial

Surprisingly few civil actions ever get to the trial stage. The majority of actions are settled well beforehand. Responsibility for setting a matter down for trial at the court office lies with the plaintiff, and the time limit for doing so is usually set at the directions hearing.

---

[1] *The Distillers Co (Biochemicals) Ltd v Times Newspapers Ltd* [1975] 1 QB 613.
[2] Ord 24, r 14A.
[3] Ord 25, r 1.
[4] Ord 25, r 1(4).
[5] County Court Rules 1981, SI 1981/1687, Ord 17, r 11(4), 5 *Halsbury's Statutory Instruments.*
[6] *Chancery Guide*, para 3.10.
[7] Guide to Commercial Court Practice, Appendix IV - Summons For Directions Checklist, Appendix VI Pre-trial Checklist.

Most civil trials are before a single judge. Witnesses normally confirm their witness statements and are cross-examined by the other side's advocate. The advocates for each side make submissions to the judge on the law and the facts of the case.

(xv) Judgment and interest

In complex cases, judgment is often reserved, that is the judge goes away to think about the case and write a judgment giving the reasons for his decision. In urgent matters, judgment for one side or the other may be given immediately, with a full account of the judge's reasoning at a later time.

Where the plaintiff is successful, and damages are awarded, the plaintiff will almost always have made a claim for interest. Interest at a rate previously set by a contract, which may specify that the interest is to be compounded, can be claimed.

If there is no right to contractual interest, the court has a discretion under s 35A of the Supreme Court Act 1981 to award simple interest on the sum awarded as damages. The matters of the amount of interest to award, the rate, and the period over which to award it are all at the discretion of the court. However, in most cases the court will award interest from the date or dates on which the damage occurred, at a rate equivalent to the judgment debt rate, which is 8 per cent at the time of writing. Interest at the judgment debt rate will also accrue for the period that the judgment is unpaid.

In some cases it may be possible to claim interest as damages where the plaintiff has had to borrow money as a result of the defendant's breach of duty, and this was reasonably foreseeable to the defendant.[1]

Appeals from the High Court are to the Court of Appeal, and, ultimately, to the House of Lords. Many appeals are not as of right, but require the leave of either the lower court or the appellate court.

(3) OFFICIAL REFEREE'S BUSINESS

It is quite possible that many Year 2000 cases will be started in the Official Referee's Courts. Official Referees are Circuit Judges who sit as Judges of the High Court on a permanent basis, and tend to deal with cases where there is a good deal of technical or scientific evidence. Many construction, engineering and, increasingly, computer-related disputes are heard in the Official Referees' Courts.

The Official Referee's Courts have special rules and procedures which go towards simplifying what will be rather complex factual issues as much as

[1] *Wadsworth v Lydall* [1981] 1 WLR 598; *Bacon v Cooper Metals* [1982] 1 All ER 397.

possible[1]. Interlocutory applications are dealt with the Judge himself, not a District Judge or Master, and the Judge tends to take a more robust approach to directions than is often the case elsewhere.

In the Official Referee's Courts pleadings are often directed to be made in the form of a "Scott Schedule", where each item of the claim is answered by the defendant in the same document. Evidence in chief is often limited to signed witness statements, the number of expert witnesses is often limited, and the expert witnesses are often required to meet to agree as much of the technical evidence as possible.

(4) LIMITATION ISSUES: SUGGESTED APPROACHES

(i) The "holding writ"

Among the first questions for a lawyer planning any Year 2000 litigation ought to be "is it in time?". A "contractual audit" of the type being undertaken in many organisations in respect of Year 2000 issues should help in identifying any causes of action. If it transpires that a cause of action has already arisen, then it may well be wise to issue a writ within the limitation period, even if it is expected or hoped that the problem can ultimately be solved without recourse to the courts.

Such "holding writs" are commonplace. The issue of a writ does not inevitably lead to trial as, of course, negotiations proceed during preparation for trial, and can go on "up to the door of the court". In fact, it is often the issue of a writ that ensures that negotiations begin in earnest. Potential defendants may be keen to delay negotiations for as long as possible, in the knowledge that time is ticking away for potential plaintiffs, and that, eventually, the lack of a writ will mean that the heavy artillery of litigation is no longer available. Once a writ is issued there is no incentive for defendants to stay away from the table.

However, the issue of a writ brings with it certain requirements. The courts take a dim view of those who waste their time. As mentioned above, a writ which is not served is generally only valid for four months, and pleadings and other stages in the action are subject to a timetable. Actions can be and are struck out for want of prosecution, and the courts must generally be satisfied that their processes are not being abused, particularly where there is a risk of prejudice to another party because of delay.[2]

---

[1] See, in general, RSC Ord 36.

[2] See the guidance of the Court of Appeal in *Costellow v Somerset County Council* [1993] 1 WLR 256, and *The Supreme Court Practice* 3/5/6. It has recently been held that inordinate and inexcusable delay by a plaintiff in full awareness of the consequences which amounted to a wholesale disregard of the Rules of the Supreme Court justified the striking out of the claim, even where prejudice to the defendant was not shown: *Arbuthnot Latham Bank Ltd v Trafalgar Holdings Ltd* The Times, 29 December 1997; *Choraria v Sethvia* The Times, 29 January 1998.

(ii) The "standstill agreement"

An alternative, or complement, to the holding writ is for potential plaintiffs to agree with potential defendants that time will not run against the plaintiff, on condition that the defendant will take no point on limitation if and when proceedings begin, notwithstanding the fact that the limitation period may have by then expired.

Although this practice is becoming more common, there is a dearth of authority on such agreements. In *Lubovsky v Snelling*,[1] the Court of Appeal held that an admission of liability while the action was still within time amounted to an agreement not to rely on s 3 of the Fatal Accidents Act 1846,[2] which only allowed a plaintiff 12 months from the date of the accident to bring proceedings, and the defendants were estopped from doing so. A similar agreement as to liability was found to estop the defendants from pleading limitation under the Workmens Compensation Act 1897 in *Wright v John Bagnall and Sons*.[3] However, both *Lubovsky* and *Wright* concerned full admissions of liability and short periods of limitation, and both cases pre-dated the Limitation Act 1980.[4]

In *Colchester BC v Smith*[5], the Court of Appeal held that an agreement to compromise a dispute as to the adverse possession of land estopped the defendant from relying on the Limitation Act 1980, s 15(1) to found title to the disputed land. However, this was principally because the agreement purported to be a final compromise of a pre-existing dispute, and, per Butler-Sloss LJ "the courts have an interest in upholding agreements to compromise disputes".[6]

Although all of the above authorities can be distinguished from a "standstill agreement" situation, it is thought that the Courts ought to be very reluctant to ignore an agreement, in writing, to waive limitation once a writ is issued, or to do so in cases where no writ is issued on the strength of the agreement. Nevertheless, there is at present no directly binding authority for this view, and courts are often unwilling to "revive" disputes that may have been dormant for a long time. There have been many cases in which parties who were under the impression that limitation was not an issue found that they were, in fact, out of time.[7] To be safe, one should always issue proceedings in time.

(iii) Practical steps

Either before or after the Year 2000, Thrombodirect Systems may form the view that it has a good claim against Anocomp, on the basis that the *Medinvent*

[1] [1944] KB 44.
[2] 31 *Halsbury's Statutes* (4th edn).
[3] [1900] 2 QB 240.
[4] 24 *Halsbury's Statutes* (4th edn).
[5] [1992] Ch 421.
[6] *Ibid.* at p 435.
[7] For example The *"Sauria"* [1957] 1 Lloyd's Rep 396; *Blytheway v British Steel Corp Plc* [1997] 9 CL.

system is either likely to crash or already has crashed. However, Anocomp refuses to acknowledge that the problem exists or that it has anything to do with Anocomp. Systems realises that bringing a claim will take a lot of time and effort in preparation, and that while it needs to act now to avoid limitation problems, a negotiated settlement would be preferable all round.[1] A worthwhile course of action might be as follows:

- Systems should send Anocomp a letter before action, setting out in detail what it wishes Anocomp to do (e.g. repair the millennium bugs or indemnify Systems against the cost of getting a third party to do it), and by when. The letter will usually state that failure to agree will lead to proceedings without further warning.

- If Anocomp's response is inadequate, Systems should issue a writ.

- Systems should serve the writ on Anocomp within 4 months of the date of issue.[2] If there is a good reason, such as if Anocomp has agreed in writing to extend the period for service, then Systems can apply for an extension of the validity of the writ under RSC Ord 6, r 8. However, the fact that negotiations are ongoing is not a good reason in this context.[3]

- In the meantime, if there will not be sufficient time to have pleadings, evidence etc ready within the formal time-limits, or Systems wishes to defer the expense of such in the hope that a satisfactory settlement can be reached, Systems should try to get Anocomp to agree to an extension of time. Of course, Systems must be careful that any overtures about negotiations, time-limits etc are made without prejudice to the issues of liability and/or the amount of damages which may be payable.

- If Anocomp does not agree, then Systems can apply to the court for an extension of the time required for service of the statement of claim. Such time-summonses are governed by RSC Ord 3, r 5, and are extremely commonplace. The matter is at the discretion of the Deputy Master (in London) or District Judge (outside London). Usually, they will be granted, even if time has expired, as long as the party seeking more time gives a reasonable explanation as to why there will be or has been a delay, and there is no risk of prejudice to the other party which cannot be compensated in costs.[4]

---

[1] It is assumed, for present purposes, that the agreement between Systems and Anocomp contains no arbitration clause.
[2] If Anocomp is domiciled outside the EU/ EFTA., see RSC Ord 11.
[3] *The Mouna* [1991] 2 Lloyd's Rep 221.
[4] *Atwood v Chichester* (1878) 3 QBD 722, 733, C.A. However, litigants should note a stricter mood in the courts recently. In *Beachley Property Ltd. v Edgar* [1997]PNLR 197, the Court of Appeal stated that breaches of the rules of the Court which occurred without any justification whatsoever and notwithstanding the absence of prejudice to the other party ought not to be allowed. In *The Mortgage Corporation Ltd v Sandoes, Blinkhorn & Co and Gibson*, [1997] PNLR 263, the Court of Appeal gave general guidance stressing the necessity for reasonable expedition. See also *Letpak Ltd. v Harris The Times* December 6, 1996, where a differently constituted Court of Appeal commented on the wind of change blowing in this area.

(5) JOINING OTHER PARTIES, AND THIRD PARTY PROCEEDINGS

(i) Introduction

Year 2000 litigation is an area which may involve many parties, and various different causes of action. Several companies in the Thrombodirect group may wish to sue various defendants, for different causes of action.

For instance, let us assume that B&W Agon were engaged by Systems, with or without a formal written contract, to perform a Year 2000 audit on all the systems used in the Thrombodirect group of companies. If problems were found, B&W Agon were to go back to Systems with proposals for dealing with them, and, if approved, to oversee the putting in place of appropriate solutions. B&W Agon attempts to do what it contracted to do but faces the following difficulties:

- Anocomp will not warrant that *Medinvent* is Year 2000 compliant. It will not give B&W Agon or anyone else access to the source code, although it makes an offer to Systems to check *Medinvent* itself, for a fee. Systems did not ask for, and thus did not get, a contractual right to access to the source code when negotiating the agreement with Anocomp. B&W Agon admits that it is possible for it to check Year 2000 compliance on the system in situ, but is unwilling to be responsible for the risk of the system crashing as a result of the test. In these circumstances, B&W Agon does not check *Medinvent* for Year 2000 compliance, stating that it is for Systems to do so.

- In investigating the *Debtpay* software, B&W Agon relies on a standard circular from Debtpay Inc to the effect that all *Debtpay* software bought through licensed dealers since 1 October 1993 is Year 2000 compliant. A B&W Agon consultant asks David Wytook, in his capacity as director of Systems, when the Thrombodirect group acquired the *Debtpay* software. Wytook's reply that it was January 1994 ignores the fact that that was merely the date at which he himself brought *Debtpay* with him from Hardman and Co, without procuring an assignment of the licence. In fact, the package was supplied to Hardman in April 1993, and is not Year 2000 compliant.

- No action in respect of either product is taken by any of the parties until after 01.01.00. However, at the fateful hour, *Medinvent* crashes completely, and soon *Debtpay* begins writing off the debts of Thrombodirect group companies.

The ramifications of this state of affairs could be numerous. For example, as regards *Medinvent*, Systems and Manufacturing could have a claim against B&W Agon (for breach of contract / negligence) as well as Anocomp (for failure to provide goods or services fit for their purpose/of satisfactory quality etc). As regards *Debtpay*, all the Thrombodirect companies could have a claim against B&W Agon for negligence. B&W Agon may have a claim against Systems, which may, in turn, have a claim against Wytook himself. Further, Debtpay itself could sue the Thrombodirect group companies for breach of its copyright.

The courts will be unwilling to allow for a multiplicity of actions in such circumstances. The RSC allow a group of plaintiffs to sue a group of defendants, and for those defendants to sue one another, all in respect of the same losses.

(ii) Joinder of causes of action

Different claims between the same parties in the same capacities can be, and often are joined in the same action.

(iii) Joint plaintiffs

Any number of plaintiffs may sue in one action, where there is a common question of law or fact to be decided in each of the claims *and* all rights to relief in respect of each claim arise out of the same transaction or series of transactions[1] (the "twin test").

Note that, in this context, the word "transaction" is not limited to contractual relationships, but should be interpreted liberally[2], usually to refer to the full set of factual circumstances. If the "twin test" is not satisfied, leave is required before the plaintiffs can join in one action.

However, potential co-plaintiffs should note that normally they must all make the same allegations of fact in the action, and be represented collectively by the same legal team. Co-plaintiffs will not be allowed to sever their interest, nor take inconsistent steps in the action.[3] Any breakdown in relations between co-plaintiffs which necessitates that one of them drops out or becomes a defendant will almost certainly be penalised in terms of costs.

(iv) Joinder of defendants

Any number of defendants can be joined, again subject to the "twin test" of common questions of law or fact and that the claims arise out of the same transactions. Again, leave is required should any limb of the twin test not be satisfied. However, it should be noted that the speculative joinder of

---

[1] RSC Ord 15, r 4.
[2] *Re Beck* (1918) 87 LJ Ch. 335, per Swinfen Eady MR.
[3] *Re Mathews* [1905] 2 Ch. 460; *Re Wright* [1895] 2 Ch. 747.

defendants, in the hope that "something may turn up" on discovery, is not allowed.[1]

Where joint defendants, A and B, blame each other for the damage claimed for, and A is held wholly liable, who should pay the costs incurred by B in defending the action? The outcome will depend on the circumstances of each case, but, usually, if it was reasonable for the plaintiff to join B, then the plaintiff's costs awarded against A may include the amounts paid to B by way of costs[2], or the court may order A to pay B's costs directly.[3]

(v) Consolidation/separation of Actions

The courts also have the power to order actions which have been begun separately in the same division of the High Court to be consolidated at the application of one of the parties, once the "twin test" is fulfilled, or there is some other reason that consolidation is desirable.[4] The courts may also order the separation of causes of action, counterclaims or co-litigants which had previously been in the same action.[5]

(vi) Third party proceedings

In the scenario outlined above, B&W Agon may wish to claim a remedy in respect of its potential liabilities to one or more of the plaintiffs against Anocomp, Systems, or others, who are not parties to the action already begun. This may be done by means of a third party notice[6], once the main action has been begun by writ or originating summons.[7] There is, in theory, no limit to the number of third parties a defendant may bring in. Furthermore, a third party may itself claim against a fourth party, and so on. Such a course can sometimes save costs by preventing other actions and in having all the matters in relation to what will often be a very complex matrix of events and duties resolved at the same time.

Actions by defendants against third parties follow the same procedure as actions by defendants against plaintiffs by way of counterclaim - they are treated as actions in their own right and as separate from the main action.

However, the are only certain types of claim for which a defendant can issue a third party notice.[8] These are:

---

[1] *Wilson v Church* (1878) 9 Ch.D 552, although see *Norwich Pharmacal Co v Commissioners of Customs and Excise* [1974] AC 133 which allows a limited right to sue innocent parties required to provide information as to wrongdoers.
[2] *Bullock v London General Omnibus Co* [1907] 1 KB 264.
[3] *Sanderson v Blyth Theatre Co* [1903] 2 KB 533.
[4] RSC Ord 4, r 9.
[5] RSC 15, r 5.
[6] RSC Ord 16, r 1.
[7] *Aiden Shipping Co. Ltd. v Interbulk Ltd.* [1986] AC 965, 981.
[8] RSC Ord 16, r 1.

- A claim for contribution - where the third party is said to be jointly liable to the plaintiff, for example under the Civil Liability (Contribution) Act 1978.[1]

- A claim for indemnity - which may arise under an express contract, a statute or a principle of law, such as when an act which causes the liability is done by the defendant at the request of another.[2] The latter category has been said to include a right to damages owed by the third party to the defendant which are substantially the same as the damages owed by the defendant to the plaintiff.[3]

- A claim for a remedy which is similar to the remedy the plaintiff claims and which arises out of the same facts as the plaintiff's claim.

- Where any issue relating to the subject matter of the main action should be determined not only between the plaintiff and the defendant but also between either or both of them and a third party.

The leave of the court is required for the issue of a third party notice unless the defendant issues the notice before he serves the defence in the main action, and the main action is begun by writ.[4]

In every case in which a third party is sought to be joined, and the third party has given notice of intention to defend, the defendant must request a hearing for third party directions, at which all of the parties to the action may make submissions.[5] The court has a wide discretion to direct the future management of the case, and may even order judgment against the third party if its liability to the defendant is established[6], in much the same way as it can order summary judgment under RSC Ord 14.

To return to our example, on 1 April 2000, Manufacturing, Plc, SA and SRL all sue B&W Agon for negligence in failing to check the Debtpay software. B&W Agon wishes to bring in Systems in respect of the remainder of the group's claim due to the misleading information provided in relation to when the software was supplied. Systems wishes to pass its liability, if any, on to David Wytook (who left the group on 2 January 2000). Furthermore, Debtpay has heard of Thrombodirect's unauthorised use of its software, and realises that the limitation period may cause difficulties. It issues a writ. The two actions could be structured like this:

- In *Thrombodirect group of companies* v *B&W Agon*, the first, second, third and fourth plaintiffs would be Manufacturing, Plc, SA and SRL respectively. B&W Agon as defendant would, perhaps, have a separate claim against Systems, as a third party. Systems itself

---

[1] 13 *Halsbury's Statutes* (4th edn). The Act also creates a statutory right of action for contribution in its own right. The claim is brought by the issue of a contribution notice. The claim can be useful in that a defence based on the claimant's own wrongdoing is not available.
[2] *Birmingham & District Land Co v LNW Ry* (1886) 34 Ch D. 261.
[3] The Supreme Court Practice 1997, 16/1/12.
[4] RSC Ord 16, r 1(2).
[5] RSC Ord 16, r 4.
[6] RSC Ord 16, r 4(3)(a).

might try to found a counterclaim against B&W Agon for its possible liability to Debtpay, and could join Wytook as a fourth party.

- In *Debtpay v Thrombodirect group of companies*, Debtpay would be the plaintiff and each of the companies the first, second, third etc, defendants. Depending on the (perhaps implied) terms of B&W Agon's retainer, or the nature of the duties owed by B&W Agon, the Thrombodirect companies might third party B&W Agon, which could then fourth party Systems, which might well fifth party Wytook.

(5) REPRESENTATIVE ACTIONS

There are occasions where there are so many potential plaintiffs to an action, or defendants to it, that joining each one to the action would lead to enormous practical difficulties. In these circumstances, the RSC allows one or more members of the group of potential parties to represent all the others as well as himself if all the members of group represented have *the same interest in the proceedings* .[1]

For parties to have the same interest in proceedings, they must all have a common interest, they must all have a common grievance and the relief must, in its nature, be beneficial to all.[2]

Let us extend our example scenario. Say that, because of inaccuracies in the manufacturing systems brought about by the Year 2000 failure, 200 of Thrombodirect's drug-delivery mechanisms manufactured after 01.01.00 are dangerously faulty. Dozens of hospitals and hospital trusts have useless machinery. The hospitals and trusts have come together and wish to share the costs of pursuing Thrombodirect.

In these circumstances, one member of the group might represent the whole group if all have the same interest in the proceedings. That member of the group will be the nominal plaintiff. This will have the effect that enforcement of any judgments or orders against members of the group other than the plaintiff (or, where one person represents a group of defendants, the defendant) himself can only be done with the leave of the court.[3]

In theory, group claims for damages for breach of contract and tort are possible even when the proportion of damages to be awarded to or paid by each party is different, once certain conditions are fulfilled.[4] The rule on

---

[1] RSC Ord 15, r 12.
[2] *Pan Atlantic Insurance Co. and Republic Insurance v Pine Top Insurance Co.* [1989] 1 Lloyd's Rep 568, C.A.
[3] RSC Ord 15, r 2(3).
[4] *Prudential Assurance Co. Ltd v Newman Industries Ltd. & Others* [1981] Ch 229; *Moon v Atherton* [1972] 2 QB 435; *Irish Shipping Ltd v Commercial Union Assurance Co Plc* [1990] 2 WLR 117.

representative actions is essentially a pragmatic tool to enable the Court to do justice, and should not be applied in any strict or rigorous sense but according to its wide and progressive scope (*per* Megarry J in *John v Rees*[1]).

(6) EVIDENCE

(i) Introduction

In any litigation, the claim usually stands or falls on the quality of the evidence presented. Those facing the prospect of Year 2000 litigation, and even those for whom it is no more than a vague possibility, should ensure that their evidence is up to scratch, both as to quality and quantity, if they wish to maximise their chances of victory.

(ii) Burden and standard of proof

The basic rule of evidence is that the burden of proof of an assertion lies upon the party which makes it. Thus, in the case of *Thrombodirect Manufacturing* v *B&W Agon*, the burden of proving that B&W Agon failed to properly check that the software was Year 2000 compliant lies upon the plaintiff, and the burden of proving any defences such as due diligence lies with B&W Agon.

The standard of proof in civil cases is the balance of probabilities. However, it would be wrong to say that "51 per cent proof is enough". The Court is not a calculator, and will be slow to act on evidence which will entail serious consequences unless it thinks it safe in all the circumstances to do so.[2]

(iii) Records

A In general

If a litigant comes to the court with no record of what he claims happened, he could still win his case, based on oral evidence alone. However, if he is faced with an opponent who has a written or other form of permanent record which substantiates his version of events and who can also provide convincing oral evidence, the party without records is very likely to lose.

Of course, every efficient business will keep financial, sales, personnel and other records. But those who may think they have a Year 2000 problem should not be complacent about record-keeping in respect of it. Proper Year 2000 records should be being kept now, not merely after what might be a disastrous event, which might destroy any pre-existing records. In the context of Year

---

[1] [1970] Ch 345.
[2] *Re JS (a minor)* [1981] 2 FLR 146.

2000 litigation, it will be vital to have a clear record of, at least, the following matters:

B Contracts

Although, of course, there can be a contract without writing, it is almost always very difficult to overcome a document put forward as a written record of the agreement, unless there has been manifest fraud. Therefore, at the risk of stating the obvious, it is very important that parties to a contract should keep a written record of it.

Analysis of the interpretation of contracts has been covered in Chapter 5 above. It will be recalled that, although the court will attempt to understand the factual matrix in which the contract was made, evidence of pre-contractual negotiations or post-contractual understandings is inadmissible in the interpretation of the contract itself.[1] Therefore it is always better for the contract to spell out what might seem to be obvious understandings or assumptions between the parties, so that there is no room for confusion later.

C Correspondence/telephone conversations

All written correspondence between the parties should be retained for as long as possible. Such correspondence can sometimes be vital in establishing the state of knowledge of a party of certain facts. This may be crucial, for example, in claims for consequential loss or allegations of misrepresentation.

The same is true of notes of telephone conversations. Scraps of paper bearing scribbled keywords are better than nothing, but not by much. If anything that might be of importance is discussed or agreed, it is important to try to record it in some detail, and keep that record on file.

D Meetings

Even informal meetings can have an effect on what the parties agreed or promised, or expected from each other. Sometimes the fact that a series of meetings took place without any records of agreement can be important. Any meetings which might affect the parties' relationships should be recorded. If a contemporaneous record, i.e. a tape-recording or note-taker, is not possible, then the discussion can be written up afterwards, preferably as soon as possible.

E "Bugs" and contact with suppliers and maintenance firms

Where a claim is made for defects in a product, or non-performance of a service, it is sometimes the case that there is not one enormous crash or

---

[1] See the discussion in Chapter 5 above.

malfunction, but a series of smaller breakdowns or problems which occur over time. A potential plaintiff would be well advised to keep a record of any problems with goods supplied, and/or with suppliers or contractors. Persistent problems may, over time, give rise to a cause of action, but, without a good record of these, this will be hard to prove.

When something goes wrong with a system, it is commonly the case that the first call that is made is to the supplier. In fact, many suppliers' warranties require that only the supplier or an authorised agent may carry out repairs.[1] It will be very important for customers to keep records of all contact with suppliers after the systems are in place as well as before the contract is made. If a customer can show that it has made all reasonable efforts to get the supplier to fix the bugs, this will be important evidence of attempts to mitigate its losses.

Lost working time caused, for example, by malfunctioning of a system that was supposed to speed things up should be recorded, as well as the cost, if any, of calling out engineers. Where organisations have to take remedial action themselves due to worry about potential problems on 1 of January 2000, then this work too should be recorded.

So, for example, a vague statement in court by Manufacturing's maintenance manager along the lines of "I think we were calling out the maintenance people about once a week to deal with the stock-control system crashing", will not be as powerful as more exact oral testimony, backed by written evidence, as to 20 failures of the stock-control system between January and April 2000, recorded with the date, time, callout of maintenance contractors, cost of repair, diagnosis of the problem and lost working time.

Conversely, it is clearly wise for suppliers of goods and/or services to keep a detailed record of their dealings with customers. If a customer is claiming constant problems with a piece of software, but the records of the supplier or manufacturer indicate very few complaints, or that the reason for most of the problems is errors by the customer, then these records will be useful evidence.

F "Before and after" records

In most situations, it will be important to keep records of what was on the particular computer or network, its specifications, and its capabilities before it is altered by new products or by maintenance. A regularly updated disk or tape archive of the data held on a system will be useful in substantiating claims for lost data and the cause of failures.

(iv) Expert evidence

Expert evidence is regularly used where there are complex issues of fact which are far removed from the experience of the Court. In Year 2000 cases, it is

---

[1] It is possible, of course, that such a requirement may be void or avoidable as being in restraint of trade or anti-competitive under the Treaty of Rome, arts 85 or 86.

likely that the expert evidence of computer programmers, IT consultants, and others will be necessary. There will be a great demand for people capable of going through what will often be complicated series' of events to determine causes and effects, both actual and potential, and to say what, if anything, could have been done about them. Expert evidence as to industry practices and the average costs of particular products or services will also be essential in many cases.

Expert evidence should be treated like the evidence of any other witness, and no court need accept it if it finds it unconvincing.[1] That said, expert evidence often carries a lot of weight with the court, and it will be important to choose an expert carefully.

In compiling an expert's report, it is very important to bear in mind that the expert must strive to be completely impartial in his views. The fact that he is instructed by one side or another should not affect his professional opinion.[2] In *The Ikarian Reefer*[3] Cresswell J restated the duties and responsibilities of the expert witness. These included the duty to provide unbiased assistance to the court, to state the facts and assumptions on which his opinion is based, not omitting to consider material facts which could detract from his concluded opinion, and not failing to say so if insufficient data is available.

The facts of *Cala Homes v McAlpine*[4] provide a clear example of what an expert witness ought not to do. The case concerned an alleged copyright infringement and inducement of a breach of contract in relation to the design of houses. The expert witness of the defendants was an architect, Mr Goodall, who had written an article on giving expert evidence in a professional journal. The article made an analogy between giving expert evidence and playing the three card trick on an innocent rustic. It further stated that for an expert to present the data so that it "seems to suggest an interpretation favourable to the side instructing him" was "within the rules of our particular game, even if it means playing down or omitting some material consideration".

Mr Goodall admitted in court that the principles in the article were those he applied to the drafting of the report on which the Defendant relied. The Defendant was not successful, and Laddie J added extensive comments as to the expert evidence:

At p 842, Laddie J said:

'The whole basis of Mr Goodall's approach to the drafting of an expert's report is wrong. The function of a court of law is to discover the truth relating to the issues before it. In doing that it has to assess the evidence adduced by the parties. The judge is not a rustic who has chosen to play a game of Three Card Trick. He is not fair game. Nor is the truth.';

---

[1] *R v Lanfear* [1968] 2 QB 77.
[2] *Whitehouse v Jordan* [1981] 1 WLR 246, 256.
[3] [1993] FSR 563, 565.
[4] [1995] FSR 818.

and at p 844:

> 'In the light of the matters set out above, during the preparation of this judgment I re-read Mr Goodall's report on the understanding that it was drafted as a partisan tract with the objective of selling the defendant's case to the court and ignoring virtually everything which could harm that objective. I did not find it of significant assistance in deciding the issues.'

(7) PROCEDURAL PRESSURE POINTS

(i) Introduction

During the course of litigation, the parties have various means open to them which may speed the process up, stop the process altogether or put significant pressure on the other party to settle. Three of the most important are the application for summary judgment, the application for security for costs and the making of a payment into court.

(ii) Summary judgment

If a plaintiff has a particularly strong case (or a defendant has a particularly strong counterclaim), and it seems that no credible defence is likely to be raised, then the plaintiff may apply for summary judgment in the matter under RSC Ord 14. The purpose of the procedure is to allow for a quick judgment for the plaintiff where it is clear that the defendant will not succeed and that to allow a full defence of the action will merely unjustly keep the plaintiff out of his remedy.

Say that Manufacturing fails to pay Chipsrus the amount it owes for the last two deliveries of semiconductors, due, naturally, to Year 2000 problems with the *Debtpay* software. Chipsrus have a clear agreement, expressly governed by English law, signed and witnessed delivery notes, and no complaints as to the quality of their goods. Chipsrus may be well advised to go for summary judgment.

The procedure is that, after the service of a statement of claim and filing of a notice of intention to defend, the plaintiff issues a summons, supported by affidavits setting out the facts of the claim and deposing to a belief that no defence exists to the claim. The defendant can, by affidavit, show evidence as to why there should be a trial. The court ought not to go behind the affidavits, but can ask itself "Is what the defendant says credible?".[1]

There are several orders the court may make in Ord 14 proceedings. These are:

---

[1] *National Westminster Bank Plc v Daniel* [1993] 1 WLR 1453.

- Judgment for the plaintiff.[1] This will be the result if there is no issue in dispute which ought to be tried.

- Judgment for the plaintiff subject to a stay of execution pending the trial of any counterclaim of the defendant.[2] This will be the result if the defendant has a counterclaim which has some connection to the claim and it is just to prevent enforcement of the judgment pro tem, so as take account of any amount which may be due on the counterclaim.

- Conditional leave to defend[3]—where, although there is a defence, it is "shadowy" [4], that is of little or no substance. The most usual condition is that the defendant be allowed to defend only if he pays money into court as security for the claim.

- Unconditional leave to defend—where the defendant has been able to show "an issue or question in dispute which ought to be tried" (RSC Ord 14, r 3(1)). Examples might be where there is a difficult point of law, a genuine dispute about material facts or a good defence such as satisfaction or illegality.

On the facts stated, in the case of *Chipsrus* v *Thrombodirect Manufacturing Ltd*, Chipsrus is likely to get judgment for the full amount. A claim by Manufacturing that the problems are the fault of its accounting software will not amount to a defence, not even a "shadowy" one.

What if Manufacturing alleges that Chipsrus' own accounting systems are also the victim of Year 2000 failure, and that in fact Manufacturing did not order the goods delivered, and tried to return them as soon as they realised this? If the evidence is reasonably convincing, then Manufacturing may well get leave to defend.

(iii) Security for costs

It is sometimes the case that a defendant finds himself sued by a plaintiff who has very few resources, or is a corporate "man of straw". Should such a defendant be successful in defending the claim of such a plaintiff, it will be very difficult to recover the costs of the action against him, and the defendant will suffer severe prejudice.

Where it appears that the defendant will have difficulty in enforcing any order for costs, an application for security for costs should be considered. If an order is made, and the plaintiff cannot satisfy it, the action may be dismissed.[5] However, it is quite difficult to obtain an order for security for costs. A number of conditions have to be satisfied:

[1] RSC Ord 14, r 3(1).
[2] RSC Ord 14, r 3(2).
[3] See, in general, The Supreme Court Practice, 14/3–14/15.
[4] *Van Lynn Developments Ltd. v Pelias Construction Co.* [1969] 1 QB 607.
[5] *Giddings v Giddings* (1847) 10 Beav 29.

- It is sometimes thought that the mere impecuniosity of a plaintiff is sufficient ground for an application for security for costs. This is not the case. If the plaintiff is not an English limited company, then the defendant must show that the case is within the grounds set out in RSC Ord 23, r 1. The most significant of these in practice is that the plaintiff is ordinarily resident out of the jurisdiction. Recent case law indicates that to all intents and purposes domicile or residence in another EU member State no longer counts as being "outside the jurisdiction" for the purpose of security for costs.[1]

- If the Plaintiff is a company registered in England and Wales, then by virtue of the Companies Act 1985,s 726(1)[2] the court may order security for costs if

  'it appears by credible testimony that there is reason to believe that the company will be unable to pay the defendant's costs if successful in his defence'.

- Further, and no matter what the status of the plaintiff, the defendant must show that, in all the circumstances of the case, it would be just for the court to make such an order.

Factors for the court to consider when deciding on the justice or otherwise of making an order are the plaintiff's chances of success[3], and (if the plaintiff is a company) the value of any property within the jurisdiction, whether any impecuniosity was brought about by the alleged default of the defendant, and whether an order for security is being brought so as to stifle a valid claim.[4] The defendant can be faced with the difficulty that if it proves that the plaintiff has no money, the plaintiff can object to an order for security on the ground that an order would effectively prevent it from pursuing a just claim. There is a growing awareness in the Commercial Court, and in the courts generally, that it is unfair to put plaintiffs to the sometimes very considerable cost of putting up security without an undertaking from defendants that they will pay to the plaintiff all such costs should no order for costs be made in the defendants' favour.[5]

If, say, Systems is taking proceedings against Anocomp, but is a mere "shell company" without assets of its own, it might be worthwhile for Anocomp to seek security for costs. This should be attempted, first by seeking the consent of

---

[1] *Fitzgerald v Williams* [1996] 2 WLR 447 - a national of an EU member State ordinarily resident within the EU should usually be treated as if within the jurisdiction; *Chequepoint SARL v McClelland* [1996] 3 WLR 341 - a plaintiff company incorporated in another member State and ordinarily resident within the EU should usually be treated as if it were an English company.
[2] 8 *Halsbury's Statutes* (4th edn).
[3] *Simaan Contracting Co v Pilkington Glass Ltd* [1987] 1 All ER 345, although the court should not go into the merits of the action unless likely success can be clearly demonstrated (*Porzelack KG v Porzelack (UK) Ltd.* [1987] 1 All ER 1074), and the Commercial Court is now very reluctant to deal with the strength of the claim at all, unless the plaintiff's claim is so strong as to justify a condition of payment in by the Defendant in Ord 14 proceedings (per Colman J, *Lecture To Commercial Bar Association*, 23 April 1997).
[4] *John Bishop (Caterers) Ltd. v National Union Bank Ltd.* [1973] 1 All ER 707.
[5] Lecture of Colman J, *ibid*. The practice of requiring such an undertaking is now mentioned in the *Guide To Commercial Court Practice*, 1997.

Systems, then, if that is not forthcoming, by means of an application to the court. Systems will have to provide security or satisfy the court that it would be unjust to order it to provide such. If it cannot, its claim may be struck out.

(iv) Payment in

In many actions for damages, the defendant may have denied all liability, but be aware that he is likely to have to pay something to the plaintiff in the end. The usual course will be to make a "without prejudice" offer. But what if this is refused? A common, and often very effective way to put pressure on the plaintiff to settle is to make a payment into court.

If the plaintiff accepts the payment in within the 21 days allowed, all proceedings are stayed[1], and the plaintiff will usually be entitled to his costs up to then. However, if the plaintiff does not accept the payment in, and if the amount of the judgment for the plaintiff at trial is lower than or equal to the sum paid in, then the plaintiff will have to pay all the defendant's costs since the payment in, as well as his own costs.[2] Of course if judgment is for more than the payment in, costs will generally be paid by the defendant. In reckoning the amounts of payments in, and whether the payment in has been beaten, it is right to take into account the interest on the damages, both at the date of the payment in and at the date of the judgment.[3]

The court does not know of the fact of, or the amount of, any payment in until after judgment has been given, except where the defence is one of tender before action.[4]

Obviously, from a strategic point of view, a payment into court can put considerable pressure on the plaintiff to settle. Payments in should not be so low that the plaintiff is bound to beat it, nor higher than the maximum the plaintiff is likely to get on judgment. A clever payment in is at, or perhaps a little below, the minimum the plaintiff would get in a worst-case scenario for him.

Thus, if Manufacturing are suing B&W Agon for £1 million, but it seems to B&W Agon that Manufacturing might only recover £250,000, due to contributory negligence, exclusion clauses or other factors, a smart move might be to pay in £240,000, at a relatively early stage. Manufacturing's advisers might well find it difficult to advise against acceptance, as they will not be able to guarantee that Manufacturing will beat the payment in. Moreover, both parties' legal costs will increase substantially between payment in and trial.

In cases which are more than simple money claims, there exists a similar procedure whereby a defendant makes an offer of whatever concession he

---

[1] RSC Ord 22, r 3(4).
[2] RSC Ord 62, r 9 (1)(b); *Finlay v Railway Executive* [1950] 2 All ER 969, although, *stictu sensu*, costs always remain at the discretion of the Court, subject to RSC Ord 62 (Ord 62, r 2(4)).
[3] RSC Ord 22, r 1(8).
[4] RSC Ord 22, r 7(1).

thinks appropriate in writing, expressed to be "without prejudice, save as to costs".[1] This called a "Calderbank letter", after the leading authority.[2]

(8) ARBITRATION

The principles, practice and procedure of arbitration are enormous subjects, well outside the scope of this work.[3] Nevertheless, many commercial agreements contain arbitration agreements, and these often feature in contracts for the sale of computer hardware and software. Parties to a dispute can also agree to submit it to arbitration instead of court proceedings. For convenience, some of the more important differences between arbitration and litigation are set out here.

Arbitration is consensual. An arbitration cannot be begun unless both sides have agreed to it, although once they agree, they are bound by that decision and the decision of the arbitral tribunal, known as an "award". Further, the parties can, by their agreement, set out, in as much detail as they wish, the procedural and evidential rules of the arbitration. Parties to a contract which includes an arbitration agreement are almost always bound by that agreement, and must arbitrate if they wish to settle their disputes. Any faults in a larger contract in which an arbitration agreement is contained will not affect the right and duty to arbitrate the claim as per the agreement[4] i.e. the agreement is separable from the remainder of the contract.

Any court proceedings on matters which are the subjects of an arbitration agreement will be stayed, unless the court is satisfied that the arbitration agreement is null and void, inoperative or incapable of being performed.[5] This will be rare. However, the courts still exercise a limited supervisory jurisdiction over arbitration.[6] It is possible to obtain the assistance of the court in appointing or, in the most serious circumstances, removing an arbitrator, in enforcing arbitration awards, or in support of interlocutory orders of the tribunal. It is also possible to appeal to the court on a point of law or serious irregularity.

The tribunal is appointed by the parties themselves or by an agreed person or organisation, or, exceptionally, by the court. Often, a single arbitrator is agreed to by both sides. In other cases, there is a panel of arbitrators. Where the main tribunal cannot agree, an umpire or chairman, can be appointed to break the deadlock. The rules of court do not necessarily apply to arbitration. However, it is commonly the case that tribunals can and do make many of the

---

[1] RSC Ord 22, r 14.
[2] *Calderbank v Calderbank* [1976] Fam 93.
[3] The advent of the 1996 Arbitration Act, 2 *Halsbury's Statutes* (4th edn), means that many of the current editions of standard works are now out of date. The 1997 edition of *Russell on Arbitration* deals with the new Act, as do several works of commentary.
[4] Arbitration Act 1996, s 7, 2 *Halsbury's Statutes* (4th edn); see also *Harbour Assurance Co. (UK) Ltd. v Kansa General International Insurance Co.* [1993] QB 701 for pre-1996 Act authority for the doctrine of separability.
[5] Arbitration Act 1996, s 9, 2 *Halsbury's Statutes* (4th edn).
[6] See, in general, the Arbitration Act 1996, 2 *Halsbury's Statutes* (4th edn).

familiar interlocutory orders for discovery, service of pleadings, etc, and that evidence is given orally and is subject to cross-examination. The tribunal can also award costs and interest on any damages, and make various other orders for the proper disposal of the matter.

The advantages of arbitration over court litigation are that it is private, that it can be more speedy, if both parties wish to get on with it, and that it can be advantageous to appoint people who are very familiar with the particular business in question as arbitrators. This may be a significant consideration in relation to Year 2000 issues. Arbitration can be cheaper than litigation, although not necessarily so, as the parties must pay the fees of the arbitrators and such costs as hiring rooms, etc. Many also feel that the atmosphere of arbitration is less formal and less adversarial than that of court litigation.

Among the disadvantages are that if a party wishes to drag its feet, it will often have much more licence to do so in arbitration proceedings. Further, the arbitrator will often not have the range of remedies open to him that a court has, nor the power to enforce interlocutory orders without the assistance of the court. Arbitrations must be settled in accordance with law, but the strict rules as to evidence and procedure do not necessarily apply. It is sometimes said that arbitral tribunals tend to try too hard to reach a compromise, even where, had the matter been litigated in court, there would have been an outright victory for one side or the other.

(9) ALTERNATIVE DISPUTE RESOLUTION

Litigation, including arbitration, is often not the best way to solve disputes. It is by its nature confrontational, and can be very time-consuming and expensive. In some cases, parties would be better advised to seek to resolve their problems outside the courts, or arbitration rooms.

The past several years have witnessed increasing support for Alternative Dispute Resolution ("ADR") as a method of solving disputes. The process is one whereby the parties agree to appoint a neutral who will take an interventionist approach and negotiate with all sides to seek a "business solution" which can reflect the totality of the issues between them. The solution may involve the parties working together to eliminate software faults, a remedy which is not available to them through litigation.

ADR might well be useful where the parties have, or wish to have, long-term business relationships which they do not wish to endanger by the hostility that is sometimes generated by litigation or arbitration. ADR should certainly be in the minds of those contemplating Year 2000 litigation, as it may be that long-term relationships with customers, suppliers or service-providers are at risk in litigation, and are more valuable than the potential fruits of victory in court.

The approaches taken in ADR can vary radically. It is for the parties to decide the remit and the powers of the neutral mediator. The negotiations are almost always without prejudice to the rights of the parties in any later litigation. Unlike in litigation or arbitration, a mediator cannot impose a decision on the parties. This need for consensuality and ability to "walk away" at any time, is the main reason that relationships can survive ADR better than litigation/ arbitration, but is also the main disadvantage, as a lot of time and money may be spent to no effect. If all the parties agree to the course of action proposed by the mediator, it is often embodied in a contract, which is enforceable in the normal way.

However, ADR is inherently unsuitable for cases where the parties wish to create or preserve legal rights, or get rapid injunctive or interlocutory relief. No precedents can be set. Also, the limitation clock continues running during ADR, and an unwilling party can delay and obstruct proceedings without adverse consequences for him, as there is no recourse to the courts to enforce requests of negotiators or mediators. Further ADR often involves "revealing one's hand", in the pursuit of a "creative" settlement. Caution is advisable before committing to ADR, although sometimes it will help in coming to an "all round" solution more quickly and easily than conventional settlement negotiations or a court-room showdown.

The Woolf Report on Access to Justice is enthusiastic about the greater use of ADR[1], and it recommends, among other things, that the proposed judicial management of cases involve encouraging the consideration of ADR, even to the point of penalising in costs a party who unreasonably refuses to agree to ADR suggested by the court itself.[2]

(10) THE WOOLF REPORT

As mentioned above, major changes in procedures have been proposed following a wide-ranging review of civil litigation by Lord Woolf. At the time of writing (November 1997), the government appears keen to implement at least some of the recommendations of the Woolf Report on Access to Justice.[3] The Woolf Report is a lengthy document, and what is attempted here is a brief summary of some of the most important proposals.

The main thrust of the Report is that civil procedure should be speeded up and made more efficient, while reducing costs to litigants, or at least making them more predictable. The positive attitude to ADR in the Report is dealt with above. The basic reforms proposed are that there should be three "tracks" on which cases would run:

- A small claims jurisdiction for cases worth up to £5,000

- A "fast track" for straightforward cases up to £15,000, with limited procedures, fixed timetables and fixed costs

---

[1] *Access To Justice* HMSO, 1996.
[2] *Ibid.* Chapter 5, para 18.
[3] *Ibid.*

- A "multi-track" for more complex cases or those with a value of more than £15,000.

Given that most Year 2000 claims will probably be worth more than £15,000, it is likely that, if the reforms are implemented, these will be on the multi track. Among the main proposals relating to multi-track litigation of the Year 2000 kind are:

- That the management of the case will be the responsibility of a "procedural judge" who will decide on directions, seek to narrow the issues, agree the likely level of costs and fix a timetable, including a date for trial at case management conferences.[1]

- That there will be an enlarged jurisdiction to give summary judgment, on the grounds that a case (i.e. of a defendant or plaintiff) or part of a case has no realistic prospect of success.[2]

- That there will be a more limited initial requirement for "standard discovery", limited to documents of whose existence a party is aware at the time when the obligation to disclose arises, with the possibility of ordering "extra discovery" later at the judge's discretion.[3]

- That expert evidence "be subject to the complete control of the court", with discretion in the court to call an expert of its own motion, a preference for single experts where the issue is to do with an established area of knowledge, and a co-operative approach between any opposing experts.[4]

- That where "proceedings may require collective treatment", the parties or the Legal Aid Board should apply for a "multi-party situation", and the limitation period would be suspended if the application were granted.[5]

---

[1] *Ibid*, recommendations p 301 et seq.
[2] *Ibid.,* p 310 et seq.
[3] *Ibid.* p 311 et seq.
[4] *Ibid.* p 313 et seq.
[5] *Ibid.* p 319 et seq.

Appendix 1: Model clauses

(1) INTRODUCTION

The clauses below are indications of the sorts of clauses that may be suitable for the purposes indicated. However, in every individual situation, it is advisable to consult lawyers who are specialised in the relevant area of law so that they can draft appropriate wording for the precise circumstances. The reader should therefore place no reliance on the suitability of the clauses below for its individual circumstances and the authors and publishers accept no responsibility or liability whatsoever in connection therewith.

(2) SUPPLIER WARRANTY

When using this warranty or part thereof within a contract, you must adapt the wording to fit in with the contract in question. For example if the term "Licensor" is not used in the contract, then the term which is used e.g. "The Supplier" must be adopted instead. Additionally, the wording of the warranty should be adapted to reflect the nature of the product in question.

Before you adapt the warranty in any way, you should seek legal advice as to the implications of such adaptation.

Warranty

The Supplier represents and warrants that:

i   *No error or interruption in the operation of the [software/product] will result directly or indirectly from the passage from the twentieth century to the twenty-first century or from the extra day occurring in any leap year in the twentieth or twenty-first century or from the occurrence of any other date.*

ii   *No reduction or alteration in the functionality of the [software/product] will result directly or indirectly from the passage from the twentieth century to the twenty-first century or from the extra day occurring in any leap year in the twentieth or twenty-first century or from the occurrence of any other date.*

iii *The [software/product] will not process any data which includes a date which does not specify the century.*

iv   *All date related output and results produced by the [software/product] shall include an indication of the century.*

v   *The [software/product] will produce accurate results in respect of calculations and other data processing which span the twentieth and twenty-first centuries.*

vi   *Interfaces and reporting facilities comprised by the [software/product] will support four digit year processing.*

Such a warranty should be reinforced by an indemnity of the following nature:

To the extent that the Supplier fails in any respect to comply with the 2000 compliance warranty, the Supplier agrees to indemnify completely and hold fully harmless the Customer against any loss, damage or expense (including legal fees) sustained or incurred directly or indirectly as a result of such failure. This indemnity is not subject to any limitation or exclusion clauses contained in this Agreement

(3) SOFTWARE MAINTAINER WARRANTY

The Maintainer hereby represents and warrants that it will carry out all testing and work necessary to ensure that:

i   *neither the operation nor functionality of the software subject to this agreement will be adversely affected by the advent of the Year 2000 or any other change of date; and*

ii   *the software complies fully with the definition of Year 2000 conformity set out in the Year 2000 warranty contained in the licence agreement between the parties [or the BSI Year 2000 Conformity Requirements as attached hereto].*

Such a warranty should be reinforced by an indemnity of the following nature:

The Maintainer hereby agrees to indemnify completely and hold fully harmless the Customer against any loss, damage or expense (including legal fees), costs and claims incurred directly or indirectly as a result of the breach of the warranty set out above. This indemnity is not subject to any liability or exclusion clauses contained in this or any connected Agreement

(4) YEAR 2000 SOLUTIONS PROVIDER WARRANTY

The Supplier hereby represents and warrants that prior to [31 December 1998], it will carry out all testing and work necessary to ensure that:

i   *neither the operation nor functionality of the software set out in Schedule [ ] to this Agreement will be adversely affected by the millennium change or any other change of date; and*

ii   *that the software set out in Schedule [ ] to this Agreement complies fully with the definition of Year 2000 conformity set out in the BSI Year 2000 Conformity Requirements [attached hereto].*

Such a warranty should be reinforced by an indemnity of the following nature:

The Supplier hereby agrees to indemnify completely and hold fully harmless against any loss, damage or expense (including legal fees), costs and claims incurred directly or indirectly as a result of the breach of the warranty set out above. This indemnity is not subject to any liability limitation or exclusion clauses contained in this Agreement.

(5) ACCEPTANCE TESTING CLAUSE

The sort of clause suggested here is not essentially different from a standard acceptance test clause. The Year 2000 factor should be reflected in the criteria against which the software will be tested such that if the software is not Year 2000 compliant, it will fail the test. The acceptance criteria may either be set out as a schedule to the agreement or be contained in a technical/functional specification which sets out the software development parameters.

Once the Software in the opinion of the Developer has satisfied the acceptance criteria set out in [   ], it shall notify the Customer accordingly and the Customer will then have [30] days to carry out its own acceptance tests.

If the Software fails in the reasonable opinion of the Customer to meet the acceptance criteria set out in [   ], it shall notify the Developer accordingly and the Developer shall have a further [14] days to remedy such defects. When it has completed such corrections, the Developer shall notify the Customer and the procedure set out in the clause above shall recommence.

If the acceptance is not in the Customer's reasonable opinion passed by [set the longstop date here], the Customer shall be entitled to choose between the following options:

i   *reject the Software and to a full and receive an immediate refund of any moneys paid hereunder; or*

ii   *accept those parts of the Software which it deems useful and reject those which it does not and pay only such proportion of the full price as the parties may agree .*

(6) THIRD PARTY SUPPLIER WARRANTY

All businesses are dependent on supplies from third parties. If the business of one or more of such suppliers fails totally, or even partially on account of the effect of the Year 2000 on its IT systems, the customer's own business may be adversely affected. The knock-on effect could be a relatively simply matter of late delivery or failure to deliver by companies whose own stock control and delivery systems are affected by the millennium bug. It could also be a more insidious technical affair such as in the case of the receipt of non-compliant data feeds which throw the recipient company's IT systems into turmoil.

One approach being followed by many companies is to request a statement of compliance from their business-critical suppliers. This request should be set out in such a way as to make it totally clear that you are only willing to continue business with your supplier if it satisfies you that it is or will be totally compliant. Many suppliers will not yet be in a position where they can give such an unequivocal statement. Thus, unless alternative suppliers can give you such satisfaction, you may find yourselves in a position of having to accept a declaration to the effect that the supplier's operation will be compliant before the Year 2000 and seek a more definitive warranty closer to the time. Whether such declarations might have any legal effect will depend on the exact wording and circumstances.

A standard form of request for such confirmation is set out below:

Dear [   ],

Year 2000 and Third Millennium Compliance

As you are aware, there is much concern as to the ability of software and hardware systems to cope with the millennium date change.

We are in the process of evaluating our own situation. As an extension of this evaluation, we wish to ensure that your ability to supply us with goods and services will be unaffected by the date change from 1999 to 2000 and all other date changes, including without limitation 29 February 2000.

Please have somebody with appropriate authority sign and return the attached compliance statement and warranty. This information will confirm to us your continuing ability to meet our requirements.

Compliance Statement

We, the undersigned, hereby represent and warrant to [
] that our ability to supply goods and services to [
] will be unaffected by the date change from 1999 to 2000 and all other
date changes, including without limitation 29 February 2000. We understand
that in making future orders from us, [   ] will be relying
on this representation and warranty.

Signed   ....

Position/title of Signatory ....

For and on behalf of   .... (Supplier's name)

Date   ....

(7) NCC YEAR 2000 SOURCE CODE RELEASE TRIGGER CLAUSE

The NCC contract provides that source code is released, inter alia if

'Coding in the Package is such that either the accuracy or the functionality or
the performance of the Package is or becomes or is demonstrably likely to
become significantly adversely affected by the entry or processing of data
incorporating any date or dates whether prior to subsequent to or including 31
December 1999, including but not limited to any of the following:

i   the Package crashes at any time while processing any such data;

ii   the Owner has warranted or represented that the Package is capable of
         accurately and correctly processing such data in accordance with the
         Package's current functional specification and the Licensee
         demonstrates that the Package is not so capable;

iii   the Owner has undertaken or attempted to procure the Package to be so
         capable and the Licensee demonstrates that the Package is not so
         capable;

iv   no such warranty, representation, undertaking or attempt has been
         given or made and the Licensee demonstrates that the Package is not so
         capable.'

Appendix 2: NCC guidance

MILLENNIUM SAFETY NET - MINIMISE YOUR RISK

The following text is reproduced by kind permission of the NCC

Have you considered what would happen to your business if your software supplier went into liquidation? Of the six largest major failures in the UK (by previous year's turnover), as notified in the press, a third of those were involved in the sale of computer hardware and software. The number of business failures is forecast to increase in the future. One of the major causes will be financial pressures resulting from organisations attempting to solve their Year 2000 problem.

In today's commercial world of IT, it is more likely than ever that your software supplier will be affected in some way by a takeover. The number of acquisitions in the information technology industry involving UK companies jumped by 21 per cent to 421 deals in 1996. Software and service organisations were the focus of most attention with 183 acquisitions representing 43 per cent of all announced deals (source: Regent Associates Ltd).

In the USA it is now widely accepted that there are not enough IT resources in America to resolve the Year 2000 problem. As a result, there is intense acquisition activity as large IT companies buy or merge to build up sufficient resources to sort out their own Year 2000 situation. This merger and acquisition activity will certainly require a great deal of reorganisation and rationalisation. The probable outcome will be that many supported mainstream applications will be downgraded, left unsupported or have their development programs curtailed. The current trend indicates an acceleration of the merger and takeover process as we move towards the millennium. It is vital that companies are aware of this and take the necessary action to minimise the risk of disastrous loss of trade and revenue.

Many organisations have by now recognised the importance of developing and implementing a plan to solve the Year 2000 problem. However, very few are actually stopping to consider the real consequences of failure and the action that must be taken now to ensure business continuity. Circumstances out of your control may damage your business. For example, have you considered if your business will survive should your software supplier goes into liquidation and you have not got access to the source code? Alternatively, your software supplier may fail to ensure that your software is millennium compliant, putting vital projects or even your entire business at risk.

Whatever size and type of operation you run, it is likely to depend heavily on the use of computer software. Whether you are a software user, software owner or a distributor, you need to minimise the risk to your business should problems arise.

There is a considerable amount of coverage being given to the Year 2000 problem in the press at the moment. This is coupled with an ever-growing tide of panic that the world is going to stop because computers will not work on 01/01/00. To the uninitiated, this is mostly hype. However, there is a challenging problem which could have serious business implications if left unaddressed. It is estimated that 90 per cent of the world's computer applications will either fail, or will give incorrect results in the lead up to, during and after the Year 2000.

- How Widespread is the Problem?

- The problem is real. Here are some examples of system crashes that have already occurred:

  A recent example was a multi-million pound UK hospital body scanner which would not work on 29 February 1996 because it couldn't handle leap years.

  The five year budgeting system of a US government agency failed while processing the fifth budget year (2000). The underlying COBOL compiler is no longer supported.

  A lottery (not UK) lost several million dollars revenue because the system refused to print tickets for a leap day.

  A case management system of some courts (US) will not accept a probation period of five years because '00' is flagged as an invalid date.

  A major food retailer in the UK discovered that supposedly 'time expired' produce was about to be destroyed when in fact the expiry date was post Year 2000.

  A leading organisation attempted to test Year 2000 compliance over a weekend. Dates were changed, the result being that valuable data was lost when the system reverted to the current date.

  Driving licences due to expire in 2000 are being rejected as already expired by car rental agencies.

  Some credit card transactions processing systems refuse cards which expire in 2000.

So, if your third party software fails due to a Year 2000 related problem, can you recover?

NCC Escrow International Limited, part of the National Computing Centre, has developed a Year 2000 Escrow agreement which can provide you with a strategy that will allow you to recover your application, correct or modify it, if necessary, and then continue with a sound working system. This is essential where such applications or its owners fail in their ability to handle millennium-related dates.

Escrow is an essential, practical provision as part of any Year 2000 plan. The NCC's Escrow2000 initiative provides a 'lifeboat' for major companies, SME's and government post Year 2000.

NCC Escrow International Limited is an independent organisation catering specifically for suppliers, distributors and end-users of application software. Escrow provides a business continuity security mechanism by storing source code. The storage of all third party software in Escrow2000 is an essential business practice and a provision against Year 2000 related disasters.

An escrow agreement can include any triggering event providing it is definable and legal. This could cover the failure of the vendor's business, failure to maintain application (through product change or because of acquisition), and even failing to meet certain specific Year 2000 criteria.

It is advisable to discuss escrow at the earliest stages of software procurement although you can take out an escrow agreement after a software license has been signed. You could ask your solicitor to draw up an escrow agreement, but it makes more sense to talk to a recognised escrow provider. NCC Escrow International is the world's leading escrow agent. It has the expertise and experience to provide you with a cost-effective and efficient service tailored to your needs. In-house technical and legal staff are able to deal with both standard and complex circumstances.

As well as operations in London, Glasgow and Manchester, NCC Escrow International has a number of agents around the world and has recently opened offices in Germany and the USA. As a result they can offer escrow agreements that are in the language of that country but, more importantly, binding in the law of that country. In addition, it is actively marketing its escrow service in Ireland and agreements are also available, bound by Irish law.

Like no other escrow agent in the world, the NCC's Escrow service also provides verification of the software source code as part of the standard offering. This service further reduces business risk by:

- increasing the quality of the source code deposited by your supplier

- ensuring relevant up-to-date versions of the source code are available

- peace of mind knowing that a reliable back-up source code is held with an independent third party

An optional service, FULL verification, is also available (at an additional cost) which ensures that the media deposited are not only readable, but can be built into a fully functional application. An independent verification service is also available.

NCC Escrow International Limited believes it is essential to keep abreast of new technology. It is the only escrow agent in the world currently holding Internet websites in escrow. If your organisation has invested a considerable amount of money in having your own website designed and constructed, you will recognise the importance of safeguarding this valuable marketing and sales tool.

The National Computing Centre puts you in touch with the experts. Whatever your query, contact the escrow Helpline + 44 (0)161 242 2430 for independent advice, or e-mail escrow@ncc.co.uk for your free information pack or disc containing the standard escrow agreements.

Appendix 3: Definition of Year 2000 conformity requirements

(1) INTRODUCTION

This document addresses what is commonly known as Year 2000 conformity (also sometimes known as century or millennium compliance). It provides a definition of this expression and requirements that must be satisfied in equipment and products which use dates and times.

It has been prepared by British Standards Institution committee BDD/1/-/3 in response to demand from UK industry, commerce and the public sector. It is the result of work from the following bodies whose contributions are gratefully acknowledged: BT, Cap Gemini, CCTA, Coopers & Lybrand, Halberstam Elias, ICL, National Health Service, National Westminster Bank.

BSI-DISC would also like to thank the following organizations for their support and encouragement in the development of this definition: Taskforce 2000, Barclays Bank, British Airways, Cambridgeshire County Council, Computer Software Services Association, Department of Health, Ernst & Young, Federation of Small Businesses, IBM, ICI, National Power, Paymaster Agency, Prudential Assurance, Reuters, Tesco Stores.

While every care has been taken in developing this document, the contributing organizations accept no liability for any loss or damage caused, arising directly or indirectly, in connection with reliance on its contents except to the extent that such liability may not be excluded at law. Independent legal advice should be sought by any person or organization intending to enter into a contractual commitment relating to Year 2000 conformity requirements.

This entire document or the definition section may be freely copied provided that the text is reproduced in full, the source acknowledged and the reference number of the document is quoted.

(2) THE DEFINITION

Year 2000 conformity shall mean that neither performance nor functionality is affected by dates prior to, during and after the year 2000.

In particular:

Rule 1   No value for current date will cause any interruption in operation.

Rule 2   Date-based functionality must behave consistently for dates prior to, during and after year 2000.

Rule 3   In all interfaces and data storage, the century in any date must be specified either explicitly or by unambiguous algorithms or inferencing rules.

Rule 4   Year 2000 must be recognized as a leap year.

(3) AMPLIFICATION OF THE DEFINITION AND RULES

(i) General Explanation

Problems can arise from some means of representing dates in computer equipment and products and from date-logic embedded in purchased goods or services, as the Year 2000 approaches and during and after that year. As a result, equipment or products, including embedded control logic, may fail completely, malfunction or cause data to be corrupted.

To avoid such problems, organizations must check, and modify if necessary, internally produced equipment and products and similarly check externally supplied equipment and products with their suppliers. The purpose of this document is to allow such checks to be made on a basis of common understanding.

Where checks are made with external suppliers, care should be taken to distinguish between claims of conformity and the ability to demonstrate conformity.

Rule 1

1.1   This rule is sometimes known as *general integrity.*

1.2   If this requirement is satisfied, roll-over between all significant time demarcations (e.g. days, months, years, centuries) will be performed correctly.

1.3   *Current date* means today's date as known to the equipment or product.

Rule 2

2.1   This rule is sometimes known as *date integrity.*

2.2   This rule means that all equipment and products must calculate, manipulate and represent dates correctly for the purposes for which they were intended.

2.3   The meaning of *functionality* includes both processes and the results of those processes.

2.4   If desired, a reference point for date values and calculations may be added by organisations; e.g. as defined by the Gregorian calendar.

2.5 No equipment or product shall use particular date values for special meanings; e.g. "99" to signify "no end value" or "end of file" or "00" to mean "not applicable" or "beginning of file".

Rule 3

3.1 This rule is sometimes known as *explicit/implicit century*.

3.2 It covers two general approaches:

(a) *explicit representation of the year in dates*: e.g. by using four digits or by including a century indicator. In this case, a reference may be inserted (e.g. 4-digit years as allowed by ISO standard 8601:1988) and it may be necessary to allow for exceptions where domain-specific standards (e.g. standards relating to Electronic Data Interchange, Automatic Teller Machines or Bankers Automated Clearing Services) should have precedence.

(b) *the use of inferencing rules*: e.g. two-digit years with a value greater than 50 imply 19th, those with a value equal to or less than 50 imply 20th. Rules for century inferencing as a whole must apply to all contexts in which the date is used, although different inferencing rules may apply to different date sets.

(ii) General Notes

For Rules 1 and 2 in particular, organisations may wish to specify allowable ranges for values of current date and dates to be manipulated. The ranges may relate to one or more of the feasible life-span of equipment or products or the span of dates required to be represented by the organisation's business processes. Tests for specifically critical dates may also be added (e.g. for leap years, end of year, etc). Organisations may wish to append additional material in support of local requirements.

Where the term century is used, clear distinction should be made between the "value" denoting the century (e.g. 20th) and its representation in dates (e.g. 19th); similarly, 21st and 20th.

Index